# Understanding Christian Leadership

IAN PARKINSON

# Understanding Christian Leadership

scm press

© Ian Parkinson 2020

Published in 2020 by SCM Press
Editorial office
3rd Floor, Invicta House,
108–114 Golden Lane,
London EC1Y 0TG, UK
www.scmpress.co.uk

SCM Press is an imprint of Hymns Ancient & Modern Ltd
(a registered charity)

Hymns Ancient & Modern® is a registered trademark of
Hymns Ancient & Modern Ltd
13a Hellesdon Park Road, Norwich,
Norfolk NR6 5DR, UK

British Library Cataloguing in Publication data

A catalogue record for this book is available

from the British Library

978 0 334 05874 8

Typeset by Regent Typesetting
Printed and bound by
CPI Group (UK) Ltd

In grateful memory of my father

Joseph Ernest Parkinson
(1929–88)

who gave me such a good example to follow

# Contents

# Acknowledgements

A huge number of people have contributed to the writing of this book, many without realizing it. The genesis of the book lay, in no small part, in my own frustration at the lack of a one-volume textbook on Christian leadership suitable to function as a course textbook to accompany the teaching of leadership modules in theological education institutions. The content is shaped particularly by the requirements of such modules. My own thinking around the topics covered has thus been shaped a good deal in recent years through interaction and discussion with students in the various colleges and courses in which I teach. I sincerely hope that the fruit of all our previous discussion and reflection might be useful to those who come after and might, in turn, stimulate fresh and fuller reflection and more informed leadership practice.

I am grateful to those who first modelled good leadership to me and showed a concern for my own leadership formation, especially Andrew Cornes and the late Ian Reid. My own leadership was significantly shaped by those with whom I shared leadership in the various churches I have served, and especially the outstanding team of which I was part during my years as vicar of All Saints Marple. My practice and understanding of leadership was hugely shaped and stretched during my time as a member of the New Wine National Leadership team, a true experience of iron sharpening iron. I am so grateful especially to John Coles, Mark Melluish, Mark Bailey, Chris Pemberton, Phil George, Mark Tanner, Steve McGanity and Mark Carey for so many stimulating times spent in their company reflecting on matters to do with leadership. It is an enormous privilege to have been a member, for the last few years, of the CPAS leadership delivery team. My thinking about leadership has been sharpened significantly by our shared reflection on leadership theory and practice and by the fresh and stimulating insights that continually seem to bubble up. I am very grateful to the team members – Charles Burgess, Pam MacNaughton, Emma Sykes, Di Archer, Sally Taylor and Kirstin MacDonald – and to other CPAS colleagues for their encouragement and support as I have gone about the business of writing this book, not least for allowing me to devote considerable time to the project.

I am especially grateful to our team leader, James Lawrence. Over the course of more than two decades, James has played a number of different roles in my life at different times, whether as colleague, coach, team leader, friend or wise counsellor. His wisdom and depth of reflection on Christian leadership probably exceeds that of any other person I know, and his insights have coloured especially the second half of this book. He has been a wonderfully encouraging critical friend during the writing of this book, and his suggestions for revisions and improvements have made this a much stronger volume than it would otherwise have been. Others too have been patient enough to read and offer comment on different chapters and I am particularly grateful to David Heywood, Duncan MacLea, John Dunnett and Jude Palmer for their insights. My thanks, too, to Lizzie Hare for her help in some of the initial research for Chapter 5.

Those who are subjects of the various case studies that accompany the different chapters are all people with whom I have reflected, in some instances over a considerable number of years, about the business of leadership. They are people whose exemplary practice has, in some way, inspired me and enhanced my own understanding of leadership. I am grateful to them for being willing to be interviewed and consenting to make their stories more widely available to others.

Nadine, my wife, with whom I have largely shared my leadership journey, has been, as ever, tirelessly encouraging and supportive as I have been more than usually focused on writing over the last two summers.

Finally, I am hugely grateful to the team at SCM Press, without whose efforts this book would not have seen the light of day, and especially to David Shervington for his wisdom and encouragement, Rachel Geddes for all her practical help, and to Hannah Ward for editing the finished text.

Throughout the book, when using personal pronouns, because I dislike the impersonal pronoun 'they', and because I find repeated use of 'he or she' cumbersome, I tend to use masculine and feminine pronouns interchangeably. Nothing is implied by the particular use of either masculine or feminine pronouns in any specific context.

My late father, Ernest Parkinson, was the first person who modelled Christian leadership to me, and continues to be one of the most influential role models in my life. A man of sure faith, deep wisdom and great integrity, he demonstrated what good leadership looks like in his professional life as a headteacher, in his family and within the local church. It is to his memory that this book is dedicated.

# Foreword

## *by the Most Reverend Justin Welby*

Many of us who find ourselves in positions of Christian leadership share two perspectives: the first is that we aren't quite sure how we got to the position we are in, and the second is that we frequently don't feel up to the responsibility we have been given. Because of both of these back stories, I am often amazed when people can write effectively and systematically about leadership, since for my part, I find myself knowing more about what I wouldn't say about it than about what I would. That is why I am grateful for Ian's book.

*Understanding Christian Leadership* is a tour de force. It is comprehensive and informed, theological and practical, theoretical and workable. It represents what must be years of research and academic work, of observation and conversation, and of practice and reflection. Ian knows what he is talking about. My guess is that this is his life in a book – and in writing it he has done us a great service.

That service is the work he has put in in order that we may get on and prayerfully work out how God calls us to lead. Ian has read, digested and made sense of recent and current theories on leadership, studied Scripture and researched scriptural models and concepts of leadership, and observed the practice of effective leadership in teams, communication and strategy. His book is biblical, hopeful, enabling, equipping and rigorous.

Because all truth is God's truth and all wisdom is God's wisdom, Ian isn't fearful of bringing the best of leadership ideas and practice from wherever he finds them – football, Scripture, business, the charity sector, government, church – and co-opting them for the gospel. As well as giving us information and evidence, he also brings character, vision, humility and service. But above all, this book's greatest theme is the person and work of Jesus Christ – who he was and how he led. This is because, of course, all leadership really comes from who we are. That is why the only hope any of us can have is that it might be the life of Christ in us that draws people, rather than any competency of our own. I doubt whether anyone who might read this book and act on it could fail to be helped to be a more Christlike leader.

If you are a leader who thinks you have it sorted, who can't understand why you aren't given more leadership responsibility, or who looks with contempt at everyone else who is leading, at the mess they are making of it, certain you would be succeeding where they are failing – then do not read this book. But if you are a leader who feels out of your depth, aware that you don't really have the gifts that it takes, and wondering how God might equip you for what he calls you to – then this book is for you, right now. Read it on your own, both sitting down and on your knees; read it with others, so that you can learn together and hold each other to what God calls you to; and read it for the sake of those to whom you are called.

And once you have finished reading it, you will find that the biggest challenge begins: to do it.

*The Most Reverend Justin Welby*

*Archbishop of Canterbury*

# Introduction

# Not *Another* Book on Leadership?!

The last 50 years have seen a veritable explosion of interest in leadership. Wherever we turn, leadership seems to be on the agenda. Whether reflecting on the effective delivery of public services, the productivity of businesses, the moral integrity of charitable organizations or the progress of our favourite sports team, the consensus, fuelled by various media, is that success in each of these enterprises stands or falls by the quality of its leadership. Politicians canvass for our votes on the basis of the leadership qualities they might bring to their respective tier of government if elected. Top universities recruit prospective students explicitly on the basis of their possession and demonstration of leadership skills.[1] Leadership is regarded as a valuable commodity, essential for the well-being and thriving of any organization or enterprise.

This insight has clearly been owned by the business sector, at least in the Western world: a 2012 survey revealed that US companies alone spend almost $14 billion annually on leadership development.[2] The (some might say 'misplaced') esteem with which leadership is held in the commercial sector is also illustrated by a 2018 survey in which the Equality Trust reported that 67 per cent of CEOs of FTSE 100 companies are paid at least 100 times more than the average UK salary.[3] Nor has this concern with leadership bypassed churches. Since 1993, a capacity to exercise leadership has been added to the list of criteria by which potential candidates are selected for training for ordained ministry in the Church of England, while those appointed to positions of incumbency in that Church are now required to demonstrate a range of leadership capabilities, including skills in collaboration, in leading teams, in supervising others in their responsibilities and in facilitating change. Recent years have seen significant growth in the number of business schools now located in or connected to UK universities,[4] each offering significant focus on leadership studies as part of their core curriculum, while the range of leadership resources now available to purchase or download at the click of a button[5] increases on a daily basis.

Given such a panoply of leadership resources, the question might reasonably be asked, why the need for yet another one?

I am convinced that good leadership, absolutely vital to the flourishing of any organization and its people, is fuelled by healthy reflection on good practice and sound leadership theory. I am also persuaded that, while the

Christian Church does not have a monopoly on leadership understanding, there is within the Christian tradition a wealth of leadership wisdom and insight that has currency today, not simply for specifically Christian organizations, but for any and every context in which leadership is undertaken. My aim, thus, in adding to the existing body of leadership literature, is to offer an understanding of leadership theory and practice, informed by contemporary academic thought and by Christian theology and tradition, which might serve as something of a leadership primer especially for those embarking upon or engaging in Christian leadership. Although I have in mind anyone who aspires to lead in a variety of different contexts, nevertheless, because my own experience of leading over a number of decades has been in the context of local churches, and because my current work involves me in preparing the next generation of leaders for ordained ministry, much of the application and many of the examples in what follows deal with this more specific context.

This book is written as an attempt to address what I see as three deficiencies in much of the current literature on leadership.

## 1 Theory and practice

By and large, leadership texts tend to fall into one of two categories: those written by practitioners and those written by academics. The former tend to focus on wisdom and knowledge garnered through personal leadership success, whether in the world of commerce or some other sector, and offer something of a blueprint for seeing such success replicated by the repetition of specific practices and strategies. These works are not without merit and are much beloved by those who inhabit an essentially pragmatic culture. The study of leaders, and of effective practice in leadership, and a willingness to learn from the positive experience of others, stimulates our own growth in leadership. The weakness of such works lies in the fact that not all practitioners necessarily demonstrate the capacity to reflect on their practice and on the reasons for its effectiveness. Successful practitioners often give the impression, whether intentionally or otherwise, that their own way is the only possible route to fruitfulness. Reflection on some of the principles that have informed their practice, and on other vital factors, especially those to do with the impact of context upon practice, would make these works infinitely more helpful and would enable readers not simply to replicate the practices described but, perhaps more usefully, to improvise on the basis of such principles and in the light of their own specific context. Not only might this lead to better and more creative practice, but it might also prevent some of the frustration and disappointment that we experience when assiduous imitation of methodology fails to produce identical results to those described.

At the other end of the leadership literature spectrum lie the weightier tomes written by academics analysing in great detail the finer points of a range of leadership theories. Usually based on wide-ranging research, these are vital tools for those who recognize that one of the keys to benevolent and effective leadership is proper reflection upon practice. However, although a treasury for those who are fascinated by theory, the forms of leadership ultimately espoused by these authors often appear to practitioners so ethereal, and so remote from our own lived experience, that we cannot begin to imagine how such theory might ever truly inform our practice.

My aim in writing this book is to offer a resource that might stimulate an appetite, especially among those training for ordained ministry, for reflective practice in leadership. This book aims to be practical, in that leadership is ultimately a practical matter. However, in establishing a sound theoretical base for such practice, and in drawing on some of the best of contemporary leadership theory, my hope is to foster a concern for leadership that is not simply a slavish repetition of the practice of others but a faithful, yet fresh improvisation in the light of sound thinking, helpful practice and an ever-changing context.[6]

## 2 Sacred and secular

Antipathy to aspects of a variety of Church initiatives, which are shaped by the introduction of leadership thinking and practice from secular sources, of which the Church of England's Renewal and Reform programme is a good example,[7] reveals a deep suspicion of elements, at least, of leadership and management discourses and profound reservations concerning their applicability to the sphere of Christian life and ministry. Martyn Percy has been one of the most eloquent critics of what he perceives to be an undiscerning embracing of secular wisdom and practice:

> Most denominations are not alert to the dangers of uncritically inculcating management and business-think into their systems and structures. To an organisation that is panicking, or to an institution that believes itself to be in decline, the rewards of incorporating secular managerialism can appear tantalising.[8]

While I wholeheartedly agree with Percy that managerialism, understood as uncritical reliance upon management insights uninformed by and even contradicting settled theological truths, is a curse rather than a blessing to the Church, my contention is that not every leadership insight from spheres other than the sacred is necessarily of Belial.[9] We will examine in greater depth in a subsequent chapter what lies behind some of the more compelling theological and ecclesiological reservations to do with leadership per se. A few observations at this point on the relationship between sacred and secular insights will have to suffice.

Whereas in previous eras leadership may well have been seen as a specific set of traits, skills or behaviours, the possession of which equipped a person to lead in any situation or sphere, there is increasing recognition that leadership is significantly formed by context. Maccoby[10] suggests that the relational nature of leadership implies that leaders who gain followers in one context may find it very difficult to do the same in a very different context. Leadership is not necessarily a completely transferable skill. This should alert us to the weakness in any thinking that insists that all leadership or management skills from any other sphere are automatically transferable to that of Christian ministry. However, to the extent that there is overlap between the concerns of any two enterprises, there is likely to be a degree of commonality in terms of the requirements for leadership in each.

Perhaps it is the fact that much of the leadership thinking and practice to which reference is made originates from the world of business and commerce that makes it appear toxic to those whose concern is not primarily productivity, profit and the satisfaction of shareholders. Surely, they contend, reliance on such thinking skews the focus of an essentially sacred body and tempts us towards unworthy goals to be pursued through inappropriate methodologies. Certainly it is fair to acknowledge that the aims of God's kingdom cannot be fulfilled purely through the deployment of strategies that take no cognisance of him and of his agency. However, it is unfair to drive too hard a wedge between sacred and secular insights on leadership as if each dealt with entirely different matters. One of the principal concerns of secular leadership theory is people, and specifically how people might most effectively be engaged, empowered and their skills put to good use. These concerns are central to the work and ministry of the Church, and thus all proven wisdom from whatever source which might enable the Church to fulfil its divine calling more effectively is to be welcomed.[11] Such an argument has good pedigree, being originally advanced by Origen,[12] who likened the plundering of scientific wisdom from the world as analogous to the despoiling of the Egyptians by Israel.[13] While we may well adapt and contextualize wisdom we draw from other spheres for use in the Church, we are impoverished, even hamstrung, if we neglect insights that would enable us to fulfil our calling more effectively. If all wisdom comes ultimately from God, who are we to deride such wisdom simply because it was not conceived in the sphere in which we have particular involvement?

The sharp distinction between sacred and secular leadership discourses may well be diminishing as secular thinking increasingly evidences a broadening in terms of organizational and leadership concerns. An increasing number of prominent leadership researchers point to a growing focus in companies on issues beyond mere profitability, and specifically on the development and growth of people as an end in itself, rather than as a means to secure greater productivity.[14] Banks and Ledbetter[15] highlight the way in which more and more leadership writers, as a reflection of this widening of leadership concern, are beginning to take more cognisance of, and make explicit reference to, the place of the spiritual. While the root spirituality that undergirds many of these references may well be more New Age than Christian,[16] it offers hope on two fronts. First, a focus on spirituality signals the fact that organizations exist for purposes not exclusively related to the interests of their shareholders. Such convictions are promising in terms of the possibility of more ethical and holistic approaches to leadership thinking. Second, wider awareness of the place of the spiritual, and a recognition that leadership in different spheres might have more concerns in common than was previously realized, may well result in greater openness on the part of others to receive some of the wisdom from our own Christian leadership tradition.

One of the concerns of this book is to help us formulate some criteria that might encourage us to take a discerning and constructive critical approach to secular leadership wisdom and to its deployment in the Church. Moreover, I am convinced that our own Christian tradition contains within it a vast body of leadership wisdom that has applicability in every sphere, not simply that of the Church. My concern in exploring this tradition is to grow confidence in this rich heritage so that, rather than simply being on the back foot in the leadership debate, we might fulfil our calling to be shapers of culture, including leadership culture, rather than being merely the recipients of the culture of others.

## 3 Leaders and leadership

Almost any book written on leadership before the 1970s (and a good many thereafter) would have dealt exclusively with the person and task of the leader, seen as the exclusive locus of leadership. As both leadership studies and cultural assumptions and values have developed in more recent years, so the focus of leadership attention has diversified. Leadership is now, rightly, seen not as exclusively to do with leader figures but equally to be located variously in the relationship between leaders and followers or distributed more widely throughout the processes and relationships that exist in any organization. The proliferation of leadership theories that have come to the fore in recent decades[17] have all drawn attention to different key elements of the leadership process. Careful study of each of them enlarges our understanding of the business of leadership and has the capacity to broaden our skill base and our leadership expertise. However, the weakness of many of these leadership theories is that leadership tends to be conceived exclusively in terms of the parameters described by each particular theory. Each theory serves as a lens through which attention is focused on those specific elements of leadership that are the particular concern of the theory in question, not infrequently as a corrective to the concerns and emphases of previous theories. By bringing certain aspects or dimensions of leadership to the fore, certain other important aspects are diminished or pushed to the margins, leading to an unbalanced understanding of the leadership enterprise. Moreover, an over focus on theories that deconstruct leadership to such an extent that it almost disappears entirely from view can leave a leader bewildered as to what, if any, role she might still have to play.

My principal concern in this volume is to enable individuals entrusted with leadership responsibility to construe and discharge such responsibility in a way that takes seriously the wider leadership discourse, recognizing the different elements involved in the leadership process, without compromising the distinctive role played by any of them. Following Gill, we will suggest that the different leadership theories might best be seen as individual pieces of a jigsaw puzzle, each complementing one another, as opposed to a single lens through which the whole of leadership must be viewed.[18] In seeking to avoid the twin perils of either defining leadership too narrowly in terms of the sole activity of leaders, or so broadly that we are hard pressed to discern what contribution, if any, such individuals might be permitted to make, one of our primary recurring themes will be that of the catalytic, rather than merely instrumental, role that individual leaders are called to fulfil in the life of a church or other organization.

## Charting the course

In the first part of this book we seek to establish something of a theoretical basis for the leadership we espouse. We explore something of the nature of leadership and ask where it might be located and note some of the key ways in which effective leadership contributes to the health and fruitfulness of an organization. We examine the distinctive contribution to leadership understanding offered by the wider Christian tradition as we look at biblical models of, and biblical insights into, leadership, as well as the way in which our understanding of leadership might be shaped by engagement with some of the central themes of Christian theology. In particular we will examine how an understanding of the present work of God's Spirit draws our attention both to the dispersed nature of leadership in the Church and its transformational vocation. Recognizing that leadership is not a wholly uncontested notion, we go on to review some of the various philosophical and theological critiques made of leadership in general, and of certain theories of leadership in particular.

Having established a solid theoretical base, in the second part of the book we turn our attention to some of the core practical concerns of Christian leadership. While by no means an exhaustive list, we identify some of these core concerns as to do with the culture and direction of an organization, the development of others, facilitating collaboration, and forming and articulating vision. A final chapter reflects a little on the spirituality of Christian leadership.

Appended to several of these chapters is a series of leadership case studies.

Each one gives a brief account of the way one particular leader has sought to exercise leadership in contexts including the local church, the National Health Service, the charity sector and higher education. Although each study describes specific leadership actions and assumptions, none is necessarily intended to illustrate the particular points made in the chapter that they follow. Rather, their aim is to bring to life some of the theoretical insights expounded throughout the book, demonstrating some specific ways in which these have been worked out in a variety of contexts.

One of the principal insights offered by the Christian tradition is that leadership is essentially a gift from God and a participation in his own leadership. While this insight may well raise our sense of responsibility and accountability as leaders, it is equally enormously liberating. It sets us free from the tyranny of having to be original or impressive as leaders in our own right, reminding us that leadership is ultimately concerned with discerning what God is about and submitting to being led by him. May God use this volume to deepen such understanding in us and grow us in leadership practice that is authentically Christian and that adequately serves the purposes of his kingdom.

## Notes

1 See, for example, Cain, S., 'Not Leadership Material? Good. The World needs Followers', *New York Times*, 24 March 2017, who relates the observation of one applicant to an Ivy League University 'that it was not the smart people, not the creative people, not the thoughtful people or decent human beings that scored the application letters and the scholarships, but the leaders. It seemed no activity or accomplishment meant squat unless it was somehow connected to leadership.'

2 Loew, L. and O'Leonard, K., 2012, *Leadership Development Factbook 2012: Benchmarks and Trends in US Leadership Development*, Bersin by Deloitte report, Oakland, CA: Bersin by Deloitte.

3 The Equality Trust, Pay Ratios, www.equalitytrust.org.uk/taxonomy/term/ 136 (accessed 25 November 2019).

4 The Higher Education Statistics Agency (HESA) survey of UK Higher Education student enrolment in 2016–17 indicates that the subject area attracting the largest number of students (333,425) was Business and Administration.

5 A Google search for 'leadership' on 22 March 2019 returned 4.5bn hits, a tenfold increase on a similar search five years previously.

6 Clearly I am not claiming to be the first person to attempt such a thing and there are a number of existing works that in different ways offer a synthesis of theory and practice (though few written specifically with church leadership in focus). Notable among these are, for example, Gill, R., 2011, *Theory and Practice of Leadership*, London: Sage; Western, S., 2013, *Leadership: A Critical Text*, London: Sage.

7 See www.churchofengland.org/about/renewal-and-reform (accessed 25 November 2019).

8 Taken from The Very Revd Dr Martyn Percy's guest post on the Archbishop Cranmer blog: Martyn Percy, 'How Bishop George Bell became a victim

of Church of England "spin" and a narrative of "decisive leadership"', http://archbishopcranmer.com/bishop-george-bell-victim-church-england-spin-narrative-decisive-leadership/ (accessed 20 April 2018).

9 See 2 Corinthians 6.15.

10 Maccoby, M., 2007, *The Leaders We Need*, Boston, MA: Harvard Business School Press.

11 One of the most helpful treatments of the relationship between sacred and secular leadership insights is Bonem, M., 2012, *In Pursuit of Great and Godly Leadership*, San Francisco, CA: Jossey-Bass.

12 Letter from Origen to Gregory Thaumaturgus, *c*. AD 245.

13 Exodus 12.35–36.

14 For example, Sinclair, A., 2007, *Leadership for the Disillusioned*, Crows Nest, NSW: Allen & Unwin; Laloux, F., 2014, *Reinventing Organizations*, Brussels: Nelson Parker.

15 Banks, R. and Ledbetter, B. M., 2004, *Reviewing Leadership*, Grand Rapids, MI: Baker.

16 Laloux, *Reinventing Organizations*, p. 158, would be typical in his recommendation that 'if we want to listen to the wisdom and truth of our souls, we need to find moments to slow down and honour silence in the middle of the noise and buzz of the work place'. He cites with approval companies offering, inter alia, daily group meditation sessions and regular 'mindfulness days'.

17 For a detailed exposition and analysis of the principal and most influential of such theories, see Dugan, John P., 2017, *Leadership Theory: Cultivating Critical Perspectives*, San Francisco, CA: Jossey-Bass; Northouse, P. G., 2010, *Leadership Theory and Practice*, London: Sage.

18 Gill, *Theory and Practice of Leadership*, p. 3.

# PART I

# Understanding Leadership

# Desiring Leadership:
# Why Leadership Matters

*Leadership, it seems, is increasingly becoming the panacea of the 21st century.*[1]

Describing the nature of my work to new acquaintances, whether at parties or on trains, prompts a fascinating range of responses. Some are intrigued that leadership studies should form part of the curriculum for formation for those in training for ordained ministry in the Church of England, wondering what on earth the two things might have in common. Others are heartened by the fact that the importance of leadership is being recognized in more and more spheres, reinforcing their own conviction that good leadership is vital for the health and effective functioning of any enterprise or organization. Still others express polite good wishes for my endeavours but are blunt about their own reservations about leadership in general and about the ways in which they have experienced it negatively, whether at work or in public life, in particular.

The response to the notion of leadership on the part of those who are required to sit in the various classes I teach in different theological institutions is also by no means uniform. While the majority, and especially those who have experienced leadership modelled in a constructive and moral way, and those who, perhaps, lack confidence in their existing abilities to fulfil the requirements of their future roles, have an enthusiasm for engaging with the subject, sometimes bordering on the over-optimistic and uncritical, others are far more diffident towards, and suspicious of, all that they believe leadership to signify. This may be due to poor personal experience of bad leadership in a workplace or a local church, or may be for more clearly theological reasons, many of which we will examine in the course of this book. Dugan appears to sum up the mood on leadership accurately when he suggests that, 'Few words elicit simultaneously such a wide range of conflicting understandings and feelings. It is a concept that both provokes and appeases. It is both desired and detested.'[2]

While this book is prompted by a conviction that good leadership is a desirable and positive thing, without which any enterprise is impoverished, we need to acknowledge from the outset the significant reservations, at times bordering on cynicism, expressed from different quarters to do either with leadership generally or with specific leadership theories and practices. The leadership discourse, despite its huge popularity and currency, is by no means universally embraced nor uncontested.[3] We are not for one moment suggesting that either the sheer weight and volume of available leadership resources or the widespread enthusiasm we have noted for leadership implies that the argument in favour of the positive contributions of leadership is automatically won. However, despite the fact that almost every student in every class I teach can point to a church leader of their own broad acquaintance whose leadership failure has adversely affected churches and their members, and despite the fact that poor leadership on the part of those in the spheres of commerce and politics has had a profoundly negative impact upon social well-being and material prosperity for most people in the Western world over the course of the last decade, and despite the fact that many leadership tropes beloved of previous eras would be anathema to most millennials (who make up a significant part of the classes I teach), nevertheless, the majority of people seem still to hold out hope for a benevolent form of leadership that has the capacity to be helpful to us in the achievement of goals that we deem to be important. Rather as a high proportion of children of divorced parents still aspire to being married themselves, seeing marriage as something capable of bringing good to those who enter it, even the casualties of poor or toxic leadership do not necessarily abandon their conviction that leadership is ultimately a helpful and constructive thing, nor their hope that better leadership is a realistic possibility. What is it about leadership that makes it, to many at least, appear so desirable?

## The human condition

A longing for leadership, while perhaps more obvious in today's connected world, is by no means a recent phenomenon. It is far from uncommon, in contemporary works on leadership, to come across references to writers from the classical era such as Lao Tzu[4] or Plato, to late mediaeval writers such as Machiavelli, or to Enlightenment thinkers such as Hobbes or Rousseau. As we will see in subsequent chapters, there is equally a wealth of reflection on leadership in a good deal of the biblical literature. What such writers have in common is an understanding that a desire for leadership arises out of the common wants and needs of humankind in every age, what Maccoby describes as 'conscious self-interest',[5] and that leadership is seen as in some way a means of enabling such needs to be fulfilled.

One of the most helpful discussions of this broad theme is offered by Michael Harvey[6] in a paper originating from a symposium of thinkers representing a range of different academic disciplines and charged with the construction of a grand, overarching theory of leadership. Highlighting the essentially corporate (as opposed to individualistic) nature of human life as it has generally been experienced, Harvey suggests that basic needs for physical survival and emotional well-being are best met by shared endeavour. At an early stage of development in any group or society, the realization dawns that together we have a better chance of surviving the threats that confront us than we would were we to attempt to go it alone. Moreover, by pooling our shared skills and resources, we will be better placed to secure the various things we require in order to sustain life and well-being. Different members of a community will display varying levels of expertise in the different qualities required for the achievement of such needs, whether physical strength, memory, experience, imagination and so on. Leadership, suggests Harvey, originates in these differences in skills and qualities as they are deployed in particular situations, those demonstrating such vital skills being deferred to and followed on the basis that to do so offers the best hope of shared needs being met and the common good being promoted. Of course, such differences and inequalities can be exploited for selfish or evil ends; the existence of leadership is no guarantee per se of the moral nature of such leadership.

Social contract theorists of the seventeenth and eighteenth centuries linked the emergence of leadership to the desire of societies for order and security, and to the need for certain wants and desires to be legitimized and others excluded. For Thomas Hobbes (1588–1679) this involved citizens surrendering their own individual power to a sovereign leader as the only means of ensuring that the natural human state characterized by 'the warre of every man against every man'[7] might give way to proper harmony and safety. Although we may not share Hobbes' and his successors' conviction that such surrender of freedom legitimates any and every use and abuse of power by the sovereign leader as a necessary corollary to the contract, the desire for order, and for legitimacy, are still powerful incentives towards the establishment of leadership. Indeed, Kellerman[8] suggests that the reason we continue to follow leaders with whom we find fault, even those whom we recognize to be abusive or unethical, is self-interest; we calculate that the benefits of following outweigh those of not following, or we reckon that resisting such leadership might prove to be more costly than simply acceding to it. We look to leadership to secure for us an environment in which the appropriate aspirations we have as individuals might be fulfilled through, and accommodated within, the purposes of the wider community and where competing claims for resources, priorities and values might be assessed and managed in an equitable and just fashion. Thus it is often the case that what we find even more unsettling than controlling leadership is the absence of leadership or even laissez-faire leadership.

Although many people throughout the world still today struggle to have their most basic needs for survival met, for the majority of the world's population the needs we feel most keenly have changed. However, the uncertainty and anxiety others have felt in more primal spheres of need are mirrored today for many as we contemplate the disorder and shortcomings of the world as we encounter it, the decay and collapse of former certainties, and our own need for knowledge to which we do not yet have access.

Sinclair suggests that history and public policy research both indicate that calls for leadership are heard most often and most clearly when anxiety and apprehension about the future are most pervasive, and especially when we are confronted with problems we have not previously faced.[9] The Harvard academic Ron Heifetz reflects on the growing prevalence in our times of what he describes as adaptive challenges, challenges that cannot be resolved by recourse to previous experiences or established bodies of knowledge.[10] As opposed to technical challenges, for which we already possess the knowledge and skills to provide effective solutions, adaptive challenges require a very different type of response. Indeed, simply deploying existing knowledge and understandings in the face of adaptive challenges may well be positively threatening for any enterprise or organization. Although we have some reservations about the tendency to draw too sharp a divide between leadership and management,[11] and prefer to see them as different and complementary aspects of the same enterprise, we recognize that the shift in the world of business and commerce from an emphasis on management to a focus on leadership similarly reflects a perception of being in changed circumstances. The historic management literature[12] assumed a reasonably settled state in which productivity and growth might be facilitated through the deployment of tried and tested and improving methods. Leadership is generally perceived to be distinguished by its future focus and its capacity to take us to new or unknown places. The changed circumstances in which we find ourselves, which for those in the commercial realm include, inter alia, the shift from a manufacturing to a knowledge environment, the shift from locally based to globally networked industries, and the massive acceleration in the pace of technological development and innovation, throw up for us a multitude of needs for which management, as historically perceived, is simply insufficient. What is required above all in such situations, of what Heifetz styles disequilibrium,[13] is leadership. We pin our hopes on leadership that might enable the discovery and implementation of solutions to new challenges, often through the possession of a perspective that has been denied others thus far, either because they are too immersed in the minutiae of the specific challenge or paralysed by the scale of it.

This is perhaps one of the great ironies of the postmodern era, that an age that defines itself largely by its suspicion of authority and its resistance to those who are regarded as in some way asserting themselves and their own perspective should be the age in which concern for leadership has grown at quite so exponential a rate. Rather like the adolescent, torn between the desire to rebel against parental authority and craving the existence of that very authority to provide a safe framework in which such rebellion might be made possible, the postmodern individual desperately longs for the establishment of effective leadership in order to create an environment in which restrictive authority might be resisted with impunity.

It may well be that factors such as numerical decline in local churches, the increasing exclusion of Christian faith from the public sphere, and the marginalization of faith communities generally, all of which alert us to the profoundly changed spiritual landscape we inhabit, are the very things that have thrust to the forefront of the Church's agenda a concern for leadership that might enable us to navigate our way through these waters we have not previously encountered. How readily such leadership will be embraced by those who have an emotional or other interest in holding on to the past is, of course, quite another matter.

If leadership emerges properly in response to experienced human needs and plays a role in enabling such needs to be met appropriately, it is equally clear that leadership may be desired for inappropriate or unhelpful reasons. The longing for someone to take responsibility in a crisis may simply be an excuse for avoiding responsibility oneself, an exercise in buck passing. It is always helpful to have someone else to shoulder the blame for failed initiatives rather than face up to one's own responsibility for their failure. Indeed, such tendencies are often highlighted by some critics of leadership discourse as a reason for being suspicious of all leadership aspirations. One of the noteworthy features of the adaptive style of leadership envisaged by Heifetz is its capacity to empower the whole workforce and, rather than simply solving people's problems for them, enable them to pursue their own solutions to the challenges they face through the provision of appropriate guidance and education.[14] This, we shall argue, is one of the defining tropes of authentic leadership in which leadership is seen more as a catalytic than as a purely instrumental force.

## Research and experience

It is clear from the writings of those who are generally critical of leadership as a whole that experience of leadership is both subjective and also varied in terms of its perceived benefit. Nevertheless, a number of research projects in a variety of different sectors each draw attention to the positive impact that helpful leadership effects on the organizations in which it is experienced.

Jim Collins' *Good to Great*[15] has been one of the most feted business books of the early twenty-first century. Based on extensive research among larger US companies, the study sought to discern key differentials between those companies whose performance on the stock market soared over a 15-year period and other, directly parallel (in terms of size, available resources and business interest) companies whose performance was significantly poorer. Of the seven characteristics identified by Collins' team as contributing to success and distinguishing great companies from merely good ones, the first mentioned, and to an extent the one without which the others could not exist, is to do with leadership.

What makes Collins' work especially interesting is that he set out on his research determined to exclude leadership as a significant factor affecting the success, or otherwise, of companies. To ascribe such a place to leadership, Collins believed, prevented one from gaining deeper and more scientifically accurate understandings of what were the real factors affecting company effectiveness. His eventual, reluctant change of mind came about purely as an inescapable conclusion, in the light of overwhelming research evidence, that constructive leadership of a particular kind made an immense difference to the success or failure of the companies that formed the research sample. This, he insists, is an empirical conclusion rather than an ideological one.[16]

Collins identifies a particular type of leadership, very different from the oft-celebrated, somewhat heroic form of leadership of which he himself was so suspicious, and one for which he coins the description 'level five leadership', as being that which enables an environment to be formed suitable for the flourishing of these companies, no matter what the sector in which they are located. Such leaders are characterized primarily by two complementary qualities: extreme personal humility allied to intense professional will. That is, while remaining profoundly unconcerned about their own reputation or personal advancement, these people are profoundly concerned about the flourishing of the organization, not simply for the period of their own tenure but also beyond.

> Level five leaders look out of the window to apportion credit to factors outside themselves when things go well. At the same time they look in the mirror to apportion responsibility, never blaming bad luck, when things go poorly.[17]

Such leaders are clear catalysts in the transition from good to great, without whom such a transition would not be possible. Collins' research is clear, not only in its insistence upon the need for leadership if an organization is to thrive, but also upon the kind of leadership that uniquely enables such thriving.

If Collins' research deals with contexts readily associated with the world of business and commerce, that conducted by Frederick Laloux[18] explores slightly less familiar terrain. Laloux is concerned primarily with organizational structure and form and their impact upon organizational health. For Laloux, such health is not confined merely to productivity and growth, though these are not unimportant, but extends to the flourishing of all stakeholders, including workers, neighbours, the environment and others. His research is among companies from a wide range of sectors, all of whom have adopted a more organic approach in terms of structure and identity and with whom leadership tends to be far more consciously dispersed throughout the organization. Once again, Laloux draws attention to the key place occupied by leadership in the development and flourishing of an organization.

What determines which stage an organisation operates from is the stage through which its leadership tends to look at the world. Consciously or unconsciously, leaders put in place organisational structures, practices and cultures that make sense to them, that correspond to their way of dealing with the world. This means that an organisation cannot evolve beyond its leadership's stage of development.[19]

The critical role of leadership in either facilitating or inhibiting growth is further demonstrated by the results of one of the most extensive research projects conducted into church growth worldwide. Undertaken by Christian Schwarz and the Institute for Natural Church Development,[20] this was conceived in many ways as a riposte to some of the more mechanistic approaches to church growth that had gained credibility throughout the later years of the last century. Founded on the theological assumption that only God can ultimately grow his Church, Schwarz likens the role of leaders to that of gardeners who, though powerless to create growth from seeds or plants, nevertheless can curate conditions that might make such growth more likely. Researching growing churches of all shapes and sizes from every continent and all manner of different contexts, Schwarz discerned eight quality characteristics that his research suggested were present in thriving churches but absent, or significantly lacking, in declining ones. Once again, the first significant such characteristic highlighted from Schwarz's research is empowering leadership, leadership that is focused on the equipping and releasing of all Christians for ministry. The absence of such leadership compromises the health and vitality of any local church and severely restricts its capacity to thrive and grow. One of the more interesting other findings from the research was that the particular leadership factor with the strongest direct correlation to the overall quality and growth of a church was readiness on the part of the leader to accept help from others: it is a collaborative and responsive approach to leadership, as opposed to a more heroic or solitary one, that is usually most beneficial.[21]

The importance of effective leadership as a contributory factor towards the health and growth of a local church is further underlined by some recent research conducted among English Anglican churches by Professor David Voas and Laura Watt.[22] Two findings are of particular interest to us. First, the likelihood of a church to grow is directly correlated to the presence of leadership that might be termed effective:

When asked about strengths in motivating people, more than three quarters of clergy who say they are better than most people at motivating people, inspiring, and generating enthusiasm to action, lead growing churches. Among those who admit to being less able in this respect, growth is reported by just over a third.[23]

While the role and contribution of clergy as visionary and inspirational leaders is clearly significant here, another recurring leadership motif also comes to the fore as being equally significant:

> The research shows that good quality lay leadership is linked to growth ... A church where volunteers are involved in leadership and where roles are rotated regularly is likely to be growing – especially where younger members and new members are included in lay leadership and service.[24]

Once again it seems that the kind of leadership that has a positive effect not only on the fruitfulness of any organization but also, presumably, on the sense of well-being and empowerment of its members is leadership that is releasing and enabling, and that works towards the dispersal of leadership within the organization in a manner that goes beyond those with designated leadership positions or titles.

## A leadership vacuum

Ladkin[25] suggests that it is often in the nature of leadership to be invisible or simply taken for granted. We can, she implies, understand more about leadership and the purpose it serves when it is missing and thus when we experience the lack of the contribution it is designed to make.

As we shall see when we consider more fully some common objections to leadership, an aversion to leadership is often prompted by a suspicion that any leadership must automatically involve an abusive and controlling use of power. Such a presumed inevitability leads to the conclusion that we will usually do better by rejecting leadership altogether. Western,[26] although critical of many historic understandings of and assumptions about leadership, dismisses the possibility of leaderless organizations and highlights the dangers inherent in denying the possibility of leadership. In such situations, he suggests, certain consequences follow:

### 1 *Leadership reappears under a different name*

This may be for a number of reasons. The absence of formal leadership often creates a sense of anxiety and uncertainty and a fear that activities and actions that appear important might be overlooked. Responsibility is assumed for such actions not by a properly appointed person but rather by someone who feels that something needs to be done, and done in a particular way. In churches and other voluntary organizations, custom and informal tradition begin to govern what is done and by whom, and begin to take on a leading role.

Sometimes a resistance towards formal leadership may be a strategy for concealing the ways in which power is being exercised. Those who resist the establishment of formal leadership procedures and practices may have an interest in clinging on to de facto power and influence that would otherwise be threatened. The toddler group volunteer who has presided informally over a coordinating group for a number of years and who insists that 'we get along just fine as we are without any formal constitution or leadership structure' may actually be exercising strong and directive leadership that ensures that tight control can be maintained over every aspect of the group without any accountability.

## 2 Group and power dynamics become distorted and informal oligarchies begin to form

This phenomenon often occurs, and is by no means uncommon in churches, when individual groups or ministry teams lose sight of their connectedness to the whole of the church. Rather than understanding the place they occupy within the wider organization and ordering their own life, activities and allocation of resources accordingly, they assert an exclusive right to self-determination in decision-making. This often comes about when leadership has been lacking or when there has been a habitual refusal on the part of overall leaders to challenge the group and hold it to account. One of the most important responsibilities of a church leader is to enable all those with delegated responsibility for the oversight of other groups and ministry areas to understand how their own area of responsibility meshes with other similar areas in the life of the church and to foster a collaborative and symbiotic relationship between all such groups.

## 3 People find themselves in roles with responsibility and accountability yet no authority or power

Because one of the important functions of leadership is to provide a context and framework in which others can exercise power and authority appropriately, where leadership is absent such facilitation of others often breaks down. Indeed, those with responsibility may find themselves disempowered by virtue of the fact that power has been seized inappropriately by individuals or groups in the absence of authorized leadership. This may be the case, for example, with a person entrusted with responsibility for overseeing and developing a church's work with children yet who is denied resources necessary for such work by a church treasurer who maintains an iron grip on the disbursement of church funds and who remains unchallenged in this.

### 4 Group narcissism takes hold of the organization

One of the key roles of leadership is to enable the organization to keep looking beyond itself and to maintain focus on its core purposes. As Stephen Cottrell puts it, 'The leader is the one who dares the whole organisation to stop for a minute and take time out to remember why they are there.'[27]

This is particularly critical for a church that, in the immortal words of a former Archbishop of Canterbury, 'exists for the benefit of those which are not yet its members'.[28] Christian leadership is called to deliver a church from the tendency merely to remain comfortable with the status quo, and to enable it to cultivate a more holistic concern for the needy world it is called to serve and to reach. In the absence of such leadership, churches, in keeping with any other group or organization faced with similar circumstances, tend to become absorbed with internal concerns or simply with securing their own survival, and lose sight of their wider, outward-facing purpose.

Effective leadership brings a sense of proper order and creates an environment in which others enjoy security and the opportunity to contribute appropriately. All of which explains why there is so often a particular desire for the establishment of leadership expressed by those who have suffered in a context where such leadership has been absent.

## The goods of leadership

We have considered some of the factors that make leadership seem desirable, at least in the eyes of some. What might be the specific goods of leadership that are particularly sought by others or that make leadership appear especially beneficial? The following is by no means an exhaustive list but represents a number of contributions made to an organization by effective leadership.

### 1 Sense-making

One of the most frequent challenges facing God's people in both Old and New Testaments is that of remembering who they are and the purposes to which God has called them. External threats and complacency and disillusionment from within all conspire to bring discouragement, leading the people to doubt not only their calling but even the very goodness or power of God. Today, the challenges facing the Christian community, especially in the post-Christian, Western world, as it seeks to follow and to represent Christ, are very similar. Recognizing itself to be an increasingly marginalized group whose moral values seem more and more ridiculous to a pleasure-obsessed culture, and whose founder's insistence on self-sacrifice and self-denial could not be more at odds with the unrestrained individualism that is the dominant cultural value of our age, and faced with ignorance, apathy and, increasingly, antipathy from others, it is hardly surprising that people are disheartened and confused. Stories and experience of decline make us wonder if God is still at work or if he, too, has given things up as a bad job. It is easy to find ourselves wondering if our own work and witness, our own contribution, really matters and whether the challenges we face and the effort we expend are really worthwhile.

Perhaps the most significant contribution made by many of the notable leaders we encounter in the Bible is their capacity to enable the people for whom they are responsible to recognize afresh the purposes for which they exist and to see their own work as meaningful and as somehow contributing to the accomplishment of those purposes. One of the clearest examples of such leadership is Nehemiah, appointed governor of Jerusalem in the mid-fifth century BC in the aftermath of the return of a number of Jewish people to Jerusalem after years of exile in Babylon. Given permission to rebuild their ruined city, the early attempts of these settlers to do so have been cruelly thwarted by local rulers and luminaries. Nehemiah, on his own arrival in Jerusalem, finds there only broken stones and profoundly dispirited people. Simply urging people to make another attempt would have been entirely futile. However, Nehemiah understands that a rebuilt Jerusalem is somehow central to God's purposes and that rebuilding is more than a human endeavour. Moreover, he comes with the conviction that as God has shown himself faithful in the past, so he is more than able to help his people overcome their current local difficulties. Nehemiah sets the work of the people against a wider backdrop such that it suddenly becomes the greatest imperative facing them. Thus inspired, every single sector of the population now joins together and accomplishes the remarkable feat of completing the rebuilding of the city wall within an extraordinary 52 days.

In an age that sees the Christian faith as making very little sense, the calling of the Christian leader is to enable others to see beyond the clamour of the world and to recognize that the Christian story is, in fact, the true story of human existence and that the most worthwhile enterprise in which we might expend our own efforts is that of the advance of God's kingdom. We do this by retelling the story of God in such a way that others are enabled to see their own place in it and to respond faithfully in challenging and unfamiliar life circumstances.

Other writers reflecting on entirely different contexts also remark on the sense-making role of leadership. So, Goffee and Jones comment on the longing of workers to know that what they do has meaning and significance. They desire to feel themselves to be part of something bigger: 'Leadership is not only about performance and results but also about meaning; leaders at all levels make a difference to performance and do so because they make performance meaningful.'[29]

Harvey refers to the role of leaders in framing stories and events in order to help the group understand the world, themselves and other groups,[30] a quality John Harris insists is vital for effective political leadership:

> The best politicians inspire, but part of their job is also to orientate: to survey an often confounding set of national circumstances, and tell us not just where we all are, but also what our position means and where we need to go next.[31]

Smircich and Morgan suggest that it may be this very capacity, to make sense of things in a way that enables action, that both propels people into leadership and that becomes the validation of that leadership:

> Within groups people are recognised as being leaders because they are seen to frame experience in a way that provides a viable basis for action by mobilising meaning, articulating and defining what has previously remained implicit or unsaid, by inventing images and meanings that provide a focus for new attention, by consolidating, confronting or challenging prevailing wisdom.[32]

One of the reasons for the peculiar impact newly arrived leaders are able to effect in some situations is that they are often able to own and articulate more clearly the foundational narratives or purposes of an enterprise; they are often less affected than those who have been present for any length of time by the challenges that tend to skew our own perspectives and rob our efforts of sense and meaning.

## 2 Animation

Different writers and theorists offer varying accounts of the impact of leaders on organizations and people. It is certainly the case that in some circumstances, certain forms of leadership have the capacity to exercise a coercive influence on others within the organization, deploying strong power in order to produce a particular effect. Such leadership methods almost invariably produce very limited and exclusively short-term results. The detrimental effect of the inhibition of longer-lasting and more far-reaching commitment often outweighs the gains. We prefer to see the agency of leadership as being far more catalytic than purely instrumental, and see the role of leadership as one of animating the organization and its members in such a way that each person is enabled and inspired to play a full part in the furtherance of the organization's goals. Thus James Dunn observes:

> Effective leadership provides a catalyst for action, and the Christian leader, adopting the stance of servant, focuses the attention of those (s)he leads on the purpose and plan of God as it affects them, and facilitates the actions needed to bring it about.[33]

In the same vein, Maccoby refers to the urgent need for unearthing leaders, as these are the ones who are uniquely gifted in mobilizing human intelligence and energy to grapple with threats and to respond to the vast opportunities for improvement that present themselves to us.[34] The question may well be asked as to why leadership is required in order for the contribution of others to be released and why this simply cannot happen spontaneously? There are, perhaps, two factors to consider here: the needs for affirmation and permission.

It is often the case that people are somewhat diffident when it comes to taking on responsibility, often because of their own assessment of their gifts and capabilities as being inadequate. It frequently takes another either to recognize or at least to affirm the particular qualities that a person might have to contribute, and that might add value to the work of the organization or further the work and ministry of a church. One of the striking things about the ministry of Jesus was his habit of recognizing unforeseen potential in others and giving them a vision for, and opportunity to have a go at, the ministry to which God may well have been calling them. All manner of factors, including lack of education or experience, previous disappointment or discouragement, lack of affirmation or a sense of not fitting the mould, hold people back from reckoning that they may have such a part to play. Effective leadership offers appropriate affirmation as well as ongoing investment and encouragement, which enables a person to move beyond some of the stumbling blocks that appear to block the way to fruitful service.

While, as we have noted, a lack of leadership does not always prevent the wrong people seizing power and exercising influence inappropriately, the resulting context is rarely one in which others emerge into service or leadership. Emerging ministry and leadership flourishes in a context where there is appropriate and legitimate oversight and in the knowledge that one has proper permission to exercise one's own role. Such permission creates a sense of order in which emerging leaders are able to feel secure as they step into new roles and in which the recipients of their ministry are clear that such new leaders are properly authorized by those entrusted with oversight of the church or organization.

## 3 Alignment

Anyone who has played team sport at any level understands that in almost all contexts what matters more than the individual skills of the various team members is the capacity and discipline of the team to play in a coordinated and organized manner. Clearly, to have both a high component of individual skills and a strongly coordinated team ethos is a winning combination. However, it is often the case that teams with a strong sense of alignment are able to outperform more individually skilful but less cohesive opponents.[35]

Alignment describes a concern to enable an organization to maintain focus on a clear and established purpose without distraction or confusion, and to facilitate the coordination of the efforts of those involved in the achievement of such purposes without dissipation of effort and energy. Alignment is not something that can be imposed upon a group or organization, but is rather something that comes about as individual members choose to commit to a common purpose and goals. Effective organizations often develop strategies for sustaining and maintaining alignment, but the role of the leader is critical when it comes to facilitating such alignment in the first instance.

Although usually couched in slightly different terms, the role of the leader in uniting the people of God around a common understanding, common values and enabling participation in a common mission has been central to Christian understandings of leadership from the earliest times.[36] Originating in the works of some of the Ante-Nicene fathers, and reiterated in Christian liturgies of ordination today, is the notion that the episkopos, the one exercising oversight, is intended by God to be a focus for unity, for the whole body of Christ. Such an understanding emerged at a time of immense turmoil and challenge for the early Christian communities faced with threats to their existence from without and to their identity from within. The issue of creating and maintaining alignment is a concern of leadership at all times but perhaps especially when the cohesion of any organization or body is threatened for whatever reason.

Perhaps one of the most notable illustrations of such leadership in recent memory has been that of Nelson Mandela. Inaugurated as the first black president of South Africa in 1994 after centuries of colonial rule, and in the immediate aftermath of the apartheid regime, Mandela inherited a nation still bitterly divided by resentment and suspicion. Determined to forge a new economy in which South Africans of all hues and ethnicities felt themselves equally to be full stakeholders and citizens, Mandela's inauguration speech[37] was a masterful first step in the accomplishment of what many felt to be an almost impossible task. Without compromise to the clear demands for change made by the country's electorate, and without minimizing the pain and distress of the past, especially that suffered by the black and coloured communities, Mandela refused to present himself as the champion of one, newly victorious section of the populace, 'as a conqueror prescribing to the conquered'. In his speech he called to mind moments of significance from his nation's history with particular resonance for the different groups, each of which made up the new 'rainbow nation'. As well as highlighting the struggle of the ANC, and its resistance to the evils of apartheid, and as well as drawing attention to the notorious prison of Robben Island where he himself spent so many years, visible from the place where he was delivering his speech, Mandela referenced the arrival of both European settlers and Indonesian slaves, 'among them many princes and scholars', the forbears of the Cape coloured community. In setting forth the primacy of principles such as democracy and justice, Mandela placed himself and all the South

African people under a higher authority and set before the nation the vision of a future in which the wounds of the past were healed and a new order established for all. He concluded by expressing his confidence that this was a challenge to which he was certain all would rise.

In the days that followed, Mandela's actions demonstrated that this speech was far more than merely lofty aspirations. To the horror of some of his close colleagues, the new president insisted on appointing to positions of senior responsibility in state and government not only members of his own ruling ANC party but also some of his former enemies and some of the staunchest advocates of the previous apartheid regime. He was also concerned to present himself as a president not only for his own black community but truly for the whole nation. In a remarkable symbolic act, for the final of the 1995 Rugby World Cup, held in South Africa, Mandela chose to wear a South Africa rugby team shirt. At that time the national team, the Springboks, had always been made up exclusively of white players,[38] and the Springbok shirt had been something of an apartheid era totem. Now Mandela was claiming it for the whole nation while standing firmly with the sporting heritage it represented. The crowning glory of the moment was, of course, the fact that, against most odds and expectations, South Africa won the final and were crowned world champions, Mandela presenting the trophy, resplendent in his team shirt.

The success of South Africa in the immediate post-apartheid period was significantly due to the leadership of Nelson Mandela and to how this leadership enabled a divided nation to find healing and a way forward in the light of a greater common purpose. Mandela articulated that purpose in a way that elicited widespread commitment to seeing it achieved, and also became the primary and very visible example of what it might look like to see this purpose worked out. Whatever our sphere of concern, whether a nation, a business, a church or a sports team, alignment is brought about through the agency of leadership that is able to articulate purpose and vision in a clear and compelling way and that enables others to see how their own interests and concerns might be achieved through subscribing to such a common vision. However, no matter how compelling our vision and how persuasive our language, if its articulation is not supported by actions consistent with such purpose, or if our behaviour in any way undermines our words, then we are unlikely to see real alignment come about. Leaders who facilitate alignment tend to be those who have so deeply appropriated the purpose and goals of their organization that this seeps out of every pore of their being.

As is evident from the career of Nelson Mandela, alignment is in many ways enabled by careful attention to sense-making and is a further consequence of the proper ordering of an organization. Churches or other organizations that are able to engage in common work are those in which the efforts, gifts, insights and other contributions of constituent members and workers are deployed in a coordinated and ordered fashion.

## 4 Problem-solving

One of the paradoxes of twenty-first-century Western culture is the coexistence of a deep suspicion of power and authority exercised in a direct and instrumental fashion, and the fascination with superhero movies. New movies of this genre seem to hit the cinema screens almost on a monthly basis, outperforming, in terms of attendances and gross earnings, almost every other genre of film. Although the plots, and even the principal characters, are increasingly more complex and nuanced, each share one central, common feature; there is a crisis, often of catastrophic dimension, to be averted, a world to be rescued and a superhero with extraordinary powers who is uniquely able to effect this.

Perhaps this popular recourse to escapism is a subtle acknowledgement that our contemporary world and the experience of life for those who inhabit it is increasingly fraught with problems for which we have few answers. Perhaps it is indicative of our longing for someone to step in and solve them for us. It appeared to many external observers that it was precisely such aspirations that saw Donald Trump elected to the presidency of the USA in November 2016. Dismissed as not morally fit to lead by former officials, ridiculed by younger generations for whom he represents the last death throes of the world their parents and grandparents sought to create, Trump became a hero to a significant swathe of (predominantly) white, blue-collar Americans. For them he represented the hope of the restoration of a lost world after whose return this constituency hanker, a hero figure who would 'make America great again'.[39]

In suggesting that one of the goods of leadership is problem-solving we are by no means advocating that leaders adopt a heroic leadership style in the hope of sorting things out singlehandedly through the deployment of superhuman abilities. While rescue might be effected through the agency of heroic leaders on the screen or in the pages of comic books, in real life problem-solving is somewhat more complex. Furthermore, the Trump presidency with its affinity for such a form of leadership seems, at least to many observers, to have created rather more problems than it has thus far managed to solve. Rather, we are advocating a form of leadership that enables people across the organization to work together to find solutions to the problems that confront them. Once again, the leader plays a catalytic and releasing role. However, effective problem-solving requires further contributions from the leader.

One of the leadership gifts is the capacity to recognize problems that others have failed to identify as issues. It may well be because leaders are unashamedly future focused, always paying attention to where the organization is heading and never quite satisfied with its current state of development, that they experience a higher level of dissatisfaction with the status quo than do other people. As Keith Lamdin observes:

Leaders know what is not right about their organisations. I call this discontent, and it is discontent in the heart of anybody that stirs the desire to lead. Knowing that something is not right often brings with it an idea about how it could be better.[40]

And if leadership involves, as we have advocated, a deep and intimate connection to the very heart of an organization and its purposes such that these become embodied in the very being of a leader, then, as Cottrell suggests:

Of all the upside-down wisdom that the Christian Church offers to the world, perhaps the greatest is that the leader should so embody the purposes and values of the organisation that he or she feels the pain more keenly than anyone else.[41]

It is often such pain and discontent that enable leaders to uncover problems and then articulate them to the wider organization. It is equally a conviction that such problems are not insoluble that enables leaders to impart confidence to the wider organization and to galvanize that organization into uncovering or devising appropriate solutions.

## 5 Hope

Stanley McChrystal[42] suggests that leaders may well be recognized and embraced not primarily on the basis of past or present achievements but rather on the basis of future promise. Followers see leaders as credible because they represent the hope of a better future, or because what they appear to promise resonates with the hopes and aspirations of that group of followers. Perhaps it is their capacity to lift others to attempt things they would not have otherwise contemplated, through the telling of stories and the alignment of people and groups around a shared purpose, that means that positive leadership is associated with the gift of hope and why leaders are often described as 'dealers in hope'. Given the contemporary spiritual climate in the UK and the challenges facing local churches and individual church members, one of the most valuable contributions church leaders are called to make is that of bringing fresh hope to their congregations. The biblical narratives are a rich resource for us in this task. Emerging mainly from contexts in which God's people were experiencing profound challenges and difficulties, not only do they point us to God and to his great works in history, they also contain some wonderful personal reflection and meditation on these works from the perspective of those for whom such challenges were intensely personal and focused. Hope grows as leaders rehearse these stories, tell of their own personal experience of God's trustworthiness, and equip others to reframe their lives in the light of these truths. Hope stimulates a belief that things could be different and that change is possible.

Perhaps it is this understanding of leadership as providing hope that lay behind Henry Kissinger's famous definition of leadership as being 'the art of taking people where they would not have gone by themselves'.[43]

Our brief exploration of some of the contributions made by good leadership, and of the dangers of neglecting leadership, may have gone some way to answering the question of why leadership is, at least in some quarters, seen as desirable. This may in turn explain why there is such a proliferation of writing on and about leadership. However, despite this plethora of literature and other resources, there is little real agreement therein on what we mean by leadership. Indeed, on occasions, we have already had to explain what we do not mean when we speak of leadership. Perhaps, before we go any further, we need to attempt some definition of leadership and spend some time exploring the anatomy of leadership and unpacking some of the ways in which it has variously been explained. This will be the subject of our next chapter.

## Excursus: leadership and ministry

It is, perhaps, at this juncture worth a short excursus on the relationship, and differences, between leadership and what we might describe as *ministry*. These two phrases are often used interchangeably, not least because, in the life of the Church, the same people have historically been likely to be expected to perform both functions, and because it is fashionable to refer to those selected for church leadership as being called into the ministry. The danger in such a confusion of terms is that it almost inevitably leads to the neglect of leadership as it is edged out by the demands of ministry.[44] And the consequent danger of this, as we shall see, is that neglecting leadership always leads to a diminishing in the capacity of the whole Church to engage in ministry.

We understand ministry to refer to any activity performed in some way at the initiative of, on behalf of or out of obedience to God and that serves the needs of others. The objective is the blessing of others. Given our description of leadership as somehow to do with the enabling and mobilization of others, we distinguish it from ministry by suggesting that leadership is any activity that directs, influences or facilitates ministry by others.[45] The mark of effective ministry is that others are helped; the mark of effective leadership is that others are enlisted and enabled to share in the work of ministry. As Simon Walker observes:

I want to suggest that the only proper goal of leadership is this: to enable people to take responsibility. Leadership is concerned with the task of helping people to move towards fully mature, responsible personhood. Everything else is secondary.[46]

One of the reasons that many church congregations remain static numerically, never quite growing beyond the 100-member ceiling, is that this is the number, it has been estimated, that one more than fully stretched minister can just about care for. New people may be added to this church, but existing people will certainly leave as their own pastoral needs are neglected. If a church leader expends all or most of her time on serving the needs of others, she will experience exhaustion through overwork, and frustration that there is always more to do and yet little obvious fruit from her labours. The leader who is prepared to embrace the work of neglecting some of the pressing pastoral needs for a season in order to envision and equip others to fulfil these and other ministry tasks not only, ultimately, sees far more accomplished but is also freer to engage in some of the core leadership activities for which others long and which we have explored in this chapter. Such a leader is far more likely to see growth and health in her church, and the church becomes far better placed to fulfil its calling to be a blessing to the wider community.

Although Jesus engages in a good deal of what we have termed 'ministry' throughout his public career, from the very earliest stages of that career he is concerned to develop others and enlarge his kingdom workforce. In the later stages of his career he spends a much greater proportion of his time enabling a small group of others to take responsibility. This, above all, provides a pattern for productive Christian leadership.

## Notes

1 Bolden, R., 2004, *What is Leadership?*, Leadership South West Research Report, Exeter, www.leadershipsouthwest.com (accessed 25 November 2019).

2 Dugan, J. P., 2017, *Leadership Theory: Cultivating Critical Perspectives*, San Francisco, CA: Jossey-Bass, p. xv.

3 Detailed examination of some of the most prevalent objections to the idea of leadership, and proper engagement with some of the key dissenting voices, is to be found in Chapter 5 below.

4 Perhaps the best-known leadership dictum attributed to him is, 'A leader is

best when people barely know he exists, when his work is done, his aim fulfilled, they will say: we did it ourselves.'

5 Maccoby, M., 2007, *The Leaders We Need*, Boston, MA: Harvard Business School Press, p. 7.

6 Harvey, M., 'Leadership and the Human Condition', in Goethals, G. R. and Sorenson, G. L. J. (eds), 2006, *The Quest for a General Theory of Leadership*, Cheltenham: Edward Elgar.

7 Hobbes, T. and Tuck, R. (eds), 1991, *Hobbes: Leviathan*, Cambridge: Cambridge University Press, p. 90.

8 Kellerman, B., 2008, *Followership*, Boston, MA: Harvard Business Review Press, p. 49.

9 Sinclair, A., 2007, *Leadership for the Disillusioned*, Crows Nest, NSW: Allen & Unwin, p. 8.

10 Heifetz, R. A., 1994, *Leadership without Easy Answers*, Cambridge, MA: The Belknap Press of Harvard University Press.

11 See p. 219 below.

12 We include here leadership literature in which leadership is perceived as simply deploying tried and tested strategies for the solution of established problems.

13 Heifetz, *Leadership without Easy Answers*, p. 35.

14 Heifetz, R. A. and Linsky, M., 2002, *Leadership on the Line*, Boston, MA: Harvard Business School Press, p. 127.

15 Collins, J., 2001, *Good to Great*, London: Random House.

16 Collins, *Good to Great*, p. 22.

17 Collins, *Good to Great*, p. 35.

18 Laloux, F., 2014, *Reinventing Organizations*, Brussels: Nelson Parker.

19 Laloux, *Reinventing Organizations*, p. 41.

20 The principal research is written up in Schwarz, C. A., 1996, *Natural Church Development Handbook*, Moggerhanger: British Church Growth Association.

21 Schwarz, *Handbook*, p. 23.

22 Voas, D. and Watt, L., 2014, *The Church Growth Research Programme*. The most substantial findings of this research were published in The Church Commissioners for England, 2014, *From Anecdote to Evidence*, London: The Archbishops' Council.

23 *From Anecdote to Evidence*, p. 10.

24 *From Anecdote to Evidence*, p. 12.

25 Ladkin, D., 2010, *Rethinking Leadership*, Cheltenham: Edward Elgar, p. 46.

26 Western, S., 2013, *Leadership: A Critical Text*, London: Sage, p. 72.

27 Cottrell, S., 2008, *Hit the Ground Kneeling*, London: Church House Publishing, p. 42.

28 William Temple (1881–1944).

29 Goffee, R. and Jones, G., 2006, *Why Should Anyone be Led by You?*, Boston, MA: Harvard Business School Press.

30 Harvey, 'Leadership and the Human Condition', p. 42.

31 Harris, J., 'Where's Jeremy Corbyn? Lost in a Rose-tinted Vision of Labour's Past', *The Guardian*, 25 June 2018.

32 Smircich, L. and Morgan, G., 1982, '"Leadership": The Management of Meaning', *Journal of Applied Behavioral Science* 18 (3), p. 258, quoted in Ladkin, *Rethinking Leadership*, p. 103.

33 Dunn, J., 1995, *The Effective Leader*, Eastbourne: Kingsway.

34 Maccoby, *The Leaders We Need*, p. xv.

35 A fascinating insight into this is provided by De Rond, M., 2012, *There Is an I in Team*, Boston, MA: Harvard Business Review Press, pp. 1–23.

36 It is articulated clearly, for example, in Cyprian's *The Unity of the Church*.

37 Delivered in Cape Town on 9 May 1994: www.southafrica.to/people/Quotes/NelsonMandela/Nelson-Mandela-inauguration.htm (accessed 25 November 2019).

38 Despite the existence of black and coloured rugby teams and leagues, players from these teams were not eligible for selection for the national side.

39 This was the campaign slogan of the 2016 Trump presidential campaign.

40 Lamdin, K., 2012, *Finding Your Leadership Style*, London: SPCK.

41 Cottrell, *Hit the Ground Kneeling*, p. 66.

42 McChrystal, S., 2018, *Leaders: Myth and Reality*, London: Portfolio Penguin.

43 Quoted in Gill, R., 2011, *Theory and Practice of Leadership*, London: Sage, p. 117.

44 The 2015 FAOC Senior Church Leadership Report (s85) stresses the importance of distinguishing between 'the specific task of *leadership* and the varied ministry tasks that church leaders have accumulated over time'.

45 Jagelman, I., 1998, *The Empowered Church*, Adelaide: Openbook, p. 9.

46 Walker, S. P., 2010, *The Undefended Leader*, Carlisle: Piquant Editions, p. 153.

# 2

# Defining Leadership

*'When I use a word,' Humpty Dumpty said, in a rather scornful tone, 'it means just what I choose it to mean – neither more nor less.'*[1]

Sir Alex Ferguson has good reason to be described as possibly the most successful football manager of all time. Not only did he win every trophy for which any English club team might compete, and some several times over, he sustained success at the highest level for his football club for more than two decades. In an era when the average tenure for an English football manager is 15 months,[2] and when most managerial careers end without the team having won any competition, his was a remarkable career in every way. His book, *Leading*,[3] is a description of the methods and strategies, and personal traits, that lay behind his remarkable career. It is hardly surprising that the book is offered as something of a blueprint for how success might be achieved in the high-octane world of professional sport, and for the kind of leadership required to bring this about. A final chapter uses Ferguson's experience to frame some more generic leadership principles, which are offered as being applicable more widely.

On the same shelf in my study where *Leading* resides are two other books, each one also purporting to deal with the broad topic of leadership. Both are written by academics, one a leadership consultant with a background in the health and social care industry, the other an anthropologist. The word *leadership* is used widely in all three books. Yet the activities and emphases described by this word and its cognates in the different books seem at times to have little in common with each other. Indeed, at times it is hard to tell whether what is described as leadership in Ferguson's book would actually pass muster as leadership in the terms set out by the anthropologist. By the same token, I imagine that Ferguson himself would dismiss the social care leadership consultant's exposition of leadership processes as not the way one wins trophies.

## A multifaceted phenomenon

Given the importance we have accorded to leadership in the previous chapter, it would seem to be a matter of some importance to be able to define what exactly we mean by leadership and to be able to describe accurately what effective leadership looks like. However, this appears to be far from straightforward. Although there is no shortage of leadership definitions in the abundance of leadership literature, such definitions as do exist are by no means all in agreement when it comes to the essence of, or basis for, leadership. Indeed, some definitions are so profoundly contradictory and critical of others that they almost appear to be describing entirely different activities. This is by no means due to a deficiency in terms of empirical research into leadership, or to a lack of accumulated data to shed light on different facets of leadership practice and experience.[4] Indeed, Burns offers the view that leadership must be one of the most observed and least understood phenomena on earth.[5] What are we to make of this diversity? Perhaps it should serve to alert us, above all, to the fact that the leadership process is somewhat more complex and multi-layered than might initially have been assumed, and that it resists any tendency to oversimplification. We will need to identify some of the several considerations that give rise to variety in the different accounts of leadership and examine the ways in which they shape and influence different approaches to leadership. What might some of these considerations be?

## 1 Context

One of the principal motivations for defining leadership is to arrive at a set of key features, disciplines or dispositions that are integral to good leadership and whose adoption and practice will thus guarantee effectiveness in any and every situation. This is certainly the approach taken by many past and present leadership manuals. The differences in approach manifest in the three excellent books we referenced at the beginning of this chapter, each born out of proven experience, alert us to the fact that leadership may well not be a 'one size fits all' exercise and that the context in which leadership is located may play a significant role in determining the shape of that leadership. A number of factors draw our attention to the contextual nature of leadership.

First, we might say that leadership does not have an identity or purpose independent from that of the organization[6] in which it is located. To this end, leadership might be described as *teleological*, shaped by the end, purpose and intentions (*telos*) of its host organization. If an organization is primarily concerned with success in the world of sport and with winning rather than losing, then there may be many dissimilarities between the leadership it adopts in order to achieve such purposes and the leadership required by an organization that exists to provide social care or other services. By the same token, it is profoundly unhelpful to import uncritically into the sphere of church leadership styles and practices from other contexts whose aims and intentions are at odds with some of the purposes or values of a church, and that have impacted and shaped those styles to such a degree that they are designed to further goals bearing little resemblance to those espoused by a church.[7] The unhelpful consequences of such borrowing are perhaps most clearly seen in the ways in which this affects attitudes to people, and especially to those undertaking responsibility in the church, whether as paid staff members or unpaid office holders. Some business approaches tend to treat staff in a somewhat commodified manner, regarding them as devices to facilitate productivity or profit. In this view, staff are dispensable, and should certainly be removed as efficiently as possible if they fail to meet requirements or if a better alternative might be found. While we believe it to be imperative that churches and their leaders provide proper, structured supervision and performance management for all staff members and others occupying positions of ministry responsibility, and while we recognize that in some cases this might well include helping those not best suited to their current roles to move on well, any tendency to commodify people or to have regard purely for their capacity to contribute must be rejected. Because the Christian Church is concerned for the flourishing of all people, Christian leadership will always be shaped around the furthering of this goal and will refuse leadership styles that threaten this.

Second, a number of later twentieth-century leadership theories began to draw attention to the impact of *situation* upon leadership. Situation in this context might refer to the current state of development of the organization in which leadership was located or the current needs or capacity of those being led. Associated principally with the work of Hersey and Blanchard,[8] the situational approach to leadership posits that different situations require a leader to adapt her leadership style according to the levels of competence and commitment of those whom she is called to lead. Given that the skills and motivations of others are not fixed but change over time, a leader must respond accordingly. Further, followers may well act differently, and thus require different styles of leadership, as they perform different tasks or even during different phases of the same task. Specifically, situational approaches to leadership have in mind the relative emphasis placed by the leader upon directing and supporting followers. Hersey and Blanchard conceived four different leadership styles, each reflecting a different combination of high or low levels of directive and supportive behaviour. They call these delegating, supporting, coaching and directing.[9] Other later writers, not necessarily building on Hersey and Blanchard's work, have similarly recognized that the state of development of an organization and the mindset and experiences of its members shape significantly the kind of leadership that might be required at that moment and have developed even wider ranges of leadership styles. Goleman et al.[10] differentiate between resonant styles of leadership – visionary, coaching, affiliative and democratic – all of which serve to create a harmonious organizational environment in which those involved experience significant motivation to perform. These are the styles that a sensible leader will seek to deploy most of the time. However, especially in moments of crisis or at times when an urgent turnaround is required, it may be necessary to deploy what the authors refer to as dissonant styles of leadership

– pacesetting or commanding leadership styles. This is equally the case in a local church, diocese or voluntary sector organization as it is with, for example, a manufacturing business or other commercial enterprise.

Walker[11] develops the range of available styles further with the addition of two further leadership styles – serving and self-giving.[12] The latter is exemplified supremely by Jesus, by many who have followed him in subsequent ages, by Gandhi and others who have surrendered life, liberty or safety in the face of injustice and evil. Far from being the passive submission to opposing forces that such acts might at first glance appear, in situations of oppression they may well be the most effective way of disarming and undermining superior political and physical power and of exposing immorality and injustice. The surrender of Jesus to crucifixion was the very act that turned the existing world order upside down, while Gandhi's peaceful demonstration against colonial rule and his submission to the brutality of those who held an interest in maintaining the status quo was ultimately the very thing that brought down that rule and resulted in independence for India. The acts of both men were supreme acts of leadership and leadership of a style that was uniquely capable of achieving the ends they had in mind in the particular situations in which their leadership was enacted.

Many prominent leaders have achieved recognition and are celebrated because of their impact in companies, nations, churches or other contexts at a time of crisis, or when urgent action was required in order to halt decline or attend to threatening circumstances. Such leaders are rightly hailed as being good examples of how to act in such situations and much can be learned from them by others facing similar challenges. The danger lies in assuming that such leadership is the best style to adopt in any and every situation and that success in leadership consists in imitating the practices and principles of these commanding or pacesetting leaders at all times and in all places. Some leaders have come unstuck by adopting far too directive and heavy-handed leadership styles in situations calling for far more resonant styles of leadership to be deployed.

Already we are beginning to see how essentially anecdotal leadership writings, arising from contexts in which entirely different styles have been appropriate and productive, might almost seem to be describing completely different activities. For our own purposes, we do well to take seriously the impact that a situation might exert upon our leadership and the ways in which we may be called to act as leaders. A church that has experienced significant disappointment, decline and loss over a period of time may well require leadership styles that are highly supportive, at least in the first instance, and may not respond quite so favourably to more directive approaches. Equally, in the first stages of a pioneering or start-up situation, a more pacesetting approach may be exactly what is required in order to give confidence and to set an example that others might then be empowered to follow. On a more personal note, understanding that leadership has many different styles sets us free from the tyranny of feeling that we have to subscribe to a universal style of leadership modelled or commended by another and yet that feels alien to us. Understanding our own preferred leadership style may well enable us to make more informed choices about the kind of context in which we might choose to exercise our own leadership calling.[13] It may also cause us to be a little more circumspect about any unqualified exhortation to others simply to replicate a previously effective form of leadership without reference to specific context. Semple's warning is clear: 'Leadership is always highly situational and contingent: the leader who succeeds in one context at one point in time won't necessarily succeed in a different context at the same time, or in the same context at a different time.'[14]

## 2 Perspective

If leadership is shaped by the context in which it is located, the way it is described will also be significantly affected by the perspective of the person describing it.

Dugan,[15] among others, draws attention to the fact that every leadership theory is born out of a cultural paradigm whose particular assumptions shape perceptions about the nature of leadership. Thus, one of the tasks for those who wish to enquire into the nature and potential contribution of different leadership theories is first to exegete the cultural and philosophical paradigm and its 'taken for granted' assumptions that undergird such theories. Such paradigms are in one sense neither right nor wrong, but tend to operate as filters that determine which features of any phenomenon (including leadership) we are more or less likely to notice and treat as significant.

An insight into the way in which such assumptions lead to diversity in leadership theory is provided by the series of papers collated by Goethals and Sorenson[16] arising out of a lengthy shared journey undertaken by a group of academics in the early years of this century. Brought together at the instigation of Pulitzer prize-winning author and feted leadership scholar James MacGregor Burns, and representing a number of different academic disciplines, these scholars were charged with the task of formulating a Grand, Unifying Theory of Leadership, which might provide a set of universal leadership principles capable of application in any context or situation. While the quest for such an integrative theory of leadership remains as elusive for these scholars at the end of their five-year journey as it was at the beginning, the bringing together of academics from a range of disciplines, each with a concern for leadership, serves to clarify some key issues to do with the nature of leadership itself. One of the fascinating contrasts in terms of approach to the subject was that evident between those from a social science background, and who adopted, by and large, an empiricist approach, and those from a humanist background, who tended to be more constructivist in approach. For the former, leadership was something 'given' and to be observed. Those in the latter camp were far more concerned to see leadership as somehow socially constructed and thus to probe those phenomena that precipitated and contributed to its construction.

The collection of papers is significant not just for the different leadership insights they offer, but also for offering a window on to what dialogue between different paradigms might look like and how joint learning can lead to a richer and more nuanced understanding of leadership. To neglect the valid insights of others whose essential paradigm may differ from our own may impoverish our own understanding of leadership and thus create limitations in the way in which we engage in leadership practice. So, drawing on the insights of the contributors to this particular symposium, overlooking the social dimensions of leadership, and specifically the ways in which leadership is permitted and enabled by groups of people, may well put us at risk of failing to secure or maintain legitimacy for the leadership in which we engage. By the same token, failure to take into account empirical evidence or data relating to observable good practice in leadership disciplines may result in ineffectual leadership or a tendency towards organizational narcissism.

Maccoby[17] suggests that perspective on leadership may also be shaped significantly by formative personal experiences. Drawing on the Freudian notion of transference, described here as the emotional glue that binds people to a leader, he explores what it is that prompts us to idealize particular leaders or notions of leadership. In the era of modernity, suggests Maccoby, the experience of most people was that of growing up in a father-led household. The sense of stability experienced (even in dysfunctional households) caused people generally to idealize the paternalistic and hierarchical notions of leadership, which were largely unquestioned in the modern age. By contrast, Maccoby observes, those who have grown up in more recent decades have had very different family experiences. For an increasing number of people, the significant person from their formative years may not be a parent but a sibling or a close friend. Our idealized leader thus becomes not someone to whom we might defer without question but one with whom we might collaborate in an interactive manner. Such preferences for leadership are not offered up as having either a positive or negative impact, but simply as a phenomenon that must be properly observed and taken into account. In common with any socially constructed belief, transference functions as a powerful framer of reality for people, which resists being changed. Developing Maccoby's ideas further, we might add that transference may well be fuelled by positive or negative experiences of leadership from churches or other organizations with which people have been involved in the past and which have thus shaped what they expect from current leaders. It is far from uncommon for people joining a new church to project on to that church and its leadership unrealistic hopes, fears and expectations imported from elsewhere, and which may remain hidden under the surface while nevertheless significantly shaping attitudes and behaviours.

### 3 Tendency to oversimplify

There is an understandable human tendency to want to simplify complex entities and this is evident in a good deal of leadership writing. The drive towards simplification may well be motivated by a desire to enable greater understanding and, in the case of leadership, is certainly motivated by a concern to identify core insights, activities and dispositions that can be imitated as a means to securing better leadership practice. However, a concern for simplicity and a fear of complexity can easily result in a tendency to reductionism and oversimplification. The usual consequence of this is an overemphasis on those features of the leadership process that are more immediately evident and a neglect of features that are more hidden or less easily defined. This is very likely the reason why so many early, and not a few current, leadership theories tend to focus almost exclusively on the person and activity of the leader, usually the most visible actor in the leadership process. This may further be encouraged by what Meindl[18] and his colleagues refer to as the *romance of leadership*, the tendency on the part of others to believe that a single leader has the power to change reality by virtue of their own agency, and the desire for such powerful leaders to exist. A realization that leadership is a rather more nuanced process and that, for example, a leader may perhaps not truly be a leader if they do not have people following them, has led more recently to a proliferation of writing on *followership*. For some writers, followers are those who authorize, empower and shape leaders,[19] and thus any description of the leadership process might best be undertaken from the perspective of the relationship that exists between followers and leaders. The precise nature of such a relationship is clearly much harder to define and quantify, which may be why it has been overlooked previously. While followership must be added to the mix in constructing any cohesive leadership theory, it is worth noting that it is equally possible to oversimplify leadership theory by stressing the place of followers to the detriment of other key features.

The difficulties we encounter in defining leadership should not alarm us unduly. To this extent, leadership finds common ground with most other significant intellectual disciplines, few of which, it has been noted, have a widely accepted overarching theory.[20] That said, what are we to make of the existence of such a range of different, and at times apparently competing, theories of leadership and of the various leadership insights they represent?

We have already referred to Gill's insight that the various leadership theories might be likened to complementary pieces in a jigsaw. While this insight has much merit, even this perhaps does not adequately reflect the tension that exists between some conflicting theories. Ladkin[21] offers the more helpful metaphor of a *cube* as a means to understand the essence of leadership. A cube, Ladkin notes, has six sides, not all of them visible at the same time. However, the lack of visibility of one side at any time does not prevent it from existing in one's imagination, of our being aware of its existence. Thus, the sides of leadership might include the person or people conceived of as leaders, followers, the community in which leadership takes place, and the historical situation that has brought all this about. Even Ladkin's offering may have limitations in helping us get to the heart of leadership. Elizabeth Faier[22] argues against any tendency to atomize the leadership process through focusing on elements or parts of leadership that even together cannot hope to encapsulate its essence. Rather, leadership must be seen as a process, 'something greater than the aggregate of its parts'. Perhaps, as Joanne Ciulla[23] has suggested, the difference in leadership theories derives not so much from the different elements of leadership referenced in each theory but rather on the way in which these elements are put together and allowed to bleed into each other.

Each different leadership theory has tended to focus on one particular leadership element, one of Ladkin's 'sides', as a lens through which the whole process is viewed. The different theories can be roughly grouped into three broad categories according to the particular lens employed. Some view leadership through the person of the leader, others through the relationship between leaders and followers, while still others view it as a more complex social process, the property of a wider group or organization. Let us explore some of the key contributions and insights of these different theories in a little more depth.[24]

## Leader-centred theories

Leader-centred theories tend to see leadership as being in some way related to a property residing in the leader. Different theories, and different eras, have variously identified different properties as being foundational in terms of leadership roles and identities.

### 1 Trait-based leadership

The earliest Western leadership theories sought to identify those innate, and often immutable, qualities, abilities and characteristics that were possessed by the great leaders in every age. Effective leadership, it was assumed, is predicated on having a leader who possesses a certain set of traits. One of the underlying premises of these early approaches was, of course, that leaders are generally born rather than made. Thus, early trait theory is designed to identify those with a particular predisposition for leadership and who are thus most likely to emerge as leaders in any situation.

The assumptions of early trait-based approaches were called into question by the growth of situational theories of leadership in the mid-twentieth century[25] and the recognition that different contexts called for different leadership skills and activities. Although falling out of favour, trait theory has resurfaced in a revised form in some more recent leadership theories. Transformational theories[26] suggest that a leader's capacity to inspire followers, to commend and communicate vision, to solve problems and to create culture are each critical for the creation of effective leadership. Theories of emotional intelligence[27] describe a range of leadership competencies to do with self-awareness and relational capabilities that are seen as crucial and tend to be identified as innate qualities: 'As we have pointed out, emotional intelligence accounts for 85 to 90 per cent of the difference between outstanding leaders and their more average peers.'[28]

Often described now as leadership competencies rather than traits,[29] and usually presented as qualities that, although coming more instinctively to some, can be learned by others, the contribution of contemporary trait-based approaches is in identifying factors that are able to shape leadership outcomes positively.[30] Northouse[31] identifies a number of traits that are consistently identified in research as being of most significance (intelligence, self-confidence, determination, integrity and sociability) and that are thus commended as worth cultivating and developing by the leader who would be successful.

The positive contribution made by trait theories is the way in which they shed light on the role of the leader in the wider leadership process and the way in which they provide a focus for leadership learning and development. By the same token, the weakness of these theories is the way in which they can serve to over-idealize or overemphasize the role of the leader to the detriment of other sides of the leadership process. It is also, of course, the case that the more innate or instinctive (as opposed to learned) is a particular trait, the less able we are to reflect on it, hone it and adjust when we experience failure or setback. Thus those who have learned particular competencies may well have the capacity to develop them much more fully and reflectively than those who are more naturally competent.

Trait theory is frequently criticized for its tendency to subjectivity: the particular traits that tend to be celebrated at any one time are either those that are especially feted by the particular culture or those that have proved effective for the author whose book we are reading!

## 2 Leadership as activity or behaviour

Although it is sometimes hard to discern whether a specific leadership requirement is best understood as a trait or as a behaviour or skill, the essential difference between behavioural and trait-based approaches is that, whereas traits tend to be regarded more as innate qualities and thus to an extent given, skills or behaviours are seen as qualities that can, and should, be learned and practised. Some of the earliest work in developing such theories[32] drew attention to the different types of skills required for leadership at different levels in an organization, suggesting that leaders needed to master a range of technical (informed proficiency in key work areas), human (the capacity to get along with and motivate others) and conceptual (the ability to work with ideas) skills in order to facilitate desired leadership outcomes. Subsequent work associated with Blake and Mouton[33] explored how leaders impact their organizations through the interplay of two concerns, concerns for people and task. Optimal leadership results from paying proper attention to both concerns.

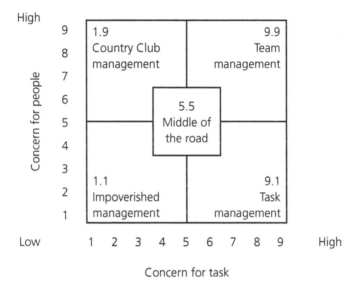

Figure 1. Blake-Mouton Leadership Grid

The Blake-Mouton Leadership Grid has been an extremely influential diagnostic tool in terms of identifying styles of leadership and facilitating the development of such optimal leadership. Although criticized to an extent as being essentially descriptive rather than predictive (little explanation is offered as to precisely how a person's skills or behaviours result in effective leadership performance), behavioural approaches to leadership have remained extremely popular for a number of reasons, not least that they make leadership widely accessible, and provide a basis and syllabus for leadership development. Some of the more influential thinkers from a business perspective who reflect such an approach include Kouzes and Posner,[34] Senge,[35] and Bennis and Nanus,[36] while this approach is reflected in a variety of works written from the locus of local church leadership.[37] Although not always acknowledging the ways in which context might affect and shape leadership expectations and expressions, style approaches are helpful in drawing attention to practices that generally contribute to effectiveness in leadership and that promote positive outcomes for groups.

## 3 Leadership as charism

Although *charisma* in a general sense has become an increasingly recognized trope in secular leadership writings, especially those from the transformational leadership stable,[38] here we use the word in its more original and narrowly theological sense to imply something enabled by the initiative of God and owing its origin to the operation of God's grace (*kharis*). This gracious activity has two implications for understanding Christian leadership.

First, we may say that leadership can be understood as a spiritual gift (*kharisma*), something that is rooted not primarily in any innate personal trait, behaviour or skill, but rather in qualities and abilities that we possess purely by virtue of the agency of God's Spirit who indwells us. The apostle Paul, highlighting some of the practical ways in which this grace of God is outworked in local church ministries and activities,[39] includes in his list of ministries inspired by the spirit several associated with leadership, such as *diakonia, didaskon* and *proistamenos*.[40] Numbers of those who emerge into leadership in both Old and New Testaments do so after an experience of being equipped by God and receiving new gifts and qualities from him. This may be through an inner experience of God's presence and power,[41] as a result of a longer process of formation,[42] or through being commissioned by those who somehow represent God.[43] Indeed, we might reflect that the Bible is full of examples of those who, naturally, had little obvious leadership potential, but whom God gifted and equipped to be most effective leaders. Paul is at pains to impress upon the Christians at Corinth, with their love for the humanly impressive, the truth that God uses the ordinary and those whom the world might dismiss as foolish to further his purposes,[44] and that, despite all human expectations, it is through our own acknowledgement of our limitations and weaknesses that we are enabled to discover and appropriate God's power.[45] Spiritual gifts, like other skills and abilities, need to be developed and honed. However, understanding this charismatic dimension of leadership reminds us that the pool from which leadership may be drawn might be rather wider in God's mind than we sometimes allow and that leadership is not restricted to those with particular innate talents or learned skills.

To treat leadership as a charism is not simply to acknowledge its origin from God but also, second, to understand the way in which leadership may be made possible as a consequence of, and response to, the activity of God in the life of a person, irrespective of whether they receive from God a specific spiritual gift of leadership. To this extent, charismatic leadership, in the sense in which we intend it here, has a good deal in common with the styles of leadership described as *charismatic* in the transformational leadership literature. In the secular field, charisma in a leader refers to an ability to inspire followers and exercise influence through embodying qualities and dispositions that are idealized by followers and that give them hope of their aspirations being achieved. In exploring here the charismatic nature of Christian leadership we are suggesting that others may be moved to follow or give credence to another as a response to God's activity in that person's life, and because such a person becomes idealized in the eyes of followers. This may come about as a person's character is shaped by God, such that qualities we might describe as holiness, integrity or authenticity grow in followers not only an inclination to trust the other but also raise the hope in followers that association with such leaders may be the best way of seeing similar qualities reproduced in our own lives. This, we assume, was a significant part of the appeal of Jesus, especially to those whose lifestyles and circumstances led to their being shunned by the formal religious establishment and by traditional community leaders.

Equally, a willingness to follow another, or to conceive of them as a leader, might be provoked not so much by their character but rather by their capacity to evoke faith and hope in God and in his present activity. It seems that Nehemiah's capacity to galvanize a thoroughly disheartened people into attempting a seemingly impossible and doomed task, and to sustain their confidence in the face of immense threats and overwhelming odds, was based on a personal confidence in God, personal experience of God's provision and intervention, and the fruit of a rich inner life with God.[46] The willingness of the people of Jerusalem to follow him is as a response to observing the impact of God's work in and around Nehemiah.

It is often worth reflecting on the Christian leaders whom we have, in the past, been pleased to follow and, perhaps, whom we aspire to be like. When we begin to identify what it is about them that disposed us to following them, we might express it in terms of their capacity to foster hope in God, the fact that when we were with them we felt God's presence more keenly, or that we felt that they might somehow enable us to enter more fully into God's purposes and to fulfil our own calling. This, we would say, was as a result not of anything innate within them but rather was authentically *charismatic*, brought about by the presence and working of God's gracious Spirit. The clear implication for us and for our own leadership is that potential for fruitfulness will be directly linked to the depth of our own relationship with God and our willingness to follow and obey him.

Although we will always want to recognize the importance of the charismatic, especially in the spheres of Christian leadership, we also recognize the unique dangers associated with such leadership. Indeed, some fascinating research conducted by Jasmine Vergauwe et al.[47] suggests that, while having a moderate level of charisma is important, having too much may hinder a leader's effectiveness. The more charismatic leaders are, the higher they are likely to rate their own effectiveness and the less accurate their own perceptions become, especially around areas of weakness. The research suggests that this tends to lead to inattention to detail and to proper process necessary to implement vision and strategy. Self-confidence can easily, the authors suggest, turn into overconfidence while risk tolerance and persuasiveness may tip over into eccentric or manipulative forms of behaviour. Without proper accountability, and without a commitment to seeing leadership primarily as an act of service towards God and others, such charismatic leadership runs the risk of becoming attention-seeking and narcissistic.

Although we will repeatedly stress throughout this book the importance of understanding God's work in the leadership process and the necessity, for the Christian leader, of receiving the empowering of God's Spirit, we also recognize the danger of underplaying other dimensions to the work of faithful leadership. Many of the biblical leaders whose careers ended badly or who proved to be unreliable had themselves experienced powerful charismatic endowment. This alone proved to be insufficient. Without the capacity for self-reflection, proper accountability and, above all, a sense of leadership as being for the benefit of others, the greater our charism, the greater our capacity will be for causing harm through our leadership.

In many ways, the leader is the most visible side of the leadership process and it should not surprise us therefore that not only did the earliest theories deal almost exclusively with leaders, but that leaders continue to remain front and centre in most contemporary leadership theories. The danger of focusing too exclusively on leaders is that they tend to become over idealized, and too many hopes and expectations are placed inappropriately upon them. As a consequence, the role of followers and others tends to be underestimated, and other players in the leadership process end up being effectively deskilled.[48] We understand why, in response to this, some more contemporary theories of leadership deconstruct the role of the individual leader almost, in some cases, to the point of extinction. A proper balance needs to be found that recognizes the vital role played by leaders without evacuating other sides in the process of their own importance. Simon Western, himself an advocate of a more holistic approach to leadership generally, and a critic of many more traditional approaches with their tendency to overemphasize the role of the leader, nevertheless sounds an important note of caution:

> It is important also to acknowledge the agency of individual leaders who can and do impact on organisational success. Individual leadership agency is often over-stated, yet individual leadership agency does matter; symbolic acts, excellent communication, personal drive and resilience, creative thinking and strategic vision do matter. Individual leaders do make a difference; they can inspire others, they can symbolise the mood of the times, and develop successful strategies with others, but they don't create cultures from thin air, and they don't ever lead alone. The mistake is to over-hype the power of the leader, creating unreal expectations that undermine the task of facing the complexities involved in leading corporate cultures.[49]

Our discussion of the place of *charisma* in leadership draws attention not only to a property in the leader but also, by virtue of the operation of this upon followers, to a more relational dimension in the leadership process. We will now give this our consideration.

## Relationship-centred theories

### 1 Early theories

Earlier, 'great man' theories of leadership may have made reference to the place of followers in the leadership process but such place was conceived entirely as that of passive conformity to the instruction and direction of the leader. Given the social character of the contexts that gave rise to such theories (predominantly military, political or from modernist manufacturing industries) and the authoritarianism that hallmarked the prevailing culture, this is hardly surprising. However, a reliance on such leadership practices today will usually not get us very far. An understanding that the leadership process is somewhat more complex than previously imagined, and a greater recognition of the significance of the roles of followers, may well have been accelerated by the shift in workplace focus from manufacturing to knowledge,[50] with its consequent requirement for very different modes of operation, and by the shift from an authoritarian towards a more collaborative ethos in the wider culture. From the early 1970s onwards, leadership theory began to take cognisance of the fact that followers had a somewhat more active role to play in the leadership process and that their compliance could not be either taken for granted or assumed simply on the basis of forceful or dynamic leadership. Associated with the work of House,[51] path–goal leadership theory is predicated on the need for leaders to focus on employee motivation in order to enhance both performance and satisfaction. Central to this theory is the notion that leaders should select specific behaviours that are appropriate for the specific needs of subordinates in specific situations. This is a significant change from more historic theories which simply required subordinates to bend their own wills to the whims and directions of capable or appointed leaders. If path–goal theory, despite its concern for subordinate motivation, continues to focus on the agency of the leader, leader–member exchange theory[52] envisages a much more symbiotic relationship between the two parties and places this at the centre of the leadership process. Recognizing that to treat all followers as a single homogeneous group is neither realistic nor accurate,[53] LMX theory advocates the recognition on the part of leaders of the need for differing relationships with different followers or groups of followers. This theory articulates the desirability of a growing interdependence between leaders and subordinates, and effective leadership is seen to happen when the relationship between leaders and subordinates is hallmarked by effective co-communication, trust, respect and commitment. Its fruit is the more direct engagement of all people in the leadership process.

## 2 The power of followers

Early relationship-focused theories nevertheless tended to be leader-centric in their focus on the agency of the leader in engaging followers. Contemporary writing on leadership explicitly acknowledges the key role of followers in the leadership process and far from viewing them as passive recipients of leadership describes them as co-creators of the leadership process itself. So Walter Wright is able to affirm:

> Leaders are dependent upon the people. They are not charismatic comets racing alone across the sky. Leadership is a relationship of dependency. Leaders need followers. Leaders are dependent upon the community because, in the end, leadership is in the hands of the followers. It exists only when someone decides to follow and decides to accept the influence … In the final analysis it is always the one who follows who determines if leadership is being exercised. It does not matter how much power or charisma you think you possess, how exciting you think your vision is. What matters is, does someone choose to accept your influence and alter his or her vision, values, attitudes or behaviours. Leadership is a relationship of influence with a purpose, perceived by those who choose to follow.[54]

Kellerman introduces her significant work on followership by referring to a short story by George Orwell.[55] Set in 1930s colonial Burma, the central character is a British police officer, responsible for upholding law and order but keenly aware of the resentment felt by the local people towards him and the empire he represents.[56] Orwell himself served in the Burmese police force and the story may well be essentially autobiographical.

One day the officer is summoned to come and deal with a normally tame elephant that has gone wild, killing a local man and damaging property. Arriving on the scene with his gun, the officer finds a large crowd has gathered to witness the spectacle of an elephant being shot. The elephant, however, has now returned to its habitual peaceable state, and the officer has neither need nor inclination to shoot it. The crowd, now numbering more than two thousand people, have other ideas. They are convinced that the elephant must be shot and that the officer should perform the task. Although feeling that to shoot the elephant would be murder, the officer realizes that he has no choice. Although being the one in the position of authority, and although the crowd pose no physical threat, he feels entirely powerless before the will of the people, 'two thousand wills, pressing me forward, irresistibly'. In the end, it is those without authority or position who exercise their own will and ensure that the elephant is killed. As Keller-man observes:

> This was the might of the many, of subordinates who, by mobilising as a mob, obliged their superior to bend to their will ... To underestimate, or to undervalue, the importance of those to whom Shakespeare once referred as underlings is to disempower them. So long as we fixate on leaders at the expense of followers, we will perpetuate the myth that they don't much matter.[57]

While we might offer the reflection that one of the key roles and callings of a leader is at all times to keep before the organization questions and concerns to do with wider moral obligations and to exert a critical challenge towards instinctive action that may ultimately be misguided, nevertheless the implication is clear: followers do matter and cannot be ignored. Indeed, there are occasions, such as that described by Orwell, in which followers may actually hold more power than leaders and may thus shape outcomes far more significantly. In some situations, leaders, especially those who are elected or appointed by others, owe their mandate or their place to the followers who have authorized them. Those same followers have it equally in their power to remove such leaders from office and to withdraw power from them. Even in functional organizations or enterprises, the capacity of leaders to exercise leadership depends heavily upon the continuing engagement of followers and their willingness to cooperate in a shared task. As Harvey observes:

> The willingness of followers to refrain from exercising certain forms of power is indispensable to stable leadership. Followers typically have more power than they employ, and more than leaders themselves – when this potential energy becomes actual ... a moment of crisis is reached, and suddenly a long-standing leadership pattern can collapse.[58]

The relationship between leaders and followers is not, however, ideally to be seen as a struggle between competing power bases. Rather, in a properly functional setting, whereas those occupying leader roles might have the prime responsibility for maintaining the focus of the organization and calling the organization back to its purpose, key tasks such as discerning the direction, allocation of resources and so on will be determined by the shared work of leaders and followers. An understanding of leadership as a relationship between leaders and followers results in a view of the leader role that is both catalytic and facilitating, enabling the (sometimes overlooked, but vitally important) contributions of a wide variety of parties with different but complementary perspectives to be heard and utilized. Thus the leadership process becomes one in which both leaders and followers exercise healthy influence on each other for the common good. Grint[59] describes the helpful influence of followers on leaders as constructive dissent, a practice that involves followers questioning leaders' decisions and providing add-itional perspectives or information to enable better decisions to be made.

> In sum, holding together the diversity of talents necessary for organi-sational success is what distinguishes a successful from an unsuccessful leader: leaders don't need to be perfect but, on the contrary, they do have to recognise that the limits of their knowledge and power will ultimately doom them to failure unless they rely upon their subordinate leaders and followers to compensate for their own ignorance and impotence ... In effect, leadership is the property and consequence of a community rather than the property and consequence of an individual leader.[60]

The wise leader will neither seek to impose her will unilaterally on others nor will she be coerced by simple majority opinion that may be unhelpful or misguided. Rather, she will seek to shape the decision-making process by facilitating proper consideration of a wide variety of insights and infor-mation, always calling the organization back to weigh such considerations in the light of its core purpose, mission and values. Although such insights might have come later to the worlds of industry and commerce, these should be second nature for the Church, with the clear preference in the biblical literature for corporate images that are more organic (the body and the family) than hierarchical. Indeed, perhaps the most insightful description of the relationship between the respective roles of leaders and followers is to be found in a 1987 paper produced by the Church of England's Advisory Council for the Church's Ministry (ACCM)[61] entitled *Education for the Church's Ministry*.[62] The authors of the report describe this relationship as inter-animative, each focusing the activity of God in each other. The role of the ordained clergy is to enable the whole people of God to understand and participate in the mission of God and to discern the specific gifts given to them by God for this purpose. The role of the people is to call into being the leadership of the ordained, both giving permission and authority to them in their leadership and sustaining them in the exercise of such leadership. Paragraph 31 of the report affirms the interdependence of the two ministries whereby 'together they can do what neither can do alone'.[63] This seems to us to be a coherent description of the true relationship between leaders and followers, a relationship of mutual trust and cooperation in which followers are active rather than passive, and leaders understand their role to be that of catalyst and steward. Kellerman arrives at a similar place in her own description of the relationship between leadership and followership, argu-ing that the two should be thought of in tandem, 'as inseparable, indivisible and inconceivable the one without the other'.[64]

One further, and frequently overlooked feature of this inter-animative relationship is that of the role of followers in determining what leadership might look like and, specifically, who might qualify to be a leader. Hollander and Julian[65] suggest that those who emerge as leaders are those who best fit the shared conceptions of followers as to what a leader should look like. The ideal leader may be conceived in terms of capacity to perform certain tasks that are seen as necessary (and that are perhaps associated with historic experience of previous leaders). Equally, it may well be that people are selected as leaders on the basis of their capacity to model behaviour or express those norms and values that are seen as most representative of the society or group. Leaders are thus seen as prototypes who model to the wider group the kinds of behaviours and attitudes that the group aspires to see represented more widely within itself. The danger for any organization is that it may, in simply perpetuating existing patterns of leadership behaviour, maintain gaps in thinking and skills that prevent it from tackling some challenges or responding to particular opportunities. Historic Christian denominations have tended to select their own leadership on the basis of the likely capacity of a person to maintain existing practice and uphold tradition rather than on a capacity to improvise afresh and in faithful but innovative ways in the light of that tradition. Thus, leadership in these churches, at least until very recently, has tended to be pastoral rather than apostolic in focus, and entrepreneurial leadership has been feared and thus all too often shunned.

## 3 Transformational theories of leadership

Transformational theories of leadership rest squarely on a solid understanding of the relational nature of leadership and have exercised the most significant influence, over the last 40 years, in terms of shaping leadership understandings. Transformational thinking lies behind most of the especially significant recent works from the arenas of business or commerce[66] and has been the catalyst for a growing concern for leadership in the Church and in other voluntary sectors.[67] Associated most significantly with the political scientist James Macgregor Burns,[68] although subsequently developed and adapted by Bernard Bass and colleagues,[69] two particular features of this theory have caught the imagination. First, and in contrast to many earlier theories that were motivated primarily by the driver of greater productivity or efficiency, Burns' theory sought to establish higher and more moral aspirations at the centre of leadership thinking. Organizations, and thus the leadership that they host, had to be focused on, inter alia, satisfying the needs and aspirations of employees, the development of followers to their fullest potential, and wider moral and ethical concerns leading potentially to social change. Indeed, for Burns, one of the key definers of true leadership is a focus on raising the level of morality in others. Thus, influential figures such as Adolf Hitler or Pol Pot would, despite their influence, under Burns' definition be denied the title of transformational leader. Bass devised the term 'pseudotransformational leadership'[70] in order to describe such inauthentic yet influential leadership which is hallmarked by warped moral values and narrow self-interest, rather than the common good. Second, this was a theory that took seriously the relational dynamics between leader and follower and especially the need for leaders to exercise particular influence to stimulate within followers an inner desire or conviction to own particular shared goals. Whereas previous understandings of leadership might have recognized the sufficiency of compliance on the part of followers with goals set by leaders, transformational leadership aspires to stimulate commitment to shared goals across the organization.[71] Thus Burns defines leadership as a process of, 'Inducing followers to act for certain goals that represent the values and the motivations – the wants and needs, the aspirations and expectations – *of both leaders and followers*.'[72]

It is not difficult to see how points of resonance can easily be found between transformational theories and Christian understandings of leadership. Christian leadership is set within a strongly moral framework, takes seriously the development of all people and the pursuit of the common good, including the good of those outwith the immediate family of the Church, is committed to the transformation of people and structures, and recognizes the power both of a compelling vision of an ideal future not yet realized and of inner compulsions to strive towards such a vision fuelled, in the case of Christian leadership, by the motivating power of God's indwelling Spirit. It is, perhaps, for such reasons that this has become one of the dominant leadership paradigms for those involved in leadership in overtly Christian contexts.

The transformational writers identify four particular leadership qualities that are deployed by transformational leaders:[73]

### (a) Idealized influence

Sometimes described as *charisma*, this refers to the quality of a leader to act as a compelling role model for others, and to commend a vision or a course of action by virtue of their own convictions and integrity. By deploying admirable qualities, such as consistency, courage, altruism and humility, a leader builds emotional attachments with followers that lead to followers idealizing the leader as one who is worthy of emulating. Many of the Transformational theorists draw attention to the importance to a leader of building trust with followers, signalling the fact that followers are far more than passive agents whose compliance can be taken for granted.

### (b) Inspirational Motivation

Bass and Riggio suggest:

> Transformational leaders behave in ways that motivate and inspire those around them by providing meaning and challenge to their followers' work

... they create clearly communicated expectations that followers want to meet and also demonstrate commitment to goals and to the shared vision.[74]

Such leaders are associated with inspiring others to feel a connection to a wider whole through such practices as enlisting followers as co-contributors in the formation of a shared vision for the organization.

### (c) Intellectual stimulation

This disposition consists in the stimulation of creativity, innovation, and critical thinking in others as followers are enlisted in the business of problem solving and forward thinking. It signals the importance of engaging followers in order to make available to the organization insights beyond those originating from the person of the leader alone.

### (d) Individualized consideration

This discipline refers to the leader's willingness to coach and develop followers, helping them to learn through personal challenges, and to create a climate in which the individual needs and concerns of those followers can be addressed. Often learning opportunities are provided through the delegation of tasks to followers with appropriate subsequent feedback and reflection. The role of the leader is critical in establishing and reinforcing a culture in which others understand how their own contribution makes a difference to the wider purposes and aims of the organization.

Transformational leadership theories are not without their critics and we will consider some of the reservations expressed about such theories in a subsequent chapter. However, for the purposes of our current discussion, the extensive influence that such theories have gained in recent years has firmly established the role of followers as central to the leadership process.

## Leadership as a social process

Some of the most recent developments in leadership theory shift the focus entirely away from leaders, whether operating alone or in relationship with followers, and on to leadership, seen in this light as a shared, social process to which many people contribute and that is distributed across, and emergent within, an organization. Leadership, on this account, is generated through the interactions of different people throughout the organization, no matter what their specific place or role might be within that organization. The emergence of such theories has been fostered by a number of different developments.

The changing nature of work, particularly the shift from manufacturing to knowledge work, has resulted in a climate in which new forms of leadership are far more suitable. Whereas in previous eras knowledge and expertise tended to be concentrated in the upper echelons of the firm's hierarchy, and thus leadership was exercised by those with such superior knowledge, today knowledge is far more dispersed, with different people located variously across any organization, possessing different pieces of knowledge and expertise. Indeed, the complexity of most businesses, and the growth in volumes and types of knowledge, means that it is impossible for any one person to be the sole repository of all knowledge and expertise. Thus, different people may well be called upon to take a lead at different times and in different situations. The scope of work undertaken by many organizations also means that a more rigidly hierarchical approach is inappropriate. The work undertaken, for example, by hospitals, schools or many other service providers, requires leadership to be widely dispersed if such work is to be performed effectively, with people at different levels in the organization invited to contribute to decision-making processes and to take appropriate initiatives in their own spheres of influence and concern.

The realities of a changing environment in which work takes place, and the appreciation that many organizations are facing uncharted territory and entirely new and previously unimagined situations, raises the requirement for leadership that is adaptive and innovative. Once again, leadership that is dispersed and thus able to harness the capabilities of all people irrespective of their place in the organization is seen as much better placed to respond to such new situations.

The prevailing cultural mindset is far more sympathetic to more collaborative approaches to leadership than to traditional, more hierarchical approaches. Postmodernity is suspicious of the embodiment of authority and power in individual leaders and prefers to see leadership as something that is co-constructed through the interactions of numbers of people. As we have observed previously, this preference for collaboration may well be prompted by formative influences such as experience of family life.[75] It may also be fuelled by a concern for more ethical leadership and a distaste for lack of concern for human and environmental casualties of more hierarchical practices of leadership. Leadership becomes, from a postmodern perspective, less fixed and more to be negotiated than simply received. If an appropriate metaphor for leadership under modernity might have been an orchestra with a conductor responsible for setting the time, determining the contributions of other members, and even choosing the music to be played, in the current era a more appropriate metaphor might be that of a jazz ensemble. Although there might be a given theme or chord progression that determines the broad parameters of what might be played, individual members are given freedom to improvise within this framework. Moreover, the ensemble may well not have an easily identifiable leader, the lead either passing between different players from time to time or, more frequently, the ensemble co-constructing leadership as each individual instrumentalist adjusts and develops his or her own contribution in response to, and in sympathy with, the contributions of other group members. Leadership is thus conceived as a far more organic, dispersed and less self-conscious practice than in previous eras, the property of a social system as opposed to a shared idea located in people's minds or a quality located in a single individual.[76] Ospina and Sorenson reflect that, whereas in simpler systems leadership may be located in the person of the leader,

> more complex systems may rely on interpersonal influence, a formula where the source of leadership shifts from a single individual to the roles of actors in negotiation and competition to influence each other ... leadership emerges by way of dialogue and collaborative learning to achieve a shared sense of the demands of collective work.[77]

Western offers one of the most compelling descriptions of such dispersed leadership, a phenomenon he describes as eco-leadership.[78] In this paradigm, organizations are likened to ecosystems in which leadership is generated throughout the organism as the organism itself subscribes to core aims and values. Translating this into practical terms, such organisms progress as each individual member or constituent group bases its actions around such aims and values that have been sufficiently owned and internalized to enable informed and good decisions to be taken. Like any ecosystem, these organizations are inherently more adaptive and thus better able to deal with the challenges of new situations. Western is at pains to point out that such organizations have not abandoned leadership or marginalized its importance. Rather, leadership has been genuinely distributed and internalized within the organization. Neither does Western underestimate the role of the individual *leader* within such a leadership discourse, even if this role is conceived somewhat differently to some more traditional understandings.

> The Eco-leader is a generative leader, who creates organisational spaces for leadership to flourish. Eco-leaders think like organisational architects, connecting people and creating networks using processes and technology ... Successful Eco-leaders embody generous and generative leadership ... Creating spaces for others to lead, they recognise that leadership is a collective effort. They constantly connect others in the network, allowing mutuality and creativity to blossom.[79]

There is, for Western, something of an irony about the development of such dispersed leadership across an organization. This does not come about either by accident or by simply letting go of the reins of leadership. Rather it comes about by the very deliberate activity and intention of leaders:

Another paradox exists. Sometimes it requires a 'Messiah leader', a charismatic and visionary individual or team, to drive change and create new collaborative cultures with distributed leadership. The challenge here is for the messiah leader to initiate, provoke and stimulate change and be prepared to let go of power when successful: a difficult task![80]

There is enormous resonance between the insights of Western, and other advocates of more process-orientated theories of leadership, and New Testament understandings of leadership, a resonance we will explore in much greater detail in a later chapter. The dominant and controlling metaphors for the Church in the Pauline writings, those of body and family,[81] are predominantly organic. The more detailed expositions[82] of leadership and ministry within the local church describe an economy of mutuality and collaboration. These are expressions of a key dimension to Christian experience, one that represents a radical departure from what had gone before. Whereas in the Old Testament era, leadership was exercised generally by a uniquely called and anointed (by God) individual, in the New Testament era leadership is exercised by an anointed community, the Church. Thus the apostle Paul is able to refer to the universal experience, of all Christians, of receiving the Spirit of God and thus being enlisted in the task of ministry and leadership under the Spirit's direction.[83] Perhaps it is this dimension to Christian leadership that has enabled the Church to adapt so seamlessly, over the centuries, to the demands of engaging in mission in different cultures and in ever-changing circumstances.

## Towards a definition

Our concern to find a working definition of leadership has encountered a significant challenge in the shape of the complexity of leadership and the diversity in its manner of finding expression. Can we arrive at a definition that might adequately reflect such diversity? Any such definition will have to encompass a number of different sides to the leadership cube.

Gill reminds us of the etymology of the word leadership and its derivation from the Old English *laedan*, meaning to take with one, or show the way.[84] Thus, our definition will need to draw attention to the role of leadership in enabling forward movement or progression. Our consideration of the different places in which leadership might be located will mean that we must draw attention to the fact that leadership is a relational process. The insights of transformational and some other theories alert us to the fact that, in order to be legitimate, leadership must encompass a moral dimension, and in order to avoid being abusive must take into account the hopes, aspirations and goals of all parties involved in the process.

Richard Bolden's definition appears to come close to summarizing much of our thinking thus far:

[Leadership is] a process of social influence, to guide structure and/or facilitate behaviours, activities and/or relationships, towards the achievement of shared aims.[85]

Amanda Sinclair is keen to stress the relational dimension of this process in her definition and prefers to describe the process as one in which people are inspired or mobilized, as opposed to being influenced, to act in positive new ways, thus emphasizing the motivational, rather than potentially coercive, role of good leadership.[86] In similar vein, the 2015 FAOC Senior Church Leadership report describes a leader as 'someone who assists others in the performance of a collective practice ... participating in that practice in such a way as to draw others deeper into it'.[87] Bearing these definitions in mind, here is our first stab at a definition of leadership:

A relational process of social influence through which people are inspired, enabled and mobilized to act in positive, new ways, towards the achievement of shared goals.

We will want to revisit this definition at the end of our next chapter in which we consider the ways in which the Christian tradition provides unique and distinctive insights into the business of leadership, when we will be in a position to consider what might be an appropriate summary definition of Christian leadership.

---

## Leadership on the ground

Established in the mid-nineteenth century as part of the church-planting boom that accompanied the growth of industrial towns and cities across the North of England, Holy Trinity Church Stalybridge (HTS) had been a modestly thriving church for much of its history. Consistently willing to embrace innovation whether in forms of ministry, styles of worship or in the ordering of its building, under a succession of faithful leaders it had grown in size, by the mid-1990s, to around 200 regular worshippers.

It was, perhaps, a desire for further growth that resulted, in the late 1990s, in the appointment as incumbent of a highly charismatic and gifted person who seemed to hold out the promise of taking the church forward to new levels in terms of size and significance.

A visionary leader with a strong personality and an extremely persuasive style, the new vicar, initially at least, engaged many hearts and minds as he set before the church a compelling vision for the future.

Responsibility for leadership was increasingly confined to the vicar himself, with other responsible bodies (PCC) and individuals (church officers) being encouraged to embrace and throw their weight behind the vicar as God's appointed leader.

Although there were those who found reassurance in so definite a style of leadership, the forceful, and at times iconoclastic, nature of this leadership began to unsettle some. People felt alienated by an unwillingness to listen to other voices, and an insistence on pressing on with a set personal agenda even in the face of questions and reservations. Questions began to be raised about the use of finance and about the appropriateness of some personal behaviours. Significant numbers of people began to drift away from the church, relationships within the church became strained as opinion divided more deeply about the leader's conduct and character, while the church's reputation in the wider community sank.

When, after a number of years in post, the vicar resigned, the church was broken. Financially unable to pay its way, the much-reduced congregation was split into two camps: those who had remained loyal to their departing leader, and those who felt their trust had been abused, angry at what had taken place, and, to an extent, guilty at what had been allowed to happen. Their hopes of recruiting a new incumbent were also pretty low, for who, they reasoned, would ever want to come to Holy Trinity?

### Walking with the wounded

After 12 years of very effective ministry as an associate vicar, Tom Parker had been growing in his conviction that it was time to move on from his current post. By his own admission, experiencing, at that time, a considerable sense of personal brokenness, Tom, a faithful pastor-teacher, wondered if he was up to the task of leading a church. He assumed, when asked to consider going as vicar to HTS, that the church would want a more charismatic form of leader to restore what they had once had but lost. He did, however, feel well equipped to walk with these people in their brokenness and to love them, enabling them to regain some health and confidence, and offered to commit to them for three years, seeing himself as a stopgap until they came to a place where a proper replacement vicar might be found.

The idea of a three-year term of office proved to be an inspired notion. It gave Tom a clear sense of focus as he sought to bring the church to a place where he could hand it on in better shape, and the freedom to act courageously knowing that he was not locked into a role in perpetuity. Equally it kept the church focused on the medium term and on facing up to what would happen beyond Tom's tenure.

Tom and his wife Judy have always shared a sense of common calling in ministry and it was very much as a team that they set about their new work in Stalybridge. Their first priority they described as simply sitting alongside people for God. A great deal of time was spent in having coffee with church members, listening to their stories, offering both care and also, where appropriate, challenge, and praying with people, seeking to enable them to encounter God's healing grace.

Recognizing that the church was both exhausted and overstretched, Tom understood that, especially in such situations, it takes time for people to have either the confidence or the inclination to embrace different ways. Not wanting to compound deeply felt pain and brokenness, he resisted creating disturbance by tinkering with, for example, styles of worship or other familiar practices, even though he sensed that some aspects of church life were seriously dysfunctional. He did stop the depleted evening service and other activities for which there were no longer sufficient resources but allowed others to continue.

## Changing the culture

Wanting to raise morale and looking for ways in which community might be built, relationships fostered and a renewed sense of purpose discovered, Tom initiated a series of work parties to attend to the neglected and deteriorating fabric of the church buildings. In many ways, this proved to be a practical activity with deeper, spiritual resonance. Repairing the fabric was a sign of an intention to see the spiritual life of the church restored.

Tom recalls one particular moment, which had the sense of being an enacted parable. Moving aside a worn-out banner from one corner of the church building, Tom realized that it had been positioned deliberately to conceal an area of damp wall. Further exploration disclosed that the damp had been caused by a blocked downpipe. Years of ingress of water had damaged the plaster beyond repair. As Tom set about removing the plaster, a noxious smell was released from the fetid water that had seeped into it. It seemed to be a picture of what had happened in the life of the church: unchecked seepage of unpleasant and destructive influence, which, far from being countered, had simply been covered up. It needed to be stopped at source, the damage exposed and proper remedies applied.

One of the key elements in this process was going to be the way the church was taught. Likening the church to a container filled with dirty water, Tom, a gifted Bible teacher, saw his teaching ministry as akin to pouring in clean water until the dirty was completely displaced. His first priority in teaching was that of reminding the congregation of some of the key aspects of God's character as the shepherd of his people, his kindness, generosity and care for those who belong to him. He wanted to enable the church to appreciate their new identity in Christ, and freedom in faithful Christian life and witness. Tom set out on what would be a lengthy journey of painting a fuller and less selective picture of God's story than had been presented in the immediate past, enabling people to live their own lives with greater confidence as participants in this story.

The new culture that Tom and Judy sought to introduce had to be made visible and reinforced by very intentional modelling. They looked for every opportunity to thank people for the various contributions made and publicly celebrated the good things that were going on in the life of the church. Intentional feedback to the congregation, often through the means of photo reporting of events and activities, not only made those involved feel properly affirmed but also whetted the appetite of others for participation in different ministry areas and activities.

### Stimulating participation and engagement

One of the consequences of a more heroic style of leadership is the general disempowerment of other people within the organization. The HTS PCC had at times been reduced to following the vicar's vision and being told either to get on board or get out! Tom sought to counter this by very intentionally engaging the PCC and other key people in strategic decision-making, modelling a strongly affiliative style of leadership, and seeking to create a sense of joint responsibility.

Churchwardens and others were invited to contribute to the shaping of sermon series and other key decisions affecting the trajectory of ministry. Tom sought also to open up the whole PCC process to the wider church, establishing a system whereby headlines of each meeting were reported back to the wider church immediately through inclusion in the weekly notice sheet.

Not only had the previous vicar operated somewhat autonomously within the life of HTS, he had also resisted submission to appropriate external authority from within the wider Anglican denomination. In particular under his influence the church had failed to make expected financial contributions to the Anglican diocese (the body responsible for paying the salaries of HTS clergy), choosing instead to direct monies to the church's own mission projects.

Tom challenged the PCC as to whether they wanted to be defined as a church that was supported by other churches (HTS clergy stipends were being paid from the contributions made by other churches) or as a church that gave to others. In January 2009, 15 months after the Parkers had begun their ministry in Stalybridge, the HTS PCC agreed to fulfil its financial obligations to its diocese. It was a watershed moment, and something seemed to have shifted spiritually – new people began either to join or to drift back to the church, and, after a challenging and dry initial period in the parish, the Parkers began to sense some encouragement.

For the Parkers, a church fails in its calling if good relationships, both among church members and also with its host community, are not fostered and encouraged. Having worked hard at the healing of internal relationships, Tom turned his attention to building relationships with the wider community. He joined the 'Town Team' and other local community groups and sought to involve the church in key community activities. Church members began to participate in the regular town clean-up days. The HTS building is situated in the very heart of the town, and so Tom offered the church buildings for community use. He asked the local butcher to provide a barbecue at the end of one clean-up day, while he recruited the local brass band to play as volunteers ate the food paid for by the church. Links were made with local schools, businesses and other community organizations, and HTS began to enjoy the confidence and trust of the wider community and to play a full part in the life of the town.

HTS had also begun to be perceived by other churches in the area as elitist, and Tom began to work on restoring relationships with local church leaders by hosting 'Churches Together' ministers' lunches once or twice a term and supporting and joining in with Churches Together activities.

## Organic leadership

Tom has never seen himself as a particularly strategic leader (the author begs to differ, seeing him as instinctively strategic!) but rather as an organic one. By this he implies that he seeks to recognize where new green shoots are appearing and to enable them to thrive. An observer might suggest that this capacity is enabled by Tom and Judy's steadfast commitment to a set of very clear kingdom values and to seeing them worked out in the life of a local church.

Their strongly relational style has enabled them to draw alongside people in an unthreatening way, to identify and develop a significant number of other ministry leaders, to flag up new ministry opportunities and encourage people to step into them, and to enable the dismantling of a failing set of small groups and its replacement with a far more functional and holistic structure of life groups with properly trained leaders and a missional DNA. New ministry initiatives also began to originate from a newly empowered laity.

It was hardly surprising that, as the agreed period of three years was drawing to a close, the church were absolutely adamant that Tom was exactly the leader they wanted for the long term and in 2011 he was instituted as vicar of the parish.

For Tom, the realization that the church had been rehabilitated came during his final year before retirement. On 22 May 2017, as thousands of concert-goers were making their way out of the Manchester Arena following an evening event, a suicide bomber detonated a home-made shrapnel-laden device, killing himself and 22 others and injuring over 100 further people, many of them children. News quickly spread around the Greater Manchester area.

Before long, Tom received a phone call from a community leader informing him that several hundred stunned people were gathering in the centre of Stalybridge and asking could they possibly go into church for a vigil. The church building was, at that time, under repair and out of use. Tom went down to join the vigil. It became quickly very clear that people were looking to him above all at this grievous moment. He found himself speaking to the crowd, helping them to make sense of their corporate grief and numbness, and leading them in prayer in the midst of their distress.

By immersing themselves, from the very beginning of their ministry, in the lives both of church members and of the wider community, Tom and Judy Parker were both quickly perceived by others to be 'one of us'. Their relational, empowering and affiliative style of ministry was used by God to heal a church, engage a community, and to see a culture established that is proving to be fruitful way beyond the incumbency of the Parkers.

## Questions to aid reflection

1  The recent experience of HTS highlights the impact of two contrasting styles of leadership. How have you experienced the consequences, either helpful or detrimental to the organization, of the deployment of particular leadership styles?

2  How might our personal approach to the exercise of leadership be affected, positively or negatively, by our own life experiences?

3  Tom Parker describes his own leadership approach as being organic, recognizing green shoots and allowing them to thrive. What might be the strengths and weaknesses of such an approach to leadership?

4  What particular leadership lesson might I draw from this case study?

## Notes

1 Carroll, L., 2015 [1872], *Alice's Adventures in Wonderland and Through the Looking Glass*, London: Penguin.

2 Kuper, S., 'Why Star Premier League Managers Matter Less than Ever', *Financial Times*, 12 August 2016.

3 Ferguson, A. and Moritz, M., 2016, *Leading*, London: Hodder & Stoughton.

4 See Stodgill, R., 1974, *Handbook of Leadership*, New York: Free Press, p. vii.

5 Burns, J. M., 1978, *Leadership*, New York: Harper and Row, p. 158.

6 We use the word 'organization' here and throughout this book simply as a

convenient collective noun for any group of people whose commitment to a common purpose results in some level of their being organized towards its fulfilment and thus among whom leadership might be either present or desired. No word is free from any number of helpful and unhelpful connotations that might be ascribed to it. In particular, organization tends to be associated with human agency and is thus not always a comfortable word to use of local churches. Nevertheless, although we may prefer to adopt more organic metaphors in describing the Church and its life, even churches demonstrate organizational features and thus for convenience may be included under the descriptive umbrella of this term.

7 We might well wish to question the morality of any organization whose goals either conflict significantly with or fail adequately to reflect some of the central concerns of the kingdom of God. While profitability and growth are clearly not necessarily inappropriate goals for an organization (although in a world of limited material resources, ultimately material growth has to come at the expense of another party!), to pursue such profitability at the expense of a concern for the well-being of workers or the wider environment would call into question the way in which the organization conceives its ultimate purpose. One of the roles the Christian Church may well be called to play is that of moral conscience, calling the world of business to widen its focus in order to encompass concerns such as that of human flourishing.

8 Hersey, P. and Blanchard, K. H., 1993, *Management of Organizational Behavior: Utilizing Human Resources*, 6th edn, Englewood Cliffs, NJ: Prentice Hall.

9 Situational leadership as a discrete leadership theory has not been without its critics. A helpful critique of the shortcomings and also contributions of this approach is offered by Dugan, J. P., 2017, *Leadership Theory: Cultivating Critical Perspectives*, San Francisco, CA: Jossey-Bass, pp. 125–47.

10 Goleman, D., Boyatzis, R. and McKee, A., 2004, *Primal Leadership: Learning to Lead with Emotional Intelligence*, Boston, MA: Harvard Business School Press.

11 Walker, S. P., 2010, *The Undefended Leader*, Carlisle: Piquant Editions.

12 Notwithstanding the good case Walker makes for these being two distinct and unique leadership styles, it may well be argued that service and sacrifice are of the essence of all authentic leadership, no matter what the particular style being deployed. To neglect these two key leadership characteristics is both to impoverish and undermine the leadership being exercised.

13 Contingency theories of leadership are something of a development of *situational* theories and address the issue of whether or not a leader is most likely to be effective in a particular situation, often by assessing the leader's capability in the three areas of relational skills, task focus and position power. The tools associated with these theories are helpful in matching leaders to different situations. A useful discussion of the merits and pitfalls of such theories can be found in Northouse, P. G., 2010, *Leadership Theory and Practice*, London: Sage, pp. 111–24.

14 Semple, S. B., 2002, *The Contrarian's Guide to Leadership*, San Francisco, CA: Jossey-Bass, p. 1.

15 Dugan, *Leadership Theory*, p. 6.

16 Goethals, G. R. and Sorenson, G. L. J. (eds), 2006, *The Quest for a General Theory of Leadership*, Cheltenham: Edward Elgar.

17 Maccoby, M., 2007, *The Leaders We Need*, Boston, MA: Harvard Business School Press, pp. 43–55.

18 Meindl, J. R., Ehrlich, S. B. and Dukerisch, J. M., 1985, 'The Romance of Leadership', *Administrative Science Quarterly* 30, pp. 521–51.

19 For example, Kellerman, B., 2008, *Followership*, Boston, MA: Harvard Business Review Press.

20 Goethals and Sorenson, *Quest for a General Theory of Leadership*, p. xiv.

21 Ladkin, D., 2010, *Rethinking Leadership*, Cheltenham: Edward Elgar, p. 21.

22 Faier, E., 'Is Leadership Greater than the Sum of its Parts?', unpublished MS, c. June 2002, p. 1, quoted in Goethals and Sorenson, *Quest for a General Theory of Leadership*, p. 21.

23 Ciulla, J., 'Some Thoughts on the Mount Hope Meeting', unpublished MS, c. May 2002, pp. 4–5, quoted in Goethals and Sorenson, *Quest for a General Theory of Leadership*, p. 21.

24 For a much more thoroughgoing and critical examination of a wider range of the most influential leadership theories, readers are referred to the excellent works by Northouse, *Leadership Theory and Practice*, and Dugan, *Leadership Theory*.

25 See Stodgill, R. M., 1948, 'Personal Factors Associated with Leadership: A Survey of the Literature', *Journal of Psychology* 25, pp. 35–71.

26 These are considered more fully below pp. 41–3.

27 Goleman, Boyatzis and McKee, *Primal Leadership*.

28 Boyatzis, R. and McKee, A., 2005, *Resonant Leadership*, Boston, MA: Harvard Business School Press, p. 28.

29 Bass, B. M., 2008, *The Bass Handbook of Leadership*, 4th edn, New York: The Free Press, p. 108.

30 The Strengthsfinder online tool has been an extremely popular method of assessing strengths and talents (traits) as a means of discerning which particular leadership roles might be the most suitable context in which such strengths could be deployed. Based on extensive research by the Gallup organization, its most recent iteration can be found in Rath, T., 2007, *Strengthsfinder 2.0*, New York: Perseus-Gallup Press.

31 Northouse, *Leadership Theory and Practice*, pp. 20–2.

32 Katz, R. L., 1955, 'Skills of an Effective Administrator', *Harvard Business Review* 33(1), pp. 33–42.

33 Blake, R. R. and Mouton, J. S., 1964, *The Managerial Grid*, Houston, TX: Gulf Publishing.

34 Kouzes, J. and Posner, B., 2012, *The Leadership Challenge*, 5th edn, San Francisco, CA: Jossey-Bass.

35 Senge, P., 2006, *The Fifth Discipline: The Art and Practice of the Learning Organisation*, rev. edn, London: Random House.

36 Bennis, W. and Nanus, B., 2007, *Leaders: Strategies for Taking Charge*, 2nd edn, New York: HarperCollins.

37 For example, Lawrence, J., 2004, *Growing Leaders*, Oxford: BRF; Dunn, J., 1995, *The Effective Leader*, Eastbourne: Kingsway.

38 See, for example, Bass, B. M. and Riggio, R. E., 2006, *Transformational Leadership*, 2nd edn, Mahwah, NJ: Psychology Press.

39 Romans 12.3–8.

40 As we shall see in a subsequent chapter, these are three words that summarize some of the core qualities expected of a leader in the earliest church and that refer to capacities to serve as representative of Christ, to teach and to manage a household church.

41 This would appear to have been the case for Paul himself (Acts 9.1–9), and was also the case for (e.g.) Moses (Exodus 3—4) and Jeremiah (Jeremiah 1.9).

42  Nehemiah may well be a good example of this.

43  This was the experience of David (1 Sam. 16.13) and Timothy (2 Tim. 1.6).

44  1 Corinthians 1.25–31.

45  2 Corinthians 12.7–10.

46  See Nehemiah 1—2.

47  Vergauwe, J., Wille, B., Hofmans, J., Kaiser, R. B. and de Fruyt, F., 2017, 'Too Much Charisma Can make Leaders Look Less Effective', *Harvard Business Review*, September 2017.

48  Gemmil, G. and Oakley, J., 1997, 'Leadership: An Alienating Social Myth', in Grint, K. (ed.), 1997, *Leadership: Classical, Contemporary and Critical Approaches*, Oxford: Oxford University Press, pp. 272–88.

49  Western, S., 2013, *Leadership: A Critical Text*, London: Sage, p. 239.

50  Maccoby reflects extensively on this phenomenon and his conclusion is aptly summed up in one of his chapter titles, 'From Bureaucratic Followers to Interactive Collaborators' in *The Leaders We Need*.

51  House, R. J., 1971, 'A Path Goal Theory of Leader Effectiveness', *Administrative Science Quarterly* 16, pp. 321–8.

52  This theory first came to prominence through Dansereau, F., Graen, G. B. and Haga, W., 1975, 'A Vertical Dyad Linkage Approach to Leadership in Formal Organisations', *Organizational Behavior and Human Performance* 13, pp. 46–78.

53  An idea developed much more fully some years later by Kellerman in *Followership*, who differentiates between followers on the basis of their level of engagement with the goals and activities of an enterprise, identifying five different types of followers: isolates, bystanders, participants, activists and diehards.

54  Wright, W. C., 2000, *Relational Leadership*, Carlisle: Paternoster Press, p. 17.

55  Kellerman, *Followership*, p. xv.

56  Orwell, G., 2003, *Shooting an Elephant and Other essays*, London: Penguin.

57  Kellerman, *Followership*, p. xvii.

58  Harvey, M., 2006, 'Leadership and the Human Condition', in Goethals and Sorenson, *Quest for a General Theory of Leadership*, p. 44.

59  Grint, K., 2005, *Leadership: Limits and Possibilities*, Basingstoke: Palgrave Macmillan.

60  Grint, *Leadership*, p. 37.

61  Now known as the Advisory Board of Ministry (ABM).

62  Advisory Council for the Church's Ministry, 1987, *Education for the Church's Ministry: The Report of the Working Party on Assessment*, London: ACCM.

63  A most helpful exposition of this paper can be found in Greenwood, R., 1995, *Transforming Priesthood*, London: SPCK, pp. 57–9.

64  Kellerman, *Followership*, p. 239.

65  Hollander, E. P. and Julian, J. W., 1969, 'Contemporary Trends in the Analysis of Leadership Processes', *Psychological Bulletin* 71(5), pp. 387–97.

66  For example, Kouzes and Posner, *The Leadership Challenge*; Collins, J., 2001, *Good to Great*, London: Random House; Bennis, and Nanus, *Leaders*.

67  Transformational thinking and ideas provide a framework for such works as Adair, J., 2001, *The Leadership of Jesus*, Norwich: Canterbury Press; Bonem, M., 2012, *In Pursuit of Great and Godly Leadership*, San Francisco, CA: Jossey-Bass.

68  Burns, *Leadership*.

69  Bass, B. M., 1985, *Leadership and Performance Beyond Expectations*, New York: Free Press; Bass, B. M. and Riggio, R. E., 2006, *Transformational Leadership*,

2nd edn, New York: Psychology Press; Bass B. M. and Avolio, B. J. (eds), 1994, *Improving Organizational Effectiveness through Transformational Leadership*, Thousand Oaks, CA: Sage.

70 Bass, B. M., 1998, 'The Ethics of Transformational Leadership', in Ciulla, J. (ed.), *Ethics: The Heart of Leadership*, Westport, CT: Praeger, pp. 16–192.

71 Theorists from a transformational perspective contrast such leadership with transactional forms of leadership, which are by and large defined by the exchanges that take place between leaders and followers. While such exchanges are not always inappropriate at certain levels within organizations (e.g. the exchange of appropriate remuneration to an employee for work undertaken, or the performance management of workers or volunteers by managers), taken alone they do not have the capacity to enable followers to accomplish more than what is usually expected of them nor to go beyond their own self-interests for the good of others.

72 Burns, *Leadership*, p. 19.

73 A focus on these particular leader qualities has led many to suggest that transformational theory represents a resurrection of classical trait theory in another guise. Perhaps the principal difference between the two is in the fact that transformational writers insist that such qualities can be learned as opposed to being innate, and in transformational leadership's focus on the impact of such leadership upon followers rather than solely upon the person of the leader.

74 Bass and Riggio, *Transformational Leadership*, p. 6.

75 See p. 29, where we reference Maccoby's work on transference, in Maccoby, *The Leaders We Need*, pp. 43–55.

76 Dugan, *Leadership Theory*, p. 244.

77 Ospina, S. and Sorenson, G. L. J., 2006, 'A Constructionist Lens on Leadership: Charting New Territory', in Goethals and Sorenson, *Quest for a General Theory of Leadership*, p. 195.

78 Western, *Leadership*, pp. 243–80.

79 Western, *Leadership*, pp. 275–6.

80 Western, *Leadership*, p. 42.

81 Clarke, A. D., 2008, *A Pauline Theology of Church Leadership*, London: T & T Clark, pp. 131–55.

82 For example, 1 Corinthians 12; Ephesians 4.11–16.

83 1 Corinthians 12.7, 12–13.

84 Gill, R., 2011, *Theory and Practice of Leadership*, London: Sage, p. 8.

85 Bolden, R., 2004, *What is Leadership?*, Leadership South West Research Report, Exeter, www.leadershipsouthwest.com.

86 Sinclair, A., 2007, *Leadership for the Disillusioned*, p. xvi.

87 The Faith and Order Commission of the Church of England, 2015, *Senior Church Leadership: A Resource for Reflection*, The Archbishops' Council, www.churchofengland.org/sites/default/files/2017-10/senior_church_leadership_faoc.pdf, p. 38 (accessed 25 November 2019).

# 3

# Leadership in the Christian Tradition I: Leadership in the Old Testament

*The Judaeo-Christian Tradition provides the longest continuous tradition of reflection on leadership in communities that the human culture has ever seen.*[1]

Leadership may well be a subject whose popularity has grown exponentially over the course of the last four or five decades. However, it is far from being a recent invention or discovery. While its exposition in forms associated with business-school texts may be absent from the biblical narratives, leadership, as defined in the terms we have previously posited, may be observed from the earliest periods recorded in this literature, and a concern for leadership that is both morally good and functionally effective is a recurrent theme throughout the Christian Scriptures. Given the definitive way in which these Scriptures shape our understanding of what it means to live life as those who are created by God, who are placed within the community of people belonging to God, and who seek to order their lives in obedience to God, our understanding of leadership must be informed and governed by insights provided by these Scriptures.

Our exploration into these texts will progress on three main fronts. First, we will want to analyse the different ways in which leadership is exercised and expressed in the biblical narratives. We will explore, over the course of this chapter and the next, leadership in the Old Testament era, the leadership of Jesus and also the leadership of those who played a significant part in the growth, development and establishment of the Church in the period immediately following the death and resurrection of Jesus. While we recognize that insights might be gleaned from leadership practice in each of these eras, we also recognize that the process of revelation in Scripture is progressive, culminating in the appearance on earth of Jesus, God's ultimate revelation.[2] Thus, we must acknowledge at the outset that some of the insights we discover in the earliest texts must be partial, offering an incomplete understanding of fully formed Christian leadership. Jesus is for us the definitive and peerless expression of authentic leadership and remains for us the bar against which all other expressions must be tested and weighed.

Second, we will need to examine the particular words and titles used by the community of faith, in Old and New Testaments, to describe those exercising leadership functions. Equally interesting will be an examination of those words commonly used in wider society to denote leaders and yet which were eschewed or disregarded by the early Church. Our study of specific leadership words or titles is not designed to enable us to uncover a universal, biblical blueprint for leadership, capable of being replicated, but rather to discern unchanging principles, values and emphases that are to inform authentically Christian leadership in every age, irrespective of specific situation. In this we are minded of the pertinent warning sounded by Michael Ramsay:

> To burrow in the New Testament for forms of ministry and imitate them is archaeological religion: to seek that form of ministry which the whole New Testament creates is the more evangelical way. And our view of the ministry had better be evangelical than archaeological.[3]

Our third avenue of exploration will be of some of the broader theological themes and emphases that shape the Christian narrative. As we have already established, leadership is always significantly shaped by its location within a specific context or community. Christian leadership emerges from, and is determined by, the community of faith in which it is located. This community is itself, of course, shaped by its understanding of, and encounter with, the God who uniquely reveals himself in Christ, who is present to animate that community by virtue of his indwelling Spirit, and of whose activity in Christ this community is the expression.[4] To understand, therefore, the precise dynamics of authentically Christian leadership we must examine the way in which it is directed and informed by such theological motifs as, inter alia, Trinity, incarnation, eschatology and pneumatology, the very motifs that define the community from which such leadership emerges.

If, as we have previously suggested, leadership is that process that enables people to move forwards towards the achievement of shared and beneficial goals, then leadership seeps out of the pages of the Hebrew Scriptures. How might we describe the leadership we encounter here?

## Old Testament leadership characteristics

### Contingent

The narrative contained in these Scriptures is that of God's redemptive purposes for the world, centring on God's determination to establish a particular people who will belong to him in a unique way and act as a living witness to his nature, presence and purposes for the sake of the rest of the world. In many ways, the clearest leadership in all this is exercised by God himself who is presented all along as the true leader of his people Israel. Many of the specific leadership titles that will in due course be used of human leaders are ascribed in the first instance to God, who is understood to be the Judge[5] of all the earth, the Shepherd[6] of Israel, and the one who liberates and leads[7] his people. Whatever else we might go on to say about human leadership, we must begin by signalling that any such leadership is rooted in and a reflection of God's own original leadership. Human leadership is always contingent upon God and delegated by him. Human leadership can never, thus, be construed as original either in form or intention but is intended to be a participation in and extension of the leadership of God. Nevertheless, although God never abdicates his own position and responsibility as true leader, for the most part he chooses to exercise this leadership through the agency of human leaders to whom he entrusts responsibility and with whom he shares this leadership. Although God is the one who sovereignly chooses to effect the deliverance of his people Israel from slavery in Egypt, his method of accomplishing this is through the agency of a leader, Moses.[8] At subsequent times of great crisis in the early days of the nation's life in the Promised Land, God's way of acting to come to his people's help was to raise up human leaders (judges).[9] We might say that the calling of leaders to play a crucial role in enabling the flourishing of the whole people is entirely consistent with God's habitual way of ordering his world according to his purposes, that of choosing a part in order to bless the whole. This consistent biblical theme is ably unpacked and explored in relation to contemporary Christian leadership by Graham Tomlin:

> He chooses some to be the means by which the blessing he pours out in Christ reaches the rest ... blessing the Church through particular people called out from the whole to enable the Church to be what it is called to be, and to do what it is called to do: to recall humanity to its priestly role in Creation.[10]

The entrusting of specific leadership roles to some is thus not to be seen as in any way an undermining of God's leadership but rather the way in which he chooses to express his own leadership.

### Charismatic

The earliest forms of leadership we come across in the Old Testament are charismatic in origin. That is, they come about through the direct action of God who initiates leadership through the agency of his Spirit working upon and in human beings. Such leadership often arises as a result of a dramatic encounter between the subject and God,[11] or through some other mystical experience in which the Spirit of God enters and influences a person in a wholly new way.[12] Although such endowment is no guarantee that a leader will always lead well, nor that they will be immune from moral flaws that threaten their integrity and effectiveness,[13] the charismatic nature of leadership highlights some important foundational truths concerning leadership.

Leadership clearly matters to God. His agency in calling and equipping people for leadership roles indicates his concern for the advancement of his own purposes and for human thriving, and the central place occupied by leadership in the accomplishment of such purposes. Indeed, some of his fiercest criticism is reserved for leaders and those entrusted with responsibility for others who have neglected these responsibilities and failed in their duty of care.[14] Thus, leadership is always to be exercised with a sense of accountability before God both for its effectiveness and its moral character. Moreover, to neglect the provision and stewarding of appropriate leadership is somehow to be out of step with God and with his way of ordering affairs on earth. While we may rightly recoil from leadership that is self-serving, abusive or otherwise flawed, this should not automatically lead us to conclude that leadership per se is inevitably a bad thing and alien to God's way of ordering things. When (as was all too often the case in the history of Israel) appointed leaders fall short of the ideal of their calling, God does not abandon the idea of leadership altogether, but rather acts to remove those leaders who have been resistant to his word and holds out the promise of leaders who will represent him and serve his people more faithfully. So the fatally flawed and self-obsessed king Saul is rejected in favour of another who is 'a man after God's own heart'.[15] The faithless and corrupt leaders of Judah at the time of the Babylonian exile will be stepped down and God will extend his care for his people through another leader in the tradition of David.[16]

Furthermore, we might say that proper leadership maintains a direct sense of connection with God. As the Old Testament era progresses, later forms of leadership might be described as institutional or dynastic rather than charismatic. Their origin now lies not exclusively in God but rather in family of origin. There is, at best, ambivalence about such leadership and its merits. When Israel, out of envy of other surrounding nations who seem to have more certain forms of leadership, demands an end to the rather less predictable pattern of government by charismatically appointed judges and insists on being provided with a king, this is understood to be a failure of trust in God and a rejection of his direct appointment of leaders.[17] One of the great tensions that will surface in the life of God's people in subsequent ages will be that between those who hold office by virtue of human appointment or birthright (kings and priests, leaders of state and cult respectively) and those who have been raised up directly by God (prophets) in order that God's concerns might be represented to those who have overlooked them and for whom leadership has lost any sense of accountability before God. God's response in the face of poor or corrupt human leadership is to raise up his own, more faithful, leaders.

This tension between institutional and charismatic leadership is never far from the surface in any mature or developed organization, and is a particular challenge for the Christian Church.[18] Institutional leadership usually emerges as a requirement for the preservation and maintenance of values and behaviours that are seen as integral to the organization and that have emerged in the course of its history. The institution appoints to leadership position those whose role increasingly becomes the creative stewardship of such tradition. Ideally, it is such leadership that guarantees the capacity of the institution to enable its own renewal and ongoing vitality. Two dangers, however, face such leadership and its host organization. On the one hand, the tradition can become fossilized and lose its capacity to function in a dynamic way, improvising and applying itself afresh in the light of changing context. On the other hand, the leadership itself can become self-serving, the position assuming greater importance than the tradition it was formed to steward. This latter failing was the one, it seems, to which later Old Testament leadership increasingly fell prey. When institutional leadership loses its capacity to effect its own renewal, then charismatic leadership, initiated by a more immediate work of God's Spirit, is required to enable the institution to own afresh those core emphases from its founding history that might have fallen into neglect, and to receive and act upon fresh direction from God. Positional leadership will always be necessary beyond the very earliest stages of any movement or organization. Perhaps the challenge for any such organization is to continually recognize where, and in whom, the Spirit of God is blowing, what leadership he is initiating, and to ensure that those who are the recipients of his particular charisms are those above all who are placed in positions of leadership within the institution. The charismatic nature of leadership also bears witness to the truth that leadership is not the exclusive preserve of those who are humanly talented or who have other advantages. Many of those whom God calls and establishes as leaders are unlikely candidates for a number of reasons. Moses has experienced crushing failure and disappointment in the very arena to which he is now invited to return, not to mention his diffidence in public speaking;[19] Gideon appears to be a rather insignificant coward,[20] hardly the greatest qualifications for military leadership; David[21] and Jeremiah[22] are rather too young to be taken seriously; Nehemiah lacks position and authority and is already committed to an indentured role from which escape is unthinkable;[23] Joseph is in prison with no hope of release.[24] Christian leadership does not despise natural or innate talents and qualities but will never see them as adequate solely in and of themselves. Genuinely effective leadership relies upon the agency of God working through others.

### Heroic

Many of the clearest examples of leadership in the Old Testament tend to be heroic in nature. If we were to categorize them according to the different leadership styles we referenced in our previous chapter[25] then we might define them as being generally commanding or pacesetting. This should not necessarily surprise us. Many of the situations into which these leaders are

thrust are situations either of crisis or of innovation, each requiring determined and directive leadership.[26] Often, these leaders are required to rescue
Israel from physical and spiritual challenges and threats that have come
about as a consequence of Israel's unfaithfulness or unconcern for God.
The danger, however, in drawing uncritically too many leadership examples
from the Old Testament is that we can easily fall into the trap of conceiv-
ing leadership generally as a heroic activity that consists of the direct and
directive actions of a prominent, solitary individual. While such examples
might be broadly helpful for those faced with particular crises or start-up
situations, we need to be very circumspect in extending our application of
Old Testament leadership styles more generally.

## Provisional

The Old Testament itself anticipates a coming, future era in which its own
existing leadership forms will be, to an extent at least, superseded by a more
dispersed form of leadership. Some of the exilic prophets speak of a coming
age in which the experience of being equipped by God's Spirit, thus far
the province of the select few, will be extended to the entire community of
faith.[27] The consequence of this will be that the knowledge of God, which
has previously been mediated to the community by the anointed leader,[28]
will be dispersed widely throughout the whole community who will share
in a common and direct knowledge of God.[29] Now there will no longer be a
requirement for special teachers, for 'they will all know me from the least of
them to the greatest'. The leadership tasks associated with particular individuals are now shared by the whole people. The anointed individual has
given way to the anointed community. Leadership is, at least to an extent,
now more widely dispersed among the entire community, even among those
who previously, for social or economic reasons, may have been excluded.[30]
As Douglas Stuart comments:

> For Christians the significance of this expectation should be clear. Those
> who live in the age of the Spirit cannot expect God to restrict any ministry
> of the Spirit from anyone simply because he or she is old or young, male
> or female, or of high or low standing socially. Where churches attempt to
> do this, they risk missing the fulness of God's blessing.[31]

Thus we might say that the concerns of leadership as encountered in the Old
Testament are unchanging, while the predominant styles and expressions of
such concerns are provisional and partial.

## Old Testament leadership words and titles

Among the various titles and other words associated with leadership that we encounter in the Old Testament literature, a number stand out as being of special significance and as shedding light on the wider conception of leadership. Several of the core ideas integral to these words carry over into and shape some New Testament leadership understandings.

### Judge

The earliest formal leaders in Israel, prior to the establishment of the monarchy, were designated Judges (*shofet*). Judges were concerned with the establishment or maintenance of justice, which, in Israel, was seen not simply as conformity to an impersonal moral standard but rather in more relational terms as the right ordering of society according to God's values and in order that God's peace (*shalom*) might be established.[32] Responsibility for seeing such order established involved judges in a range of possible actions including ruling, delivering the community from danger,[33] coming to the aid of those suffering injustice, championing the cause of the needy and disadvantaged,[34] and ensuring the material and spiritual well-being of the community. The judge's role is thus a clear reflection of the role that God exercises over the earth and in particular over his covenant people, is performed as an extension of this role, and is an anticipation of the ministry to be performed by God's future messianic ruler.[35] Leadership from the outset is thus seen as a participation in the work of God, at the initiative of God and in a manner that is in accord with his aims and values. Whereas much of the contemporary leadership literature stresses the creative role of the leader in determining direction, goals and objectives for her organization, the Christian leader is less concerned to be creative in this regard and more concerned to discern and champion those objectives that are already determined by God. One of the key distinctives, thus, of Christian leadership is that it is to be conceived of as contingent upon, delegated by and submitted to God who is the true leader.

In the era of the New Covenant under which the presence of the Spirit extends to the entire community, the whole Church is enlisted in the task of judging the earth in union with Christ.[36] Thus the task of the Church must always include the pursuit of God's justice, the establishment of God's shalom, the expression of particular concern for the downtrodden and disadvantaged, and opposition to those things that hinder the fulfilment of God's purposes. Christian leadership will be focused significantly on enabling the Church to perform this task faithfully and on reminding the Church of its calling when it is in danger of neglecting this.

## Shepherd

Shepherd (*ra'ah*) is a way of designating rulers, leaders and deities, with a rich history in antiquity and by no means unique to Israel. The Babylonian king Hammurabi refers to himself in his law code as *shepherd of men*, while the oldest of the Egyptian royal hymns describes the role of the king as being to act as shepherd for his flock through providing food and protection.[37] Plato[38] likens rulers of the city state to shepherds who care for their flocks.

At one level, the frequent use of this term to denote leaders is a little surprising. The role of shepherd, while widespread in the ancient Middle East, was not one that was in any way glamorous or necessarily worthy of great honour. The shepherd was very much in thrall to his master, the owner of the flock, and had very little personal status. Nevertheless, his was a hugely demanding and responsible role. Sheep and goats were valuable commodities and often in danger from the attacks of wild animals and robbers. If a sheep was lost, then, unless he could prove it was not his fault, and that he had taken all possible steps to prevent it, the shepherd himself became financially liable for the loss. Every incentive was present to the shepherd to ensure the safety and well-being of the flock. It was often the case that a shepherd had grown up with his flock since boyhood and thus had an intimate connection with and knowledge of each of the animals under his care. To conceive of leadership through the lens of shepherding is to cast it in profoundly personal and caring terms, as a weighty responsibility entrusted to one by another.

The metaphorical use of this word and its cognates to designate leaders is most commonly found in the writings of the exilic prophets. God himself is frequently referred to as the Shepherd of his people[39] who are understood to be his flock. However, the responsibility of shepherding the flock is shared with human leaders whom God appoints.[40] The Persian emperor Cyrus, whom God will use to effect deliverance of Israel from their Babylonian captivity, is introduced as God's shepherd who will 'perform all my desire',[41] while the eschatological promise of the restoration and reunification of the divided kingdoms of Israel and Judah envisages God exercising his care over his people through the agency of a Davidic ruler styled as shepherd.[42]

Not only is this word used regularly in the Old Testament to describe the work of leadership but it is also taken up consistently by the New Testament writers and, as much as any other word, shapes profoundly our understanding of the essence of both the task and character of Christian leadership. Shepherds are concerned first and foremost with the flourishing and well-being of the sheep. The corrupt leaders of Ezekiel 34 are berated by God for their neglect of their expected duties and responsibilities. They have failed to feed the flock, have not paid particular attention to the healing and restoration of those who are wounded or damaged, and have refused to go looking for those who have been scattered or become lost and endangered. Without adequate leadership the flock is seen as vulnerable to attack from hostile forces, as in danger of becoming lost and aimless, and of being deprived of those things that are essential for its well-being. By definition, leadership must therefore be other-focused and never self-serving or dominating.[43] As Walter Wright observes: 'Shepherds are there for the sheep! It is a position of responsibility and service, not status and power. The sheep do not exist for the shepherd; the shepherd was hired because of the sheep.'[44] We must always be suspicious of any leadership whose consequence is to diminish people, instrumentalize them, treating them merely as a means to achieving an end, or that refuses to take into account people's legitimate needs and aspirations. We will be equally suspicious of those who seek to use their leadership role as a means of gaining favour or accolades, or whose concern to impress others is greater than their commitment to those for whom they are responsible. To practise leadership in such a way is to be an unfaithful shepherd.

In short, the Old Testament tradition understands leadership to be primarily concerned to facilitate the thriving of people and communities through the provision of direction, especially when this might not be clear, through acting to avert danger and threats, and by exercising concern especially for those who are most vulnerable for whatever reason. While this understanding has clear and direct applicability in the context of local church leadership, leadership that has as its goal the enabling of all people to fulfil God's call to work with him in the advance of his kingdom has relevance no matter what the context. Likening the people of God to a flock of sheep is by no means to imply that our destiny is merely to be passive recipients of God's largesse. Israel in the Old Testament, and the Church in the New, are called to an active ministry, that of being a sign to the rest of the world of the truth and goodness of God, a blessed people through whom others would experience God's blessing.[45] Authentic leadership is not intended to keep the flock in lazy dependence upon its ministrations, but will always have in mind the animating and empowering of others for the specific purposes God has intended for his people.

The motif of shepherd as a metaphor for leadership is developed by the New Testament writers partly, no doubt, because of its rich history in their tradition but also because this is an image that Jesus himself adopts explicitly to describe his own ministry and that of those who will follow him. Not only is he the good shepherd who lays down his life for the sake of his sheep[46] but he is also the one who longs to gather to himself those sheep who are lost,[47] and who is heartbroken over the plight of Israel who are distressed and dispirited like sheep without a shepherd.[48] His general instructions to his apostles prior to his ascension are to continue and to replicate his own ministry and leadership. His specific and more personal command to Peter is to 'shepherd my sheep'.[49]

It is clear that this understanding of leadership gained wide provenance in the early Christian community. Peter himself urges those with leadership responsibility in the Church to shepherd the flock of God,[50] always with an eye on the fact that our leadership is to be in imitation of the Chief Shepherd to whom we will ultimately have to give account for the way in which we have exercised our leadership. The apostle Paul, in describing the fivefold leadership functions that Christ brings about for the health and well-being of the Church, includes shepherd (*poimēn* – often translated as *pastor*) in his list.[51] In his valedictory instruction to the elders (*presbuteroi*) of the Ephesian church,[52] Paul urges them to shepherd (*poimainein*) the Church of God, to be on guard for the flock, and to fulfil their calling as those whom the Holy Spirit has placed as overseers (*episkopoi*) of that flock. What is fascinating about this verse, to which we must return when we give fuller consideration to New Testament leadership words, is the juxtaposition of three words all of which will come to have huge significance for understanding the nature of church leadership in the ages to come. In this context, elders, overseers (bishops) and shepherds seem to be interchangeable terms to describe those charged with responsibility for leadership in the local church. Irrespective of the later formalization of some of these terms and their association with specific offices in the Church, we note here that each sheds light on the true nature of all Christian leadership and its particular concern to enable the flourishing of all God's people and their mobilization in fruitful service.

### Servant

The servant motif (*ebed*) has been described by John Mackay as 'the most significant symbol in the Bible and in the Christian religion'.[53] It is certainly one of the most widely used designations for leaders in the Old Testament. Its further importance for our purposes lies in the way in which Jesus' apparent reflection on particular usages of this motif in the Old Testament informed his own self-understanding and consequently shaped consciousness of the leadership calling and task in the early Church.

Schulz[54] draws attention to the breadth of meaning of which this word is capable, being used to describe both those of the lowest social status (slaves[55] and vassals[56]) and also those enjoying the highest possible privilege, that of being God's servant.[57] Perhaps it is the richly nuanced nature of this term that makes it such a useful designation for those who are called to lead on God's behalf.

No matter what the specific context in which 'servant' is used, its essential connotation is one of humility before another. In Israel it was used to describe slaves or other indentured workers, and while the Jewish system of slavery is generally held to be far more benevolent than those of neighbouring nations (let alone later practices of slavery), the servant is owned by another and his whole focus is on acting for the benefit of his master, being concerned to fulfil that person's will rather than his own. For the Christian leader, servanthood signals the importance of obedience to God and of submission to his will. David is idealized as the model servant who kept God's commands and followed God with all of his heart, doing only that which was right in God's sight,[58] while Caleb is differentiated from his peers as a servant who has followed God fully.[59] Effective Christian leaders are always followers first and never lose their commitment to discern and pursue God's will rather than their own. Such service is a duty but equally an immense privilege, and our obedience is a joyful response to this grace that has been extended to us. More than that, servants of the Lord have a clear dependence upon God leading to a proper expectation that God himself will resource them and act on their behalf. So Elijah sees his servant status and his obedience as grounds for expecting God to vindicate him before the prophets of Baal.[60]

Being a servant of the Lord may well imply occupying a privileged and honoured place. However, this is never seen as grounds for using such privilege for our own advantage. Rather, servanthood also highlights our calling to serve others and to enable their own legitimate interests to be furthered. The counsel given to Solomon's heir Rehoboam by the elders of Israel[61] is to be a servant to his people and to serve them. This will result in their being willing to be his servants for ever. True service is a blessing to those whom we lead and fosters harmony in churches and other organizations. As Wright observes:

> Leadership is for lovers of people. Servant leadership is about a relationship with God that so shapes who we are that people see in us a person of character and commitment whose influence they choose to follow ... Servant leadership is community directed and uses its power not for selfish ends but for growth of those who are being led and the accomplishment of the shared mission of the community.[62]

Robert Greenleaf's suspicions, after a career in management research, that the more authoritarian styles of leadership beloved of the institutions of high modernity were ineffective, led him to develop the more ethically driven perspective that has come to be known as 'servant leadership'. A member of the Society of Friends, Greenleaf's leadership convictions draw significantly upon the leadership practices modelled by Jesus and prefigured in the Old Testament Scriptures. For Greenleaf, the servant leader is always servant first: the aspiration to lead is prompted by a desire to see the needs of others met. The goal of servant leadership, and its best test, according to Greenleaf is:

> Do those served grow as persons; do they, while being served, become healthier, wiser, freer, more autonomous, more likely themselves to become servants? And what is the effect on the least privileged in society; will they benefit, or at least, not be further deprived?[63]

Although criticized for a tendency to encourage and condone a form of paternalism in leadership, and thus in danger of stunting the growth and development of followers, servant leadership has become influential in a number of different spheres. Although we will want to argue that true servanthood results in the personal growth of followers and in the enlargement of their own capacity to serve and lead themselves, the insights of Greenleaf and others have clear resonance with values at the heart of any Christian understanding of leadership. Most significantly we will want to affirm the truth that Christian leaders are servants first and that leadership is a consequence of our willingness to serve God and others. As Neil Cole puts it:

> Servanthood is not an adjective to describe a good leader as if it is one of the many qualities of a good leader. Servanthood is what we need, even more than leadership. Leadership is just a function for the servant.[64]

Servanthood as a motif for leadership comes into especially sharp focus in the book of the prophet Isaiah, occurring 19 times in the exilic chapters 40—55. This particular collection of texts, containing a series of passages often described as *servant songs* because of their exposition of the role of a servant of the Lord, are of particular interest because of their frequent echoes in the life and ministry of Jesus. The New Testament writers often represent his career with reference to, and in the light of, these texts,[65] no doubt prompted by the fact that Jesus himself appears to have reflected intensely upon them and understood his own ministry to be conformed to them.[66] The interpretation of the servant songs is by no means unproblematic, principally because the identity of the servant is unclear. A largely unresolved debate continues as to whether the prophet has in mind an individual (either himself, a future idealized, messianic figure, or Cyrus the Persian, who is referenced explicitly as God's anointed[67]) or the nation of Israel (either in part or as a whole). It may well be that the ambivalence is deliberate and that the calling of the elect nation, to be servant of God for the benefit of the other nations, is enabled through the servant ministry of the one particular servant. Schulz points out the shift in the servant theme in these chapters immediately following the account of the substitutionary, atoning death of the righteous servant which makes many righteous.[68] In the remaining chapters of the book, *ebed* is used exclusively in the plural and now denotes a faithful remnant within Israel acting on God's behalf: 'In terms of the thematic development within the book of Isaiah, the work of the individual servant restores the national servant so that individuals within Israel once again serve God.'[69]

Our cursory investigation of leadership in the Old Testament gives us a picture of leadership that is called into being by God as a sharing of his responsibility for a right ordering of the world. It is exercised in obedience to his direction and will. It is focused on enabling his particular people to flourish and thrive, and thus to be enabled to fulfil their own unique calling to be a light to the nations and a sign of God's living presence on earth. It is such an understanding that lies at the heart of Jesus' own leadership and that he develops further during his own earthly ministry.

---

## Leadership on the ground

When Linda and David Maslen recommitted their lives to Christ after a number of years away from faith, they were keen to throw themselves into active Christian service. With a number of years' experience of senior management in the corporate world, most recently with HMRC, where she oversaw a network of contact and enquiry centres, with responsibility for over 10,000 staff, Linda assumed that her own sphere of ministry was most likely to be the boardroom. Although this did prove to be an area where she was able to exercise influence for Christ, it seemed that God also wanted to stretch her expectation of how he might use her.

In the immediate aftermath of the financial crash, Christians Together in Calderdale had established one of the first food banks, in Halifax, West Yorkshire, as a response to the serious issues to do with poverty now surfacing in the community. Dave became involved in this ministry, serving large numbers of people, many of whom were either homeless, asylum seekers, sex workers, suffering from addiction, or a combination of the above. This was a ministry from which Linda excused herself, as she felt she had neither aptitude nor calling for it. Nor did she feel that she could even begin to identify with the groups of people who were served by this ministry. However, some months after Dave had joined the team, convicted by God over her hardness of heart towards the food-bank users, and her lack of love for those whom the Lord regarded as precious, Linda was moved to offer her own services to the work. She was asked to set up a prayer ministry team to offer prayer to those using the food bank.

### An accidental church plant

Most of the clients were entirely unchurched but some began asking for prayer for personal needs, often revealing heartbreaking evidence of personal brokenness. As clients began seeing prayers answered, sometimes in dramatic fashion, the team started to see a trickle of people

---

coming to faith. In their desire to help them to grow and to find Christian community they took them along to Sunday worship in local churches. This wasn't a huge success, not because the local churches were not welcoming but because of the immense culture gap that existed between the worlds of these new Christians and those of the predominantly middle-class local churches. Linda began to wrestle with how new converts might be enabled to settle in the Church.

The following months saw a number of reasonably unsuccessful attempts at addressing this issue. Neither a Monday evening Bible study meeting, nor a Sunday afternoon 'Church Lite' in the town centre, with a bring and share lunch (Linda is horrified today to reflect on the ways in which we fail to question the pervasive influence of middle-class cultural values on our approaches to mission and discipleship), really seemed to engage people. The issue was becoming more pressing as a growing number of people were coming to faith through the ministry of the food bank. It was then that Linda and the team hit upon the idea of Saturday Gathering.

Launched in October 2011, Saturday Gathering (SG) was intended as a six-week experiment. Linda was insistent that this was not being set up as a church, and that those serving on the team should continue to be involved in their own local churches. Holding the event on a Saturday evening meant that this would not conflict with any Sunday worship in those churches. Using the same space as the food bank, the format was shaped by the tried and tested Alpha formula of worship, teaching and prayer ministry, all in the context of a meal. Linda was clear that the focus must be on encountering Jesus. To that end, worship was of a style that was both culturally accessible and that would facilitate encounter with God, and teaching was based on narratives from the Gospels. The teaching was processed in discussion over the meal, and this was followed by further worship and opportunity to receive prayer. The format was a huge success, and the six-week experiment has continued until the present day.

As SG gained momentum and as community was formed among those involved, despite the intentions of the team, increasingly those coming along began to refer to it as their church. After some months of meeting, a number of people were now asking to be baptized. In due course, 26 candidates (17 planned and 9 more spontaneous) were baptized and confirmed by the local bishop in a glorious service. Linda now realized that she and the team had, in her words, 'planted a church by accident'. Her task was now to see a proper foundation laid for the church and to enable the team to grapple with issues around how the church might be appropriately ordered. What would it mean to order a church in a manner that demonstrated faithfulness both to Anglican theology and ecclesiology and also to the specific requirements of the missional context of the church?

Linda's wide experience in managing people, with a focus on empowering others to discover solutions to problems, proved invaluable as she now led her inexperienced team on a journey of discerning direction for the new church. In particular, the team had to be enabled to let go of some of their own inherited assumptions, both ecclesiological, in terms of what church looked like, and cultural, in terms of how people might be expected to behave. Because of the chronic personal brokenness of so many of the SG members, a large proportion of people had lifestyles and relationships that were highly chaotic. How might SG enable people to embrace lifestyles more in keeping with the pattern of Christ's calling, without making this appear to be a condition of belonging, as opposed to a consequence of experiencing the transforming power of Christ? How could they hold out the hope of forgiveness and restoration without appearing to condemn people for the consequences of their brokenness? One of the strengths of SG is the coherence of the leadership team. This was forged in those early days as the whole team worked together to establish clear vision and values, which enabled it to navigate its way through these initial murky waters.

## Building relationships with statutory bodies

As SG gained momentum, it began to come to the attention of other agencies. The police began to recognize that the ministry of SG was leading to a reduction in people living on the streets. The local council, with the approach of universal credit, were desperate to build greater financial resilience among those who would be most affected by this new policy. Recognizing the success of SG in working in this area for the benefit of those whom other statutory agencies were unable to reach, the council approached SG and invited them to apply for financial assistance in this ministry to the homeless. So keen were the council to offer resources that they were even prepared to waive the requirement that recipients would not engage in the propagation of faith.

One of Linda's key responsibilities now lay in the development and management of relationships with other statutory bodies as SG sought to be a catalyst for further kingdom initiatives in the community. What was really needed was a more permanent building, which could be open on a daily basis and operate as a centre for other much-needed activities and services. The council had a redundant former church building they could make available. This they did, even bending over backwards to remove restrictive covenants on the building forbidding its use for public worship. The provision of this building, now known as the Gathering Place, enabled the provision of daily drop-ins, a community cafe and other key services. Most importantly, it provided the facilities to open a winter shelter for the use of those rough sleeping in the community.

### Living by faith

The new SG building came also with the promise of a grant from the council of £60,000, a vital contribution towards the costs of the winter shelter. However, as the shelter was opened, news came from the council that, due to a shortfall in income, this funding would no longer be available. Linda's challenge was to encourage the SG trustees to remain confident in God's capacity to provide for the needs of a project that was being undertaken as a clear response to his direction. She was adamant that SG was a faith project and that those responsible for it must lead confidently out of faith, rather than be limited by fear. Holding firm in the face of this particular challenge proved to be a formative and faith-stretching experience for the trustees. Linda's resilience and confidence was rewarded when, ten weeks later, the council discovered a £60,000 surplus – which was donated to the winter shelter.

The convictions to do with leading others, and the understanding that relational and motivational forms of leadership are far more effective ways of bringing the best out of people than are more commanding and controlling styles, which Linda gained through her experience in the corporate world, have been very fruitfully deployed in SG. Over the last eight years, SG has seen close to 200 people baptized. A not insignificant proportion of those who have come to faith are now engaged in productive activity, whether voluntary or paid employment, or are serving in some way in SG and its associated ministries. Linda herself has now moved on from SG, having been ordained as an Anglican minister, and is currently the incumbent of a new church in a neighbouring city. The team she trained and developed is now doing an extremely effective job of leading SG and its associated ministries, continuing the vital work of enabling those on the furthest margins of society to experience the transforming love of Christ.

## Notes

1 Croft, S., 2016, *The Gift of Leadership*, Norwich: Canterbury Press, p. vii.

2 Hebrews 1.1–3.

3 Ramsay, M., 1990 [1936], *The Gospel and the Catholic Church*, London: SPCK, p. 69.

4 Ramsay, *The Gospel*, p. 7.

5 Genesis 18.25.

6 Psalm 80.1; Psalm 23.1.

7 Exodus 3.8 – the Hebrew word here is יצא (*ys'*), which has a strong overtone of causing something to happen through personal agency.

8 Exodus 3.10.

9 For example, Judges 2.16–18; 3.9–10.

10 Tomlin, G., 2014, *The Widening Circle*, London: SPCK, p. 113.

11 For example, Moses (Exod. 3—4), Samuel (1 Sam. 3), Gideon (Judg. 6.11–24), Ezekiel (Ezek. 1—2).

12 For example, Jephthah (Judg. 11.29), Samson (Judg. 13.25; 14.19), David (1 Sam. 16).

13 Samson lived an extraordinarily colourful life and would have been unlikely to satisfy those who select potential candidates for ordained ministry! Gideon, David and others who started well all ended badly, and even Moses fell short in his capacity to trust God and was unable to complete his commission. Saul, the first king of Israel, came into office through an exceptionally dramatic experience of God's call, yet a host of significant character flaws and inappropriate ambitions completely undermined his career, rendering him a liability.

14 This is especially the case with the oracles of God delivered by the prophets of the pre-exilic and exilic era: for example, Isaiah 1.23 and Ezekiel 34.1–10, in which rulers are castigated for their corruption, self-interest and lack of concern for justice.

15 1 Samuel 13.14.

16 Ezekiel 34.23–24.

17 1 Samuel 8.4–9.

18 An exceptionally helpful reflection on the mutual relationship between the institutional and charismatic in the life of a church or movement is offered in Snyder, H., 1997, *Signs of the Spirit*, Eugene, OR: Wipf and Stock, pp. 267–85.

19 Exodus 2—4.

20 Judges 6.11–15.
21 1 Samuel 16.7.
22 Jeremiah 1.6–8.
23 Nehemiah 1.11—2.8.
24 Genesis 40.23.
25 See above pp. 26–7.
26 There are, of course, some examples of leadership in a more settled time (e.g. the early career of Solomon in 1 Kings 3—8, or the social leadership of Boaz in the book of Ruth), but the Old Testament narrative is more concerned to relate the critical events of Israel's history than to give an account of settled life under the Judges or the monarchy.
27 Ezekiel 36.26–27.
28 Being privy to otherwise unknown knowledge of God and of his ways, and communicating this to others, has been a key part of the role of the leader.
29 Jeremiah 31.33–34.
30 Joel 2.28–29.
31 Stuart, D., 1987, *Word Biblical Commentary: Hosea–Jonah*, Waco, TX: Word Books, p. 262.
32 See Schultz, R., 1996, 'שׁפט', in VanGemeren, W. A. (ed.), 1996, *New International Dictionary of Old Testament Theology and Exegesis*, vol. 4, Carlisle: Paternoster Press, pp. 213–20.
33 Judges 2.16.
34 Psalm 68.5.
35 Psalm 96.13; Isaiah 11.3–4.
36 1 Corinthians 6.2.
37 Eichrodt, W., 1970, *Ezekiel*, London: SCM Press, p. 469.
38 Plato, 2007, *The Republic*, London: Penguin Classics, 4.440d.
39 For example, Jeremiah 31.10; 50.19; Ezekiel 34.11–16.
40 For example, Ezekiel 34.1–10; Jeremiah 3.15.
41 Isaiah 44.28.
42 Ezekiel 37.24.
43 Ezekiel 34.4.
44 Wright, W. C., 2000, *Relational Leadership*, Carlisle: Paternoster Press, p. 24.
45 Genesis 18.18.
46 John 10.11–18.
47 Luke 15.1–7.
48 Matthew 9.36.
49 John 21.16–18.
50 1 Peter 5.2–4.
51 Ephesians 4.12.
52 Acts 20.28.
53 Mackay, J., 1958–59, 'The Form of a Servant', *Theology Today* 15, p. 304.
54 Schultz, R., 1996, 'עבד', in VanGemeren, W. A. (ed.), *New International Dictionary of Old Testament Theology and Exegesis*, vol. 4, Carlisle, Paternoster Press, pp. 1183–98.
55 For example, Leviticus 25.39, 44–45.
56 For example, 2 Samuel 8.2, 6, 14.
57 For example, Numbers 12.6–8.
58 1 Kings 14.8.

59 Numbers 14.24.

60 1 Kings 18.36–37.

61 1 Kings 12.6–7.

62 Wright, *Relational Leadership*, pp. 12–13.

63 Greenleaf, R. K., 2002, *Servant Leadership: A Journey into the Nature of Legitimate Power and Greatness*, 25th anniversary edn, New York: Paulist Press, p. 27.

64 Cole, N., 2009, *Organic Leadership*, Ada, MI: Baker, p. 204.

65 For example, Matthew 12.18; Romans 10.16; 1 Peter 2.23.

66 For example, Mark 1.11; 10.43–45; Luke 4.18–21; 22.42.

67 Isaiah 45.1.

68 Isaiah 53.11.

69 Schultz, 'עבד', p. 1195.

# 4

# Leadership in the Christian Tradition II: Leadership in the New Testament

*Only with great care and caution can the church's ordained leaders take their cues from secular models of leadership, because our leading is to be congruent with the leadership of Christ himself.[1]*

*One of the greatest ironies of the history of Christianity is that its leaders constantly give in to the temptation of power ... even though they continued to speak in the name of Jesus who did not cling to his divine power but emptied himself and became as we are.[2]*

## The leadership of Jesus

Our reflection on the leadership of Jesus will lead us along two related paths. On the one hand we will seek to learn from the example Jesus sets for us in leadership and explore what it might mean for us to follow. We acknowledge that in so many ways Jesus' own ministry and leadership is unique and there are elements of it that it would be impossible for us to imitate (we are neither divine in nature nor are we capable of reconciling the world to God by our death, or by any other means). Nevertheless, Jesus' final commission to his disciples involved him impressing upon them that he was sending them out in exactly the same way that he himself had been sent by the Father, with the same commission and in the same power of the Spirit.[3] This came hard on the heels of an earlier assurance that disciples would, by virtue of the indwelling of that Spirit, do exactly the same works that Jesus had been involved in during his own earthly ministry.[4] On the other hand, we will, therefore, pay attention to some of the specific instructions and teachings Jesus gives, often as a way of contrasting the nature of leadership in God's kingdom with those contrary leadership understandings espoused by the culture of his time.

It should come as little surprise that we find many of the leadership themes and emphases that were to the fore in the Old Testament era reiterated and intensified in the leadership of Jesus. Jesus views his own ministry as one of seeing God's just rule established on earth. He sets out his stall for his future career by affirming to those gathered in the synagogue in his home town that his calling is one of proclaiming God's good news of liberation and restoration to those who are disadvantaged, sick, oppressed and overlooked.[5] In this he stands not only in the tradition of the mysterious servant of Second Isaiah but also of the Judges of the pre-monarchical era.

Like those leadership types from earlier ages, Jesus understands his own leadership to be charismatic in both inception and execution. It is because the spirit of the Lord is upon him, as he explains in his inaugural sermon, that he is now embarking upon his career. When, later, in conflict with other religious leaders concerning the nature of his authority, he points out that this authority is not something innate or counterfeit but rather something resulting from the working of the Spirit of God within him. Any understanding of Christian leadership must always take seriously the activity of God both in bringing such leadership to birth and in sustaining and energizing it. Neglecting this vital dimension to leadership may well result in us merely engaging in activity that is at best an imitation of God's true work. Nevertheless, given all that has been already observed in earlier chapters, we do not believe that such an experience exempts the recipients of grace from the imperative to apply themselves to cultivating and developing received leadership gifts, nor from the responsibility to adopt practices, habits and disciplines that will provide a helpful framework in which those gifts might flourish.

Given that leadership is, for Jesus, initiated by the activity of the Spirit within him, it is also, consequently, utterly contingent upon the will, empowering and directing of the Father. Jesus' career begins with an experience of a heavenly call and an affirmation in the direction of his future ministry.[6] He frequently stresses the imperative of only doing the Father's will[7] and is prepared to move on from otherwise fruitful spheres of ministry in order to fulfil the purposes of the one who sent him.[8] Leadership is simultaneously both a participation in the work of the Father and a response to his bidding. In this, the example Jesus sets draws attention to a sometimes overlooked dimension to leadership generally and Christian leadership in particular. That is, the understanding that leadership involves modelling to others what good followership looks like, both setting an example of how to follow as well as enabling and empowering people to follow another. Given the fact that the Christian experience is one of discipleship, Christian leaders are called to enable and encourage discipleship by modelling in their own lives the practices and dispositions of which such discipleship consists. Leaders may well be best described as leading followers.

While it is relatively unexceptional for those called to leadership in the context of church or other ministerial sphere to frame their own leadership in the light of the model offered by Jesus, we are convinced that he exists as a type for any Christian involved in leadership in any sphere, whether sacred or secular. Jesus' concern, under the direction of the Spirit, is to work for the advance of God's just rule on earth and to enable human flourishing through the overturning of structures, practices and conditions that militate against this. Whether our calling is to lead in the sphere of business, health care, education, or any other sector, and whether our role gives us extensive, organization-wide capacity or very restricted, and even informal, influence, our concern must be to use such influence for the furtherance of those aims that are important to God and that reflect his just care for his creation.

Jesus expressly owns for himself familiar titles and themes from the history of his people in order to describe himself, subtly reinterpreting them through the way in which he inhabits them. Thus, Jesus describes himself as the true shepherd[9] with proper authority over the sheep. Authentic leadership of such a kind consists, according to Jesus, in a willingness to lay down his life for the sake of the sheep. Such leadership can never be self-interested but is focused on the ultimate welfare and security of the sheep and is motivated by a deep love for them and a desire to serve them on God's behalf.

Perhaps the motif that most significantly shapes Jesus' own self-understanding in leadership is that of servant. This is most graphically illustrated in the dramatic incident of Jesus washing the feet of his disciples on the eve of his betrayal and execution.[10] For the purposes of our current discussion, this incident is noteworthy for a number of reasons. Most significantly, it stands as a powerful reminder of the calling of leaders to be servants of others; even the one who is rightly referred to as teacher and Lord, for the sake of his followers, is prepared to take the place of the lowest servant.[11] Jesus is explicit about his intention to teach a leadership lesson and to model authentic leadership: if leadership is not concerned first with service of others, then it is not true leadership. Second, we might say that such leadership can only be exercised by one who is secure in their calling, and for whom significance and security is grounded in their relationship with God rather than in their status as leader. John leads us to understand that such an act of service was uniquely possible for Jesus because of his sense of security in the Father's love and provision.[12] It may well be the case that the reason the other disciples, conveniently flouting accepted social custom, refused, in the absence of a household servant, to stoop so low as to wash each other's feet, was that throughout their supper appointment the atmosphere was somewhat tense given the existence of an ongoing, simmering dispute about who was the greatest among them.[13] An obsession with status and reputation, often driven by personal insecurity or hunger for recognition, may well be the very thing that keeps leaders, or potential leaders, from fulfilling the responsibilities God might be requiring them to perform. More than anything, Jesus models here the importance of experiencing true freedom in leadership, the freedom to please God rather than others, and to be utterly unconcerned for our own reputation and status. This may well be one of the more radical leadership insights hosted by the Christian tradition and offered to the wider leadership discourse.

We have suggested that Jesus' self-understanding was, no doubt, formed through reflection on the servant songs of Second Isaiah. Such reflection may itself have been encouraged by Jesus' own experience at his baptism: the words spoken over him include an overt reference to the first servant song.[14] Matthew in his Gospel is particularly keen to explain Jesus' life and ministry with reference to these and other similar Scriptures.[15] It is highly likely that this instinct was prompted, in the first instance, by Jesus' own conviction that his life and ministry were in fulfilment of such texts. The notion of sacrifice as an essential part of leadership, which was prominent in Jesus' exposition of shepherd, is even more prominent here. Jesus is explicit in his affirmation that servanthood, for him, in fulfilment of Scripture,[16] will involve the laying down of his life as a redemptive offering for the salvation of others.[17] Thus, after the model of Jesus, we must affirm that authentically Christian leadership involves a willingness to lay down our own lives for the sake of others and for their legitimate interests. This is powerfully expressed by Jeffrey Greenman:

> Jesus teaches that the Cross determines the nature of authentic leadership – New Testament leadership is literally cruciform ... Christian leaders are people who live the Cross – humbling themselves; voluntarily divesting themselves of their rights and privileges; trusting not in their own wisdom; insisting not on their own way; doing nothing out of selfish ambition; seeking not their own advantage but the benefit of others; in humility, considering others better than themselves; giving up their lives for the sake of the lost, the vulnerable and the neglected ... If this is the normative pattern for leadership, it means that the crucial question for each leader is: how far are you willing to go in your discipleship?[18]

One of the most striking features of Jesus' leadership was the extent to which it was focused on the calling, growth, development and releasing of others into ministry and leadership. More than any other biblical leader, it seems that, from the very outset of his ministry, Jesus is sharply focused on multiplying his own ministry through the empowering of others. This, we will suggest, sets the tone for all leadership and may well be the most authentic hallmark of truly biblical leadership. All four canonical Gospels record one of the earliest acts of Jesus' career as being that of inviting others to follow him and journey with him. Each has Jesus giving at least one of these first followers a vision for a fuller life of ministry and leadership as a consequence of involvement with himself.[19] After observing Jesus in action, these early followers are themselves trained and sent out to do exactly the same things they have seen Jesus do.[20] Ultimately, the entire body of disciples are commissioned, in the power of the Spirit, to continue the works of Jesus and to exercise leadership on his behalf and in his place.[21] In preparation for this, it seems that, at least in the final months of his time on earth, Jesus spent the majority of his time with this small group of closest followers, very intentionally preparing them for the time when he would no longer be with them. We have already made a distinction between leadership and ministry, suggesting that the latter is concerned to meet the needs of others while the former has a focus on releasing and developing others. While Jesus engages in ministry, his real legacy consisted in those whom he left behind and whom he had trained to continue his own work. Leadership after the example of Jesus is identified by the legacy that it leaves, those who have been developed under its influence. As Cottrell puts it:

> The secret of effective leadership seems to involve having an eye on a larger goal: the affirmation, training and mobilization of others. In which case one of the main tasks of leadership is to identify and nurture those who will not only take the organization forward but in due course take it over.[22]

## Leadership in the early Church

The New Testament writers who deal with those who picked up the leadership baton passed on to them by their Lord and teacher are generally far more concerned to expound the manner in which leadership is to be exercised than they are to posit a specific blueprint for leadership as a practice. Although, especially in the sphere of the local church, we encounter practices and offices that will inform and shape leadership throughout the centuries that lie ahead, many commentators point to the fragmentary, evolving and varied approach to church leadership that is reported in Scripture.[23] Despite this variety in form, it is nevertheless possible to discern a reasonably consistent understanding of the nature of leadership and of its essential values.

Leadership, whether exercised in the Church or the world, is generally seen by these writers as a good and positive thing, a gift from God to enable the right ordering of the world and so to provide a safe and secure context in which people might flourish. Thus the apostle Paul is able to write positively about the very Roman regime (*exousia*) by which he will be imprisoned and ultimately martyred, describing it, along with other similar jurisdictions, as 'established by God'[24] and 'a minister of God to you'. He similarly urges Timothy[25] to encourage intercession for all rulers and those in authority (*huperokhē*), 'so that we may lead a tranquil and quiet life in all godliness and dignity'. Equally, the writer of the Epistle to the Hebrews urges his audience to obey their church leaders (*hēgoumenois*) for they are accountable to, and presumably thus appointed by, God, in the work of keeping watch (the connotation here is that of pastoral oversight) over them. Despite this positive welcome for leadership and authority generally, leadership in the Church is, nevertheless, significantly different from that practised by worldly rulers and leaders. Jesus has already warned his apostles that leadership in his kingdom is after an alternative pattern, focused on service rather than status.[26] Perhaps the biggest clue as to how leadership was conceived in the earliest Christian communities is provided by the specific words chosen to describe such leadership and by the titles given to those who shared in this leadership. Of equal significance might be the words that were *not* used. Essentially these are words that connote status and privilege or that elevate the position of the leader.[27] It is to these that we turn first.

## Refusing privilege

### arkhōn – leader/ruler

This was the most commonly used word to describe leaders in the New Testament era, and is the one used by Jesus of those rulers with whom he contrasts his own leadership and that of his followers.[28] It is a word frequently used to describe civic or public authorities, and is also used of synagogue rulers[29] and other Jewish authorities,[30] including Herod[31] who colluded with Pilate in the crucifixion of Jesus. Jesus notably uses it to describe Satan, the prince of this world,[32] while the apostle Paul refers to the whole of the present world order as being subject to ruling spirits (arkhontōn)[33] who are under judgement and passing away.

Given the variety of uses of this term, even in the sacred sphere, it would be no surprise if the early Christians adopted it for their own use in recognition of the power and authority of Jesus now made known through his resurrection and ascension and bestowed upon his Church. That they did not is most striking. It is not that they were unaware of the extraordinary authority now entrusted to them in Christ, and they were by no means afraid of exercising this both for the benefit of the sick and oppressed[34] and as a counter to the illegitimate threats and demands of secular or religious authorities when they were seen to conflict with the requirements of faithful obedience.[35] However, this is a descriptor that so emphasizes the standing and rank of the office holder that it cannot have sat well with those who wanted to point away from themselves to another, and who saw their leadership as existing for the benefit of others rather than themselves. As we shall see, the titles they preferred to use defined the holder more in terms of the relationship they enjoyed with their Lord than in terms of any inherent personal status.

### hiereus – priest

Given the prominence of this particular title for some spiritual leaders in the culture out of which the early Church emerged, and given the fact that the earliest Christians saw themselves as in continuity with the historic Jewish community of faith, it is, on one level, surprising that 'priest' was not a term adopted by the early Church to describe their own leaders. Its complete absence from the literature[36] may be explained by a number of factors.

Perhaps the most obvious reason this was not a word to be used was that, in the minds of the earliest Christians, it was a role that had already been filled. The Christology of the Epistle to the Hebrews in particular, but of the New Testament as a whole, presents Jesus as having fulfilled and made obsolete the role previously played in part by the Levitical priests of the Old Testament. While the Church as the body of Christ is happy to understand its own identity to be a priestly people,[37] representing God to the world and the world to God, the designation 'priest' belongs to the whole people rather than to any particular individual from among the people. As Schillebeeckx points out:

> It emerges above all from the pre-Nicene literature that the ancient church had difficulty in calling the church leaders 'priestly'. According to the New Testament, Christ and the Christian community alone were priestly; the leaders were at the service of Christ and the priestly people of God, but are themselves never said to be priestly.[38]

It would be another 150 years before the word 'priest' would begin to be used regularly to describe those holding specific office in the life of the local church.[39] It may well be that 'priest' seemed an unsuitable word to describe Christian leaders because of its connotations of status and privilege and its association with particular types of positional and dynastic leadership. Perhaps the reluctance of our first Christian forebears to use this term to describe their leaders might lead us to be a little more circumspect about its widespread usage today and to question the impact of its deployment both upon those who are so described and those whom they are called to serve. As the FAOC's *Senior Church Leadership* insists:

> Leaders are not *above* others, even if their calling often requires them (literally and metaphorically) to stand up in front of others. Any of our language and practices that embed attitudes of superiority need to be resisted, as do ways of living that tend to separate those with leadership responsibilities from the shared experience of the 'ordinary' church.[40]

## How the first Christians described their leaders

We have established that leadership is generally seen by the New Testament writers as a positive gift from God, though, in the light of the Christ event, must be redefined in ways that differentiate it from leadership as previously conceived. As we turn to examine the particular words used to describe early Christian leaders, we must understand at the outset that these are words that, at least in the earliest Christian decades, referred primarily to functions exercised in the church as opposed to titular offices or positions held. The key question to be answered thus becomes, 'What did leaders do?'

## Exercising oversight

### proistamenos

This is one of two words used in antiquity to describe those who occupied some position of secular leadership and that the New Testament writers were comfortable in adopting for their own purposes. In classical Greek, *proistamenos* is often used of military or political leaders but has the clear overtones of taking responsibility for, supporting or protecting those over whom one is set.[41] In the LXX it is used to describe the head of a household.[42] Paul refers to those who labour in the Church and 'who are over you in the Lord' (*proistamenous*) as being worthy of special honour and love.[43] The *proistamenos* is mentioned in Romans 12.8 as part of a longer list of spiritual gifts and callings and set in company with those who are called to teach, exhort and show mercy. We assume that this juxtaposition of roles is deliberate rather than accidental, implying some overlap between them. There is a more explicit connection between this word group and the role of *presbuteroi* (elders) in 1 Timothy 5.17, where the latter are instructed to rule (*proestōtes*) well. Above all, the use of this word group implies an understanding of leadership that involves responsible care and oversight with a particular concern for the spiritual edification and nurture of others. The borrowing of words from the setting of family and domestic life[44] may well have been particularly suitable to describe the work of leaders because the primary setting for the life of the first congregations was that of a home. This would be particularly the case if, as Clarke suggests, each house church was led by the person in whose house it met.[45]

### hēgoumenos

Less frequently used to denote leaders is the noun *hēgoumenos* and its cognates. Although sometimes used of civic or military leaders or city governors, in classical Greek the word was used primarily of one who acted as guide in showing the way or setting an example to follow. The word occurs in 2 Chronicles 18.16 (LXX) as part of the prophecy of Micaiah ben Imla. Here the prophet describes Israel as 'like sheep without a shepherd', of whom the Lord says, 'they have no master (*hēgoumenon*)'. The parallelism of this verse implies that a master or leader is associated with oversight for the flock, to guide them and ensure their security. It may well be that it was the capacity of this word to reflect nuances both of holding responsible position and yet serving the interests of others that led Jesus to use this in his own exhortation to his disciples to see their leadership as expressed through service.[46] This nuance is picked up by the authors of the 2015 FAOC report *Senior Church Leadership*,[47] who observe that while Jesus does not forbid the use of the term leader, he offers a radical redefinition of what leadership means in the light of his own ministry and sacrificial death. The paradox of leadership in the New Testament church is that there is plenty of leadership in evidence, but equally a sensitivity about some leadership language and especially about the status associations that often accompany it.

The word is used with approval in Acts 15.22 to describe those who are regarded as exercising leadership within the Church. It is a word used most extensively by the writer of the Epistle to the Hebrews and is found three times in the final chapter of that letter. Here the recipients of the letter are urged to imitate the faith of those who led them[48] and to obey their leaders and submit to them.[49] The motivation for such obedience is that the leaders are the ones who keep watch over those in their charge and who are ultimately accountable to God for discharging this responsibility faithfully. While leadership is never to be equated with ruling over others in an overbearing manner, the fact that leaders are accountable before God for the well-being of their charges means that faithful leadership will, at times, involve taking steps to induce and persuade others to act in particular ways, though not to coerce them.

The use of words whose provenance lay in the world of civil government may well give an insight into the self-understanding of the first leaders of the early Christian community.[50] They saw their role as social, rather than purely religious. Their conviction was that, as a consequence of the work of Christ, a new humanity (rather than a new religion or cultus) had been brought to birth, of which they were the first fruits. Their role, as leaders in this community was one of formation, of socializing new believers into a new society that was the Church,[51] habituating them to life under God's new way of ordering things. To belong to the new community of Jesus, in the days of the early Church, a person was mentored in practising change in habits.[52] This was the key responsibility of the leadership of these new communities and was akin to the role of those who shaped the life of other communities through their leadership. Christian leadership will always have as a primary concern the shaping of individuals and communities after the pattern of Christ, albeit in a manner that is focused on serving others rather than oppressing them.

### kubernēsis

This word occurs only once in the New Testament, in 1 Corinthians 12.28, where it finds its place among a list of various gifts and ministries in the Church. Although often translated as administration (and thus connoting for later generations practical organization or desk work), the etymology of the word suggests a rather more nuanced meaning. The cognate kubernētēs is used on two occasions[53] in the sense of helmsman or one who steers. A similar use of the word is found in the LXX of Ezekiel 27.8, 27ff., where it is translated as 'pilot'. Coenen suggests that this background, and the particular placement of this word in the list of spiritual gifts in 1 Corinthians 12 (between gifts of healing, giving help and tongues), implies that it is a term for a mediating function keeping order within the whole life of the Church.[54] We suggest that the particular contribution this word makes to our wider understanding of New Testament leadership is to highlight the way in which oversight was understood to be directional, steering and guiding the Church in its life and ministry, and ordering and coordinating (administering) the exercise of the spiritual gifts of the whole body.

### episkopos

Although this word became associated from the early second century onwards with the presiding office in the Church, its less than universal deployment in the New Testament to denote leaders in the local churches should make us wary of associating it with office holders as opposed to describing functions of certain leaders. In classical literature words of this group were used to denote the act of paying attention to, inspecting or supervising an activity or person, and were applied to deities as well as to public officials. This usage is carried over into the Old Testament, where *episkopos* is used both of governors and their associates[55] and of God's loving care of people[56] and of the land.[57] That this was a role that was understood to be authoritative is indicated by the parallelism of Isaiah 60.17, where the LXX relates together the roles of *arkhontes* and *episkopoi*.

We have already noted[58] the implication from Paul's farewell speech to the Ephesian elders[59] of a close relationship in meaning between the functions of overseer and shepherd. A similar linking of the two terms is found in 1 Peter 2.25, where Jesus is described as 'the Shepherd (*poimēn*) and Guardian (*episkopos*) of your souls'. The work of leadership, in imitation of that of Christ himself, is to exercise loving, pastoral care over those in our charge, enabling them to grow in faith and in their capacity to engage in fruitful service of Christ. From the list of qualifications required of an overseer laid out in the Pastoral epistles,[60] in addition to a number of qualities to do with personal character, two particular aptitudes are required that give some insight into the expected role of a Christian *episkopos*. First, such a person must be able to manage their own household and oversee its members, demonstrating good personal, pastoral skills, and, second, must have an aptitude for teaching God's truth. Authentic oversight involves paying attention to the growth of others through enabling them to hear and understand God's word and being equipped to act upon it.

### presbuteros

The word usually translated 'elder', and its cognates, was originally used simply to distinguish those who were older from those who were younger.

In classical literature the word gradually began to be associated with the dignity or rank that came as a result of age, and was subsequently used of those who filled responsible and respected positions such as, inter alia, ambassadors, members of official committees, etc. Coenen suggests:

> Although their role was in origin neither religious nor cultic but socio-political, the existence of elders *as an institution* was of considerable significance in the life of Israel and the Jewish synagogue community, as it was among other peoples of the ancient world ... and is assumed in every strand of Old Testament tradition.[61]

The elders of Israel are prominent at key moments of decision-making at the time of the Exodus and during the wilderness wanderings,[62] and emerge as those who direct the judicial, political and military affairs of local communities in the period after the settlement of Canaan.[63] In the period of the monarchy, the elders appear as a form of ruling class whose influence is seen both in the inception of the monarchy,[64] at times of crisis,[65] and at other significant moments in national life.[66] Following the exile, the elders assume the role of guardians and representatives of the Jewish community both among those remaining in the land[67] and those who have been taken into exile.[68] As the post-exilic age progresses, the elders of Israel are increasingly identified with lay members of the ruling Jewish council,[69] while the title of *presbuteros* is also regularly associated with those having responsibility for governance in the local synagogues.

Christian elders are referenced by Luke as exercising responsibility in the church in Jerusalem,[70] possibly after a pattern that replicated that of the Jewish synagogues, and Paul and Barnabas are reported as extending this pattern by appointing *presbuteroi* in the various churches they founded in Asia Minor.[71] Coenen and others regard it as probable that the terms *presbuteros* and *episkopos* are interchangeable, especially in the light of Acts 20.28 and Titus 1.5.[72] However, a compelling alternative understanding is suggested by Campbell[73] in a comprehensive study of this topic. Campbell's contention is that *presbuteros* was an honorific title given by the wider community to a respected, older member of that community (very likely a household head) who would serve as a member of a council of elders, a group who exercised influence on behalf of the community. Such a council would give wise advice and make appropriate decisions on behalf of the community. Clarke suggests that while some *presbuteroi* might have churches meeting in their homes (and would thus also be overseers who would additionally be involved in teaching), this would not, in the earliest instances, be the case with all.[74] This makes sense of the implication of 1 Timothy 5.17 that not all elders teach, and of the suggestion in Titus 1.7 that overseers are drawn from among the ranks of the elders. Following Campbell, he suggests that whereas a single overseer in the first instance would preside over the church meeting in his or her home, as more house churches emerged in a single community so these overseers would be formed together into an eldership for the sake of the wider Christian community. In due course it would be necessary for a single overseer to emerge with overall responsibility, the monarchical bishop of later centuries exercising leadership as *primus inter pares*.

For our current purposes, perhaps more than anything, the existence of a council of elders serves to remind us that leadership in the New Testament is always a corporate and collaborative exercise, as opposed to the work of a solitary, and often heroic, individual. We will have cause to explore further the ongoing significance of this insight in a subsequent chapter.

## Representing Christ

One of the striking things we note from reading the New Testament is the clear understanding on the part of the earliest Christians that leadership was somehow both in imitation of Jesus and exercised at his behest and on his behalf. Thus, the apostle Paul sees himself as 'a bond-servant of Christ Jesus, called as an apostle, set apart for the gospel of God',[75] and is keen to encourage his protégés to be imitators of him as he is of Christ.[76] Peter, James and Jude each begin their own letters to the churches in similar terms, expressing their own indenture to Christ. Explaining the dramatic healing of a man who had been lame from birth, Peter insists that, far from this being the result of any personal power or piety on the part of Peter or his companion John, 'it is the name [literally *authority*] of Jesus which has strengthened this man whom you see and know; and the faith which comes through [Jesus] has given him this perfect health.'[77] Leadership consists, in no small part, in passing on to others what has been received from the Lord Jesus.[78] Dunn[79] suggests that this sharing directly in the leadership of Christ is a consequence, for the earliest Christians, of their consciousness of being 'in Christ'; we never experience such leadership independently of him. This sense of leadership as being somehow on behalf of Christ is reflected in some of the other New Testament words associated with leadership.

### diakonia

This word and its cognates are perhaps the most widely used words to describe those exercising leadership in the whole of the New Testament. With the exception of the Thessalonians correspondence, they are to be found in every one of Paul's letters, as well as in the Synoptics, Acts and Revelation. This extensive use indicates the central importance of these words for Paul, especially in terms of understanding the nature and work of leadership.

In classical literature *diakoneō* is used first to describe the work of waiting at table. Its meaning subsequently develops to encompass caring for household needs and then to serving more generally.[80] Many earlier studies of the use of this term in the New Testament suggested that the dominant understanding of the word here is to do with menial, practical service, though subtly altered from its use in classical literature by virtue of it being now seen as shaped by the example of Christ, the perfect *diakonos*.[81] However, more recent studies have advocated for the widening of this basic understanding. The earliest classical uses of this word are thoroughly examined by Collins,[82] who argues for a much broader general usage than merely domestic service. Collins suggests that over one-third of uses in classical literature are to do with the conveying of a message or the delivering of an errand on behalf of another, concluding that central to the notion of *diakonia* is the idea of being a go-between or representative of a master. Even where the context in which the word is used is that where slaves are concerned and where the activity in question is the performance of household chores, Collins argues that the dominant motif is that of acting as an agent of another, activity he describes as being 'of an in-between kind'.[83] The broad sense of Christian usage, he then goes on to suggest, was generally in line with earlier uses of the word, and implied involvement with agency on behalf of or representation of another. It is in this sense that Paul is able to describe his own ministry as being that of a *diakonos*,[84] a term that directs attention not to the menial nature of Paul's service but rather to the fact that his authority derives from his being an agent of Christ. Georgi[85] suggests that the phrase *diakonos Khristou* is used by both Paul and by his opponents in Corinth as a term of respect rather than servility, and that, in keeping with classical usage, words of this group were associated with the work of sending a message via an appointed envoy. Arguing for a close relationship between the two notions of humble service and representation on behalf of another, Georgi concludes that both overseers and deacons[86] should be seen as those who are occupied in missionary proclamation, and that despite later ecclesiastical developments, in the New Testament at least, there should be no sense of either office being seen as in subordination to the other. Whatever our conclusions as to the relative weight to be given to the different facets of these words, we can be reasonably clear that the frequency with which *diakonia* words are used throughout the New Testament indicates the conviction that Christian leadership consists in speaking and acting on behalf of Christ, of representing his interests fully and ensuring that his will be done, and of conducting such an embassy in a manner that authentically reflects his own commitment to serve God and others.

### apostolos

The precise question of to whom the title of apostle can legitimately be attributed (whether this is a description exclusively of the Twelve originally appointed by Jesus, plus, somewhat later, Paul, or whether it extends to a wider group of people) is beyond the scope of this book. What can be said with confidence is that the early Church saw itself, and thus its leadership, as apostolic in nature. Cognates of this word are used extremely frequently in the LXX, almost exclusively with the meaning of to send someone out to act with the full authority of the one who sends.[87] A number of commentators have drawn attention to the Jewish legal institution of the *saliah* (shaliach), a proxy representative of another who was commissioned by that other person to act with his full authority and who, to all intents and purposes, stood exactly in the place of the sender as an extension of that person. In the New Testament, apostleship in its widest sense is tied up with the missional notion of being sent by Christ to make known the good news of his kingdom to others. For our purposes, it further underlines our understanding of Christian leadership as being tied up with representing Christ to others and particularly of furthering his missional aims of making his gospel known more widely. Moreover, it is given, according to Dunn,[88] for the enabling and equipping of the whole Church for the work of ministry. This identification with Christ, however, does not give the Christian leader licence to bask in the reflected glory of her master. Both *apostolos* and *diakonos* are words that draw attention away from the person exercising leadership and fix it firmly upon the one being represented. The Christian leader is never at liberty to draw attention to themselves or to seek status or favour in their own right as a consequence of the ministry entrusted to us by Christ. The consistent self-understanding of New Testament leaders is that we are under the authority of another and are called to serve and please him by extending nurture and oversight towards those for whom he has made us responsible, working for their formation and flourishing as if in the place of Christ.

This desire to imitate Christ also has implications for the way Christian leaders exercise the oversight entrusted to them. The oversight envisaged by the New Testament writers as being consistent with authentically Christian leadership is evidenced not merely by the specific words used to describe overseers but also by the way this oversight was actually exercised. Paul, who has a clear self-understanding as an apostle appointed by Christ and a strong sense of the responsibility incumbent upon such a position, despite the strength of his appeals at times to those whom he is addressing, refrains from imposing himself upon others or simply asserting his authority.[89] He prefers exhortation and appeal to command or decree, appealing, for example, to a common experience in Christ,[90] an experience of the grace and mercy of God,[91] the calling we have received,[92] the name of Jesus,[93] or the meekness and gentleness of Christ.[94] Banks suggests that in this Paul is simply seeking to imitate the example of Jesus, whose own authority was exercised with gentleness and in weakness.

In this respect, Paul not only proclaims the gospel message and all that flows from it but *embodies* it, conveying its life through both his words and deeds. Christ's identification with humankind also affects the manner in which Paul can speak to his converts. For God draws people not through the exercise of power, but through the demonstration of *weakness* – or so it seems from a human point of view – in the cross ... In the death of Jesus, Paul finds an understanding of his own authority with the churches he was called to serve.[95]

Interestingly, similar convictions about the roles of leadership and of the relationship between those appointed as leaders and the wider Christian community, are expressed in the Church of England's Faith and Order Commission report on *Senior Church Leadership*:

> From earliest times, the Church has sensed a need for order and focus, for a clarity of vision that looks to the needs of the whole body. This leadership is consensual. The social world of the New Testament was intensely hierarchical; authority was instantly recognized and respected (Luke 7.8). It is all the more striking that leadership in the church is accorded by mutual recognition rather than imposed by external authority: it has to be 'recognized' (1 Corinthians 16.15, 1 Thessalonians 5.12). Effective leadership depends on co-operation between leaders and led (Hebrews 13.17; 1 Peter 5.2).[96]

## Animating the body

A third dominant motif for leadership in the New Testament is that of empowerment or animation. Leaders are not primarily those who do things instead of others but rather so that others might be equipped to play their own full part in the life and service and advance of God's kingdom. To this extent they are stewards of and catalysts for God's work.

Perhaps the clearest expression of this dynamic is to be found in Ephesians 4.7–16. Here, the apostle Paul,[97] having in previous chapters sketched out a picture of the calling and destiny of the Church of Jesus Christ, now explains something of the ways in which God orders and equips this Church in order that it might fulfil its purpose. God's grace is given to every member of the Church[98] so that the whole Church (all the saints) might share in the work of serving God and his kingdom.[99] God's intention is that the Church grows,[100] presumably both in the quality and purity of its life and also in terms of its scale and influence, as each member of the body plays their full part. God's way of equipping and animating the whole body through the mobilization of every member is to provide the Church with gifts of leadership,[101] diverse in function but that together reflect the fullness of the ministry of Christ.[102] As Howard Snyder observes:

The chief priority of pastoral leadership is discipling people for the king-dom ... essentially, the pastor's first priority is so to invest himself or her-self in a few other persons that they also become disciples and ministers of Jesus Christ. It is so to give oneself to others and to the work of discipling that the New Testament norm of plural leadership becomes a reality in the local congregation. In other words, it is to bring the ministry of all God's people to functioning practical reality.[103]

Stephen Pickard laments that this animative dimension to Christian leader-ship has all too often been neglected or even rejected by those occupying positions of leadership within churches.

It is remarkable how poorly formed are the habits for collaborative prac-tices among clergy and lay people. Indeed, I would go so far as to say that clergy generally evidence minimal aptitude for such a way of ministry ... A truly collaborative approach to ministry seems to require something of us that we lack the spiritual capacity and will to deliver.[104]

In a fascinating unpacking of Paul's assertion that in the body we are all 'members one of another',[105] Pickard explores the precise interrelationship between the priesthood of the whole body of Christ and that of its ordained leaders, advocating a relationship that he describes as inter-animative; that is, each brings into being and enables the precise ministry of the other.[106] Such an understanding delivers us from both a rigidly hierarchical approach to leadership, in which laity are merely passive recipients of the ministra-tions of others, and from an overly egalitarian approach in which leadership roles disappear as they are collapsed into an amorphous mass in which no distinction exists between people and between their respective roles. The animative role of those appointed to leadership is described by Pickard as being that of 'pointing the community to its fundamental energy and resource and how to facilitate the release of the *dunamis* of the Spirit of Christ in order that true praise of God may overflow in the world'.[107]

Christian leadership will always have as one of its primary concerns the envisioning and equipping of all God's people for service and witness in the world in order that the whole Church might fulfil its calling to be God's priesthood on behalf of the world. Thus Christian leaders will be especially concerned with the ministry of teaching, building up an ever-expanding picture of God's kingdom as a backdrop against which people are enabled to improvise the acting out of their own lives and to help others discover their own particular gifts and calling and grow in confidence and experience in deploying those gifts.

## Leadership after God's likeness

Our study of New Testament leadership practice and our examination of some of the words used (and rejected) by the earliest Christians to describe their leaders has painted for us a picture of Christian leadership and its key concerns. One of Pickard's principal contributions to our discussions is to highlight the impact of theological themes and assumptions upon any understanding and practice of leadership. Leadership is inevitably shaped by the context in which it is located, and the Church, the context from which Christian leadership takes its form, is shaped by the God to whose image and likeness we are called to conform. It has not been difficult to see evidence of this already in our discussion of biblical words for leadership. Christian leadership will always be defined most significantly, in terms of its identity, emphases and objectives, by the nature and character of God as reflected in some of the central motifs of Christian theology. Our consideration of biblical leadership must be undertaken with reference to these theological motifs, and it is to some of these that we now turn by way of conclusion.

### Creation: leadership as stewardship

A conviction that the world and everything in it is created, that it exists as a consequence, in some way, of the agency of God, as opposed to some random set of circumstances, changes the way we view everything, including the work of leadership. Most significantly, it reminds us that we alone do not ultimately have the authority to determine the trajectory for the world nor for any group of people for whom we have responsibility either in the Church, the workplace or in a voluntary capacity. That authority belongs to God, and our task is to exercise our own leadership responsibilities in a way that conforms to his express will and that is in accord with his character. We are not, in this way, to be completely original thinkers, but rather those who seek to discern his way and to do our best to enable his will to be done. However, God's intention in creating humankind in his image is for us to exercise stewardship over his creation, ruling and overseeing things on his behalf. Creation reminds us of our proper place in God's economy, but also of our special calling and of the responsibilities that come with this. The created order is not a commodity for us to use merely for our own pleasure, but rather a gift to be stewarded.

Perhaps, most significantly for our own purposes as those with an interest in leadership, the Christian understanding of creation has profound implications for the way in which we will treat others. One of the criticisms rightly levelled at certain leadership understandings, and at a good deal of business practice, is that when we lose sight of the created nature of the world, then it becomes easy for people to be commodified and treated in a purely instrumental manner, as means to the achieving of ends conceived by leaders or other stakeholders. The leader who sees herself as primarily a steward of God's creation will have a far more benevolent and concerned approach to people, recognizing that they too, no matter what their place in any organization, are to be stewarded and nurtured along with every other part of creation. Thus, Peter urges his audience to be good stewards (*oikonomoi*) of the grace of God, serving one another in the use of their gifts,[108] while Paul employs the same word to describe the ministry of the *episkopos* who stewards the Church of God.[109]

## Incarnation: leadership as engagement

Perhaps the most striking truth about God's way of exercising influence is that, at the most critical moment in his engagement with the world, rather than dispensing instruction and influence from a distance, he enters into the very stuff of creation, becoming a human being and living among us.[110] Not only is Jesus the perfect model of leadership for us by virtue of his own leadership practice, but the very manner in which he laid aside heavenly privilege and immersed himself in the arena of human life, involving himself in the most thoroughgoing way with those whom he sought to lead back to God, is paradigmatic for authentically Christian leadership. Christian leaders are not those who lord it over others from on high or at a distance. Rather, they are called to be those who lead from alongside others, from below, certainly leading with strength and authority, but an authority rooted in an appeal that gains credibility from a commitment to those whom they lead and that is manifest in their choice to identify with them. The incarnational leader, following the pattern of Christ, will be willing to serve in unfashionable and overlooked places, to live in communities that, given the choice, he might prefer to avoid, to draw alongside those who are profoundly different, all for the sake of exercising the leadership entrusted to him by Christ for the benefit of such people.

The incarnation further bears witness to the importance of integrity in leadership. Jesus' authority and influence flowed from the quality of his life, from the fact that the kingdom values that he sought to inculcate in and commend to others were manifestly worked out in every dimension of his own life and were most evident in the ways in which he interacted with others. Leadership influence relies upon there being a congruity between what we advocate and what we practise, between our espoused values and the realities of our lifestyles. Christian leadership is integrated leadership, in which the vision and strategies we commend are most powerfully communicated by the habits and attitudes we cultivate, the choices we make and, especially, by the way in which we treat others. It is, no doubt, for this reason that while the New Testament has comparatively little to say about leadership practices, it has an enormous amount to say about the way in which disciples, and especially leaders, are to conduct themselves. Paul commends himself to others not on the basis of his extraordinary teaching or other aptitudes but on the basis of his gentleness,[111] his refusal to profit financially from others[112] and his reliance upon God.[113] Roxburgh and Romanuk remind us:

> The process of becoming a leader is no less than the process of becoming a fully integrated human being. It is first about the leader's character and formation. Character is a matter of personal habits, skills and behaviours that engender confidence and credibility. Character is the place where one's deep hunger, personal identity, and calling merge to generate the confidence that allows people to trust a leader and agree to journey together in a new direction.[114]

## Trinity: leadership as collaboration

If leadership is a reflection of the very nature and being of God, then the way in which we conceive God will have a profound impact upon the ways in which we conceive leadership. This point is made clearly by Pickard, who traces the roots of specific understandings of ordained ministry back to particular espoused theological emphases. Because God is Trinity, he argues, our leadership models and practices must be constructed in a way that bears proper witness to God's trinitarian nature. More individual and heroic models of leadership and, for Pickard, theologies of priesthood that set ordained ministers apart as a separate 'caste', are attributed to viewing leadership through the lens of other theological motifs[115] and failing to pay proper attention to the requirements of a thoroughgoing social trinitarianism.[116] Pickard's understanding of the relationship between leaders and the whole body of Christ as being inter-animative derives wholly from his understanding of the nature of the relationships that exist between the persons of the Trinity. For Pickard, the persons of the Godhead exist not in independence of each other but rather in dynamic relationship, whereby each is co-presented by the others. None can be properly understood or experienced other than in the context of their relationship with one another. Thus, he argues:

> The ministries of the ecclesia are called to recognise and call attention to the trace of God's energetic and holy order. As the ministries of the church serve this implicit divine order they enable the church to realise itself as the embodiment and witness to the reality of God in the world. But the ministries cannot do this if they are not properly coordinated as instantiations of God's own ordering, i.e., intrinsically related in a 'mode of togetherness' such that they raise each other to the fulness of the ministry of each.[117]

The fact that at the heart of God is a relationship of persons and that this relationship works together in a collaborative fashion[118] bears witness to the fact that Christian leadership will always similarly be collaborative. Although the outworking of this will be explored much more thoroughly in a subsequent chapter, suffice it to say here that one of the principal concerns of any leader will be to identify others with whom leadership responsibility might be shared, who might particularly reflect strengths in areas where that leader is weak, and in collaboration with whom joint working might achieve far more than merely the sum of individual contributions.

## Pneumatology: dispersed leadership

In our study of Old Testament leadership motifs we noted the provisional nature of much leadership of that era, recognizing that some of the exilic prophets spoke of a coming age in which the anointed individual would give way to an anointed community. With the coming of the Spirit at Pentecost this new era was inaugurated, with a number of consequences for the way leadership might be viewed.

In many ways, the leadership that is most evident in the earliest Christian community is that of God, often attributed to the work of the Spirit. It is the Spirit who directs the earliest Christians and leads them into new and unforeseen situations, such as ministry to Samaritans,[119] to an Ethiopian eunuch,[120] to Gentiles[121] and to unreached groups far from the first centres of influence.[122] When faced with challenging and contentious decisions, the early leaders look to the Spirit to lead them and to give them wisdom and a common mind.[123] An understanding of the Spirit's leading is not, however, confined to particular officers of the Church but is widely spread among the whole body of Christ. While the Church might be ordered by particular people appointed as stewards and overseers, their calling is to cultivate and affirm the wider working and leading of the Spirit through the members of the body. It is such an understanding that underlies Paul's treatment of the gifts of the Spirit in his correspondence with the Corinthians, Romans and Ephesians. By the same token, the leadership exercised by particular individuals within the Church is recognized and validated by the body of Christ itself (1 Cor. 16.15; 1 Thess. 5.12) as opposed to being imposed upon the body by some external authority.[124]

Christian leadership seems to consist far more in enabling the whole body to share the mind of Christ and to be led by his Spirit than in receiving revelation from God on behalf of and instead of the body as a whole. This understanding of the dynamics of the work of the Spirit may well be the most distinctive thing that marks out Christian leadership from Old Testament leadership. It is a matter of some concern that the Christian Church has all too often demonstrated a preference for Old Testament models that are now superseded by the Pentecost event, resulting in over-elevated leaders and disempowered and passive followers.

## Eschatology: leadership as catalyst for change

Our study of biblical leadership thus far has been an exploration, in a sense, of where we have come from. We have been concerned to go back into our history as the people of God in order to unearth the earliest and most formative traditions that have shaped us in order that we might improvise afresh, in a very different context from the first century, in the light of certain fixed convictions and values. However, the Church is not simply shaped by understanding of where we have come from. We are to be equally shaped by an understanding of where we are going. That is, we need to understand what is the future to which all things are heading, to be defined by God, and thus how might we be conformed ahead of time, in part at least, to that future identity in which we will one day participate. Lesslie Newbigin expresses this well:

> The Church is the pilgrim people of God. It is on the move – hastening to the ends of the earth to beseech all men to be reconciled to God, and hastening to the end of time to meet its Lord who will gather all into one. Therefore the nature of the Church is never to be finally defined in static terms, but only in terms of that to which it is going. It cannot be understood rightly except in a perspective which is at once missionary and eschatological.[125]

To describe the Church as eschatological is to affirm that the final page of history has been written and that the whole of creation is hastening towards the end set for it by God, 'the summing up of all things in Christ'.[126] The Church is, to use another phrase from Newbigin, 'the sign, foretaste and instrument' of this coming new age. We are called, and enabled by the eschatological Spirit, to represent the new life of this coming kingdom in all that we are and do. The age in which we now live, the provisional age between the inauguration of the kingdom on earth in the ministry of Jesus and its consummation that will take place on his return, is not an age of passive waiting for something to happen, but active participation with God in the proclamation and demonstration of the presence, ahead of time, of that eschatological kingdom. Our confidence in a God who is 'forever making all things new' leads us to hope for the transformation of people, structures and communities and to play our part in seeing the release of God's presence and power for such transformation to take place. This understanding of the context in which the Church is set has profound implications for our understanding of the role of its leadership.[127]

First, we must say that leaders are not simply called to be custodians of the past (the guarding of foundational tradition *is* a legitimate concern of leadership) but also catalysts for the embracing of God's future. By signalling to the Church, and the world, its ultimate destination, we encourage others to lay hold of this future now and to become increasingly habituated to the realities of the age that has come in Christ and that will fully come at his parousia.

Second, given the transformative nature of God's kingdom we must say that leadership will always be directly concerned with being a catalyst for change. By this we do not simply mean that leaders are always to be concerned with novelty for novelty's sake. Rather, leaders are those who enable others to move forwards with God and to restructure their lives and the lives of churches and other organizations in line with the preferences of God's kingdom. Newbigin is correct to describe the Church as a pilgrim people. Pilgrims are always on the move, never content to settle in their current location, restless to arrive at their ultimate destination. Part of the calling of a leader is to enable others to experience godly dissatisfaction with the status quo and then help them to discern appropriate steps to take in order to bring the future increasingly forward into the present.

Third, the eschatological nature of the Church reminds us that those who exercise leadership do so on behalf of a returning master to whom they are ultimately accountable.[128] This sense of accountability may well explain the fondness of New Testament writers to describe leadership and ministry in terms of stewardship. Thus, Paul describes himself as a 'steward (*oikonomos*) of the mysteries of God', not the master of the household, 'but a fellow employee, tasked with supplying his fellow servants with all they need to carry out the master's orders'.[129]

Fourth, and finally, we might also observe that it is this eschatological tension that makes leadership such an uncomfortable vocation at times. Part of the calling of a leader is to experience a greater restlessness than others. We occupy the place of tension between maintaining tradition and adapting for a new context, between preserving the past and innovating for the future, between ensuring stability and enabling change. These are experiences that are by no means unique to Christian leadership, but from which authentically kingdom-focused leaders will never be immune.

## Concluding reflections

At the end of our initial foray into exploring what we mean by leadership, we came up with this tentative definition:

> A relational process of social influence through which people are inspired, enabled and mobilized to act in positive, new ways, towards the achievement of shared goals.

In the light of our examination of biblical patterns of leadership, we now need to ask whether or not such an understanding will serve the purposes of defining Christian leadership. Is there anything here that clashes with biblical leadership as we have understood it, and, equally, is there anything missing from this definition when applied to the exercise of *Christian* leadership?

We have sought to stress the collaborative and distributed nature of leadership in the New Covenant era, an insight that is accommodated in our definition of leadership as a process, as opposed to being the instrumental actions of one or a few leading individuals. We have also understood leadership to be a process of influence leading to the mobilization and enabling of others to act positively. We have also recognized the dynamic nature of God's kingdom and recognize that leadership is somehow about facilitating new ways forward. So far so good! Perhaps the one thing lacking is an understanding that leadership is about the facilitation not simply of shared goals conceived by participants but rather the accomplishment of those kingdom goals set out by God. Here then is our modified, working definition of Christian leadership:

A relational process of social influence through which people are inspired, enabled and mobilized to act in positive, new ways, towards the achievement of God's purposes.

Our understanding of what such leadership might look like will be enhanced as we examine some of the key responsibilities and practices that lie at the heart of good leadership. This we do in Part 2 of this volume. However, before we can shift our focus to the work of leadership, we need to acknowledge some of the significant reservations expressed towards the very notion of leadership. It is to these that we must now turn our attention.

---

## Leadership on the ground

What is distinctive about a *Christian* organization? Specifically, what might be the difference in approach to international development undertaken by a Christian development agency as opposed to that adopted by a secular counterpart? These were questions that had engaged Matthew Frost's imagination for some time. Surely, he reasoned, those wholly committed to Jesus Christ would meet the needs of the least, the last and the lost in a different way than others might do? The prospect of exploring them further was at least one factor in his sense of call to take up the role of UK CEO of the international development organization Tearfund in 2005.

---

## Active listening

Founded in 1968, Tearfund had, for more than three decades, been at the forefront of disaster relief in some of the world's most impoverished places, and was increasingly concerned not simply to provide aid but also to facilitate the development of local communities. Although doing a good deal of effective work, Matthew was aware that what was most lacking, at this stage in the organization's development, was a sharper sense of focus and a more clearly articulated and widely embraced vision, capable of bringing greater alignment and energy to the organization.

For the first three months in his new post, Matthew effectively left the day-to-day running of Tearfund to his deputy and undertook a lengthy process of listening to God and to others. With a sense of call to discern what God was doing already, Matthew split the organization's staff up into groups of about eight people, and met with each group in turn, asking them three simple questions:

- Why are you here? (What is your motivation for being here?)
- What is your vision? (What do you long to see Tearfund accomplish?)
- What do you think the challenges will be to seeing this happen?

Several things emerged from this process. One of the most wonderful, for Matthew, was the sense of passion evident in all the staff members. Even those who were involved in support roles, such as facilities maintenance, had a deep engagement with Tearfund's goals and spoke of their roles in terms of a vocation. Equally vital was the way in which people began to speak about integral mission; the mission in which we are called to participate recognizes the indivisibility of both the proclamation and the demonstration of the gospel, and rejects any dualism in which either dimension is separated out from the other, or its centrality in any way diminished. One other recurring theme was an ambivalence about the role of the local church (as opposed to other agencies) in the accomplishment of development.

As this process of listening took place, two further pieces of evidence landed within Tearfund. Prior to Matthew's joining, an annual organizational review process had been initiated. Fifteen leaders of some of Tearfund's partner organizations (those who delivered the work on the ground) from around the world had been invited to spend two weeks in the Teddington offices, asking questions and examining all that was going on. Under the leadership of Rene Padilla, the group now submitted its report. Its primary recommendation was that Tearfund embrace more fully the role of the local church in development. The report also recommended greater accountability towards those whom Tearfund served and a greater willingness to empower them to take initiative. At the same time, the then Tearfund Churches Training and Development manager, Tulo Raistrick, had made an extensive survey of the role of the local church throughout the world and had uncovered many stunning examples of local church-led development that had hitherto been taking place under the radar.

## Strategic leadership

With the fruit of these various listening processes to hand, Matthew selected six people from across the organization to work with the leadership team on a six-month strategy review. This group was charged with studied reflection on questions to do with Tearfund's identity, distinctiveness and vision. Their task was threefold. First they were to bring to the organization a set of values that would shape its future trajectory (Tearfund did have 9 existing values and 12 guiding principles, but no one seemed to pay any attention to them). Second, and in the light of these values, they were to produce a compelling, high-level, time-bound (a critical factor according to Matthew) vision statement that might then become the framework for determining future actions. Third, the group must form a high-level strategy to enable the realization of the vision.

With all the insights from the various listening processes to hand, the group came up with a distinct set of five values:

We are Christ-centred, courageous, truthful, compassionate, servants.

Reflection on the organization's purpose and identity in the light of these values resulted in an exciting vision statement that would shape the next decade of Tearfund's ministry:

To see 50 million people released from spiritual and material poverty in the next ten years through a worldwide network of 100,000 churches.

Matthew was concerned that the strategic planning be deliberately high-level and not too detailed so as not to inhibit innovation and improvisation, especially at the front line of Tearfund's work. He was also insistent that strategy be constructed around a confrontation with the brutal facts that threatened the accomplishment of the vision. How might we use our scarce resources to address the problem of poverty? The resulting high-level strategy had four particular elements.

- Getting behind local movements of integral mission and working to shape theology at a grass-roots level, such that this approach to integral mission and development becomes more widely owned across local partners and networks.
- Working through the local church in long-term development work and relief work, recognizing that the local church, rather than Tearfund, are the answer to a community's challenges.
- Working more in advocacy both locally and nationally, working to challenge the things that perpetuate poverty.
- Identifying inspired individuals, local missional entrepreneurs who are already functioning as change-makers within their communities.

As the vision and strategy were communicated throughout the organization, excitement as well as focus grew. What was now required was to tackle some of the challenges to do with organizational effectiveness, and to ensure that Tearfund's organizational culture had the capacity to enable, rather than hinder, people acting to accomplish the vision. Two particular things were identified as needing change.

## Organizational design

First, Tearfund needed to become more agile and more responsive to the leading of the Spirit and to rapidly changing contexts. The organizational structure, as far as Matthew was concerned, needed to be one that encouraged and facilitated improvisation and creativity, especially among those at the frontline of Tearfund's work. Second, Tearfund needed to rediscover the entrepreneurial courage that had been so much at the heart of its founding DNA. Matthew felt that Tearfund had become somewhat risk-averse and had thus lost its capacity to be super-responsive, a quality he saw as vital if the vision were to be accomplished. He knew the process of organizational design would be a long one. There were, perhaps, four things that were key in the changes that came about over the next ten years:

1 The values needed to be embedded, beginning with the Tearfund leadership team but then extending throughout the organization such that they became intuited by all.

2 Primary operational responsibility needed to be increasingly devolved to the grass roots of the organization. Whereas previously most permissions had to be granted at high level within the organization, now country representatives were given increasing responsibility along with higher levels of budgetary responsibility. Those working in local contexts who had an intuitive knowledge of their situation and particular expertise needed to be empowered to take initiatives.

3 The essentially transactional nature of current organizational culture needed to give way to a culture that was essentially relational. Matthew insists that transactional cultures are usually constructed out of fear that, left to their own devices, people will not always do the right thing and therefore some formal mechanisms are required to prevent this. In this culture people are essentially accountable to their managers. The paradigm that shapes and describes this hierarchical form of culture is that of a machine. A relational culture, on the other hand, is more organic. The controlling paradigm for this culture might be that of family or living organism. In such a culture there is a confidence that trustworthy people usually want to do the right thing for the well-being of the organization and its various stakeholders. Accountability in this culture is no less present but tends to be more mutual, is exercised between peers, and is focused on learning and growth. Relationship becomes the core building block of the organization, and every element of organizational life is analysed through the lens of its impact, for good or bad, on relationships. Such a culture may well involve a good deal of messiness, and may well be somewhat disturbing and unsettling to those who value tidiness and order. For leaders it involves giving up significant levels of control over people and systems. However, not only is such a culture usually much more

productive and empowering, but, for Matthew, it reflects one of the key values that lies at the heart of a distinctively Christian understanding of organization. One of his own priorities throughout his time at Tearfund was do everything he could to coach people in creating systems that enabled relationships to flourish.

4 The personal growth of those involved in the organization was prioritized. Matthew speaks of his own longing to help everyone to become the best possible version of themselves and to be enabled to do those things about which they are most passionate within the organizational vision. Practical ways in which personal growth was encouraged included some significant changes in HR practice. Job descriptions had previously focused on tasks to be accomplished. Now they were reframed in terms of goals and values. Training was given across the organization in such areas as giving and receiving feedback as a means to growth, in conflict management and in active listening skills.

### Outcomes

Of all the innovations that came about during this exciting phase in Tearfund's history, quite the most impactful in terms of advancing the vision was that of mobilizing local churches. As local churches and their members began to play a much fuller role in initiating and delivering development, innovation and creativity was released at grass-roots level. According to Matthew, all of the most interesting new developments came from the margins rather than from the centre, whether the emergence of self-help groups in Ethiopia as a means of lifting thousands out of poverty, or the launch of campaigns related to modern slavery or environmental concerns. These things all bubbled up to the surface because space had been given for people to pursue their God-given passions and to respond to the promptings of the Holy Spirit and the front-line realities of those whom Tearfund exists to serve.

Earlier institutional sluggishness had given way to a far more attentive and responsive culture. 'We got better at spotting things and at getting behind them', suggests Matthew.

Employee engagement improved each year, according to the annual surveys inviting feedback and comment. People especially warmed to the growing emphasis on acting with courage and being willing to take appropriate risks.

Perhaps most significantly, by 2015 Tearfund could report that, through the envisioning of over 130,000 churches to act as catalysts for the development of their wider communities, over 40 million people had been lifted out of poverty. As Matthew Frost prepared to move on from his role, he left behind an organization confident in its sense of identity and vocation, agile and responsive, committed to increasing devolution of power and influence away from the centre, and with a commitment to pursue new ways of increasing the scale of its operation, to the end that poverty and the causes of poverty might be overcome.

## Questions to aid reflection

1 How would you answer Matthew's question, 'What is distinctive about a *Christian* organization?'

2 What strikes you about the particular strategies Matthew deployed and the actions he took as a way of facilitating organizational change? Can you think of ways in which some of these might be helpful in your context?

3 Matthew was concerned that personal growth of employees and others should be seen as a priority. What do you think are the particular factors in the life of an organization that might especially promote or hinder such an aspiration?

*Notes*

1 Willimon, W., 2015, *Pastor*, Nashville, TN: Abingdon Press, p. 283.

2 Nouwen, H., 1989, *In the Name of Jesus*, London: Darton, Longman & Todd, p. 58.

3 John 20.21.

4 John 14.12.

5 Luke 4.18–21.

6 Mark 1.9–11. The words Jesus hears at his baptism are popular messianic prophetic texts, whose citation here would leave him in no doubt as to the messianic nature of his own calling and career.

7 For example, John 5.19; 6.38.

8 For example, Mark 1.38–39.

9 John 10.11–18.

10 John 13.1–17.

11 John 13.13–15.

12 John 13.3 – his action in foot-washing is entirely linked, for John, in Jesus' knowing that he had come from God and was going back to him.

13 Luke 22.24.

14 Isaiah 42.1.

15 For example, Matthew 12.18–21; 17.5.

16 Very likely Isaiah 53.

17 See Mark 10.42–45.

18 Greenman, J. P., 'The Shape of Christian Leadership' (inaugural address on 10 February 2004 as the R. J. Bernard Family Chair of Leadership at Tyndall Seminary, Toronto), quoted in Jacobsen, E. O. (ed.), 2009, *The Three Tasks of Leadership*, Grand Rapids, MI: Eerdmans, p. 88.

19 Peter (Luke 5.10) is told that he will now be involved in catching people for God, an unthinkable thing for one who, as a fisherman, was by definition no longer under the kind of instruction required for nascent religious teachers or leaders; Nathaniel (John 1.47ff.) is similarly enlarged in terms of his aspirations through an encounter with Jesus.

20 The apostles in Luke 9.1–6, and a larger group of other disciples in Luke 10.1–20.

21 John 1412; 16.7; 20.21; Acts 1.8.

22 Cottrell, S., 2009, *Hit the Ground Kneeling*, London: Church House Publishing, p. 48.

23 For example, Clarke, A. D., 2008, *A Pauline Theology of Church Leadership*.

24 Romans 13.1–5.

25 1 Timothy 2.1–2.

26 Mark 10.42–45.

27 Given the love of honorific titles that was so prevalent in both Graeco-Roman and Jewish culture, this aversion to them might represent one of the starkest contrasts between Christian and other contemporary or historic approaches to leadership.

28 Luke 22.25.

29 For example, Matthew 9.18.

30 For example, John 12.42; Acts 23.5.

31 Acts 4.25ff.

32 John 16.11.

33 1 Corinthians 2.6.

34 For example, Acts 16.18.

35 For example, Acts 4.19.

36 The sole instance of a Christian leader referring to themselves in such terms comes in Romans 15.16 where the apostle Paul describes his calling to preach to the Gentiles as being 'priestly service of the gospel of God'. This is generally understood to be a metaphorical use of this term. It may indicate Paul's own sense of his self-offering in the cause of the gospel (cf. Philippians 2.17). More likely, it may be a way of explaining how the Gentiles have now become acceptable before God through the gospel, and being likened to an acceptable offering gladly received by God and Paul, who brought the gospel to them, being likened to the Old Testament priest who makes the offering.

37 1 Peter 2.5.

38 Schillebeeckx, E., 1981, *Ministry: Leadership in the Community of Jesus Christ*, New York: Crossroad, p. 48.

39 Polycrates of Ephesus (AD 190) refers to the apostle John in this way. It was not until the early third century, as Christian worship became more exclusively centred on the Eucharist seen increasingly as a re-presentation of the sacrifice of Christ, and the role of the priest as celebrant took on more cultic overtones, that priesthood becomes more prominent as a designation for church leaders. Carey suggests that this may have been motivated by a concern on the part of early third-century Christians to express their faith in ways that might have more coherence with the prevailing pagan culture with its strongly cultic overtones and in which priesthood was revered. Carey, G., 1986, 'Reflections Upon the Nature of Ministry and Priesthood in the light of the LIMA Report', *Anvil* 3, pp. 19–31.

40 Faith and Order Commission of the Church of England (FAOC), 2015, *Senior Church Leadership*, Archbishops' Council, p. 181.

41 Coenen, L., 'ἐπίσκοπος, πρεσβύτερος', in Brown, C. (ed.), 1975, *New International Dictionary of New Testament Theology*, vol. 1, Exeter: Paternoster Press, pp. 188–201. FAOC, *Senior Church Leadership*, p. 68, suggests that it might be translated as 'the one prepared to stand out in the assembly and to stand up for the rights of weaker members'.

42 2 Samuel 13.17; Amos 6.10. This same usage is to be found in 1 Timothy 3.5 where faithful oversight (*prostēnai*) of one's household is a requirement for leading the Church of God.

43 1 Thessalonians 5.12.

44 Paul likens his own role in relation to the Thessalonians to that of a nursing mother caring for children (1 Thessalonians 2.7), refers to himself as a 'Father in the Gospel' to the Corinthians (1 Corinthians 4.15), and on numerous occasions refers to members of churches founded by him as his children in the Lord and also as his brothers and sisters in Christ.

45 Clarke, *A Pauline Theology of Church Leadership*, p. 55.

46 Luke 22.26.

47 FAOC, *Senior Church Leadership*, p. 67.

48 Hebrews 13.7.

49 Hebrews 13.17.

50 The use of *ekklēsia*, a word drawn from public life indicating an assembly or guild, to describe themselves, as opposed, for example, to synagogue, a word with more religious overtones, further emphasizes the consciousness of the early Church as being an entirely new culture.

51 Clapp, R., 1996, *A Peculiar People*, Downers Grove, IL: InterVarsity Press.

52 Roxburgh, A. and Romanuk, F., 2006, *The Missional Leader*, San Francisco, CA: Jossey-Bass, p. 119.

53 Acts 27.11 and Revelation 18.17.

54 Coenen, 'ἐπίσκοπος, πρεσβύτερος', p. 198.

55 For example, 2 Chronicles 24.11; Nehemiah 11.9, 14, 22.

56 For example, Psalms 80.14; Zephaniah 2.7.

57 Deuteronomy 11.12.

58 See p. 67 above.

59 Acts 20.28.

60 1 Timothy 3.1–7; Titus 1.5–9.

61 Coenen, 'επισκοπος, πρεσβυτερος', p. 194.

62 For example, Exodus 12.21–27; 18.13; Numbers 11.16ff.

63 For example, Joshua 20.4; 1 Samuel 16.4; Judges 11.5ff.

64 1 Samuel 8.4ff.

65 For example, 2 Samuel 17.4; 1 Kings 12.6ff.

66 For example, 1 Kings 8.

67 Ezekiel 8.1.

68 Jeremiah 29.1.

69 The Synoptic Gospels refer to this group of people in similar fashion – for example, Matthew 26.3; Mark 8.31.

70 Acts 11.30; 15.2.

71 Acts 14.23.

72 Coenen, 'επισκοπος, πρεσβυτερος', p. 199.

73 Campbell, R. A., 1994, *The Elders: Seniority within Earliest Christianity*, Edinburgh: T & T Clark.

74 Clarke, *A Pauline Theology of Church Leadership*, p. 58.

75 Romans 1.1.

76 1 Corinthians 11.1.

77 Acts 3.12, 16.

78 For example, 1 Corinthians 11.23; 15.3.

79 Dunn, J. D. G., 1975, *Jesus and the Spirit*, London: SCM Press, p. 92.

80 Hess, K., 'διακονεω', in Brown, C. (ed.), 1975, *New International Dictionary of New Testament Theology*, vol. 3, Exeter: Paternoster Press, pp. 544–9.

81 See, for example, Beyer, H. W., 'διακονεω, διακονια, διακονος', in Kittel, G. (ed.), 1964, *Theological Dictionary of the New Testament*, vol. 2, Grand Rapids, MI: Eerdmans, pp. 81–93.

82 Collins, J. N., 1990, *Diakonia: Re-interpreting the Ancient Sources*, Oxford: Oxford University Press.

83 Collins, *Diakonia*, p. 335.

84 2 Corinthians 11.23.

85 Georgi, D., 1987, *The Opponents of Paul in Second Corinthians*, Edinburgh: T & T Clark, pp. 27–8.

86 For example, in Philippians 1.1.

87 Von Eicken, E. and Lindner, H., 'αποστελλω', in Brown, *New International Dictionary*, vol. 1, pp. 126–8.

88 Dunn, J. D. G., 2003, *The Theology of Paul the Apostle*, London: Bloomsbury, p. 581.

89 Even to the disreputable Corinthians he insists that he is not lording it over their faith but working together with them for their joy (2 Corinthians 1.24).

90 Philippians 2.1–2.

91 Romans 12.1; 2 Corinthians 6.1.

92 Ephesians 4.1.

93 1 Corinthians 1.10.

94 2 Corinthians 10.1.

95 Banks, R., 1994, *Paul's Idea of Community*, Peabody, MA: Hendrickson, p. 179.

96 FAOC, *Senior Church Leadership*, p. 46 (para. 114).

97 I am fully aware of the debates that surround the authorship of Ephesians but it would not serve the purposes of this book to enter into discussion of them

here. In referring to the author of this letter as 'Paul', the author claims the support of his former New Testament lecturer, the late G. B. Caird, who would insist that this letter was either written by the apostle Paul 'or by someone so close to the mind and heart of the apostle that it might be best to refer to him as "Paul"'.

98  Ephesians 4.7.

99  Ephesians 4.12.

100  Ephesians 4.12, 16.

101  Ephesians 4.11.

102  I do appreciate that scholarly opinion is divided in terms of the proper inter-pretation of Ephesians 4.12 and specifically concerning the relationship of the first two prepositional phrases in this verse. Lincoln (1990) is one of a number of recent commentators arguing for a distinction between the two. On this reading, God's gift of certain ministries (or offices) to the Church constitute God's equipping of his Church, are given so that works of service may be undertaken (by the recipients of such gifts), and are God's way of building up his Church. My own conviction, both on linguistic grounds and because it has greater resonance with the argument of the whole paragraph, is that the reading favoured, for example, by Barth (1974), Bruce (1961) and Caird (1976) among others, in which the second prepositional phrase is seen as related to the first, is preferable. On this reading, which is assumed in the argument above, the equipping of all God's people for works of service (which is of a piece with the universal receiving of grace referenced in verse 7) is accomplished through, and is a function of, the exercise of the ministries given by God to the Church.

103  Snyder, H., 1983, *Liberating the Church*, Downers Grove, IL: InterVarsity Press, p. 248.

104  Pickard, S., 2009, *Theological Foundations for Collaborative Ministry*, Farnham: Ashgate, p. 1.

105  Romans 12.5.

106  Pickard, *Theological Foundations*, p. 147.

107  Pickard, *Theological Foundations*, p. 166.

108  1 Peter 4.10.

109  Acts 20.28–29.

110  John 1.14.

111  1 Thessalonians 2.7.

112  2 Corinthians 11.7–9.

113  1 Corinthians 2.3–5.

114  Roxburgh and Romanuk, *The Missional Leader*, p. 126.

115  Specifically for Pickard a distorted, Nestorian Christology, or an overdevel-oped pneumatology.

116  Further insights into the ways in which our leadership practices are directly affected by our understanding of the nature of the relationships between the differ-ent persons of the Trinity are offered by Miroslav Volf, in Volf, M., 1998, *After Our Likeness: The Church as the Image of the Trinity*, Grand Rapids, MI: Eerdmans.

117  Pickard, *Theological Foundations*, p. 143.

118  We are reminded here of Barth's assertion that 'there is a threefoldness to every act of God'. Barth, K., 1975, *Church Dogmatics* 1/1, trans. G. Bromiley, Edin-burgh: T & T Clark, pp. 295ff.

119  Acts 8.4–25.

120  Acts 8.26ff.

121 Acts 10—11.

122 Acts 13.2; 16.7–9.

123 Acts 15.28.

124 FAOC, *Senior Church Leadership*, p. 114.

125 Newbigin, L., 1953, *The Household of God*, London: SCM Press, p. 25.

126 Ephesians 1.10.

127 The impact of eschatology on leadership in different spheres of life is explored much more fully in Padfield, J., 2019, *Hopeful Influence*, London: SCM Press.

128 Hebrews 13.17; Luke 16.1–13; Matthew 25.14–30.

129 FAOC, *Senior Church Leadership*, p. 71.

# 5

# Distrusting Leadership: Critical Reflection on the Practice of Leadership

*'Leadership is, at best, a contested concept and at worst a dangerous, violent and totalitarian heresy.'*[1]

Our argument thus far has been, essentially, that good leadership makes a positive difference to any undertaking and that a concern for its establishment and development is therefore to be welcomed. We have also sought to demonstrate that such a concern is evident among the community of God's people throughout their long existence and that the Judaeo-Christian tradition bears witness to the proper place of benevolent leadership. However, it is plain from the wide-ranging criticism of leadership expressed from a number of different quarters that convictions about its helpfulness as a practice are not universally shared. While some of these criticisms are prompted by theological or spiritual concerns, whereby leadership is viewed as an essentially secular enterprise, and thus as antipathetic to the purposes for which the Church exists, others express broader reservations about leadership generally, and its inherent dangers, and are more philosophically or ethically motivated. For some of its critics, leadership is a fatally flawed enterprise that works against the very goals its proponents claim for it.[2] Leadership is thus something to be resisted rather than embraced. Whether or not we share such conclusions, the concerns that give rise to them deserve to be taken seriously, not least because they serve to alert us to some of the real dangers of engaging in or committing ourselves to leadership that is exercised in an unreflective or unaccountable manner.

It is worth sounding one note of caution as we embark upon any critical reflection on leadership. In an earlier chapter we commented upon the difficulty of settling on any universal definition of leadership. Leadership can represent very different things to different people and carry with it all manner of varying connotations. It may well be the case that the reservations expressed by an author about particular leadership theories or practices seem entirely justified and pertinent. However, given the diversity that exists when it comes to understanding and describing leadership practice, it is not always appropriate to extend such criticism to any and every practice that falls under the leadership banner. Different writers may have very different things in mind and may hold very different assumptions, despite all commenting on the phenomenon each describes as 'leadership'.

In weighing the challenges brought to bear by those who offer a negative critique of leadership discourses, we shall have to work hard to exegete the precise assumptions about leadership that underlie such criticisms.

As we reflect on some of the most commonly expressed theoretical critiques of leadership, we ought to note in passing the ways in which attitudes to leadership are so often shaped by personal experience of providing and receiving leadership. Bad personal experiences of poor leaders will often foster or exacerbate reservations to do with leadership generally. Sometimes this is as a result of having witnessed inconsistency or moral failure on the part of a leader, sometimes with an abuse of power or the feeling that a leader has behaved in a manipulative or inconsiderate way, and is sometimes prompted by having experienced leadership that is ineffectual, self-serving or frankly incompetent. It is hard to justify leadership practice that lacks integrity or proper consideration for others (and this book is written at least half in the hope that such practice might be improved). Yet the experience of poor leadership is all too common; it is, sadly, disheartening and even destructive for those on its receiving end. The mere existence of leadership is no guarantee in and of itself that such leadership will be either moral or good. As Barbara Kellerman warns:

> Scholars should remind us that ... leaders are like the rest of us: trustworthy and deceitful, cowardly and brave, greedy and generous. To assume that all good leaders are good people is to be wilfully blind to the reality of the human condition.[3]

We may rightly observe that those entrusted with leadership have a greater responsibility to order their own lives properly and to conduct themselves in a moral fashion, as their own actions have much greater consequences for others to whom they owe a duty of care. Bad leadership exercised by one or a few individuals may well make us far more cautious about receiving other leadership in other contexts, and generally suspicious of leadership per se. But in and of itself, bad leadership does not imply that all leadership is inevitably equally flawed, and the antidote to bad leadership is not no leadership but good leadership.

## Philosophical and moral reservations

### Leadership is a manipulative abuse of power

There is no avoiding the fact that leadership is inevitably an exercise in the proper deployment of power and authority, uncomfortable though this may appear to many people. Our discomfort with the notion of exercising power may well be as a consequence of the tendency to equate power with coercion, a tendency that perhaps owes its origins to Weber's somewhat contentious insistence that power is 'any probability of imposing one's will within a social relationship, even against resistance'. It may also be the case that we are most acutely aware of power when it is used in a coercive fashion. The beneficial use of power may not always be quite so obvious to the naked eye. Yet power, as Nye points out,[4] is simply a resource to enable us to achieve preferred outcomes and is neither morally good nor bad per se. In his excellent reflection on ways in which power might be redeemed, Andy Crouch goes so far as to claim that, far from being a force for oppression, power is a gift from God given to enable human flourishing and the furtherance of God's good purposes. Flourishing, he suggests, is the true test of legitimate power.[5] The trouble is that power can be used inappropriately and in a way that might be seen to hinder or prevent human flourishing. Given leadership's relationship with the use of power, as a practice it is clearly vulnerable itself to being desired, seized or deployed from less than pure motives. Concerns arise around leadership and its capacity to degenerate into a misuse of power. The suspicion grows that leadership must inevitably, even if at times unintentionally, become an abusive practice. This suspicion is variously expressed from a number of different quarters.

The current age, often defined as late modernity or postmodernity, is generally wary of any perceived assertion of power by an individual or group over others. Such power claims are seen to be located in the metanarratives and authority structures so beloved of modernity and are regarded as being threatening to the autonomy of the individual, possibly the most pervasive perceived good of the present age. Because leadership is so readily identified with the use of power to achieve one's desired outcomes,[6] it becomes discredited as a consequence of its tendency to impose upon others. Such a view is reflected in a number of radical feminist critiques[7] in which the form of power associated with leadership is characterized as 'power over', the exertion of the will of an individual over against another. For these critics, not only is leadership associated historically with what Amanda Sinclair refers to as the 'lionisation of the achievement of (usually male) individuals in powerful privileged positions',[8] but the way power is used is defined and legitimated by a social order shaped by the tendency of men to exercise power over others.[9] Many feminist theorists advocate for a different deployment of power, one characterized by the philosopher Paul Ricoeur as 'power-in-common',[10] hallmarked by cooperation and mutual support and a concern for communal action. On this account, leadership must inevitably be regarded as obstructive of the proper deployment of power, as abusive, and thus as something to be rejected as having no positive value.

The Christian writer Justin Lewis-Anthony[11] expresses similar reservations about leadership, insisting that the deployment of power that is an inevitable consequence of leadership is the antithesis of that modelled by Jesus. Leadership is for Lewis-Anthony, therefore, a heresy, a distortion of Christian truth, mired by its inevitable association with a resort to violence.

Lewis-Anthony traces the roots of much modern leadership theory back to the soil of popular North American culture.[12] Highlighting the human need for myths and metaphors, controlling stories to encapsulate and make sense of our experiences and give meaning to our lives, he puts forward the myth of the heroic individual as one of the most prevalent myths for North Americans. Two factors in particular are seen as being influential in the formation of this cultural myth. From the time of the first settlers, the frontier, understood as the limit of settlement, exercises a profound influence on the emerging American psyche as each generation has to come to terms with changing circumstances. In the words of the historian Frederick Jackson Turner:

> to the frontier the American intellect owes its striking characteristics. That coarseness and strength combined with acuteness and inquisitiveness; that practical, inventive turn of mind ... that restless, nervous energy; that dominant individualism, working for good and for evil, and withal that buoyancy and exuberance which comes with freedom – these are traits of the frontier.[13]

The frontier represented new adventure, new hope, progress and expansion, and those who developed it were inventive and resourceful pioneers who blazed a trail for others to follow. The American dream was given credibility by those, often heroic figures, who extended the limit of the frontier. Second, linked to this experience, is what Lewis-Anthony describes as 'the myth of the American Adam'. America was experienced by the European settlers as a vast wilderness to be tamed, a land to be subdued and a garden to be planted; in many ways a new Eden. Such a land was to be tilled by a gardener,

> a prelapsarian Adam, given a second chance to live as if the fall had never happened, and whose life and destiny would be limited only by the illimitable bounty of the American land and the sincerity of the American settler.[14]

Being Adam, suggests Lewis-Anthony, carries with it the social consequence of being alone, which gives a form of validity to the phenomenon of individualism, the deliberate and thoughtful withdrawal of a man from his fellows, forming a little circle of his own, in short, becoming self-sufficient.[15] Thus, in the American consciousness, those who are in any way formed by the frontier (which, because of its pervasive influence in American culture, by and large includes at least most who trace their origins to the European settlers), see themselves as self-contained individuals capable of providing for themselves.

These myths of cultural identity are writ large in, and further reinforced by, the most powerful expressions of popular culture, the movies. The central characters of mid to late twentieth-century American films were typically heroic characters readily identifiable with a mythical America of moral certainty and individual power.[16] Often saving the day, or a community from threat, through the deployment of some aspect of their personal strength and unusual skill, these figures reinforce the popular understanding of the nature of individual agency and thus of what a leader should look like. Leadership is heroic. We may aspire to be like the heroes we see on the big screen but we may equally have to admit to being unlike them and thus settle for being followers of those who truly resemble them.

There is a significant problem, however, for Lewis-Anthony with leadership in the tradition of John Wayne and his like. The movie heroes celebrated by those who pay to see them typically achieve their goals and succeed in their redemptive tasks by the use of power in a violent fashion. To be a leader in these terms means being prepared to use violence. Indeed, to an extent this is what followers expect and require of their leaders, finding reassurance in the leader being the one who will use violence on our behalf, against those who threaten us, in order to rescue us from such threats and to enable us to flourish. Leadership as a secular social dynamic is thus, for Lewis-Anthony, 'inescapably mired in the violence and individualism of ... John Wayne'.[17] It is not difficult to see how such a violent use of power must be regarded as being in direct contrast to Jesus' own strategy for disarming and overcoming that which threatens the flourishing of humankind. Jesus' way of redemption consists in suffering and sacrifice, rather than violence and the will to power. He overcomes evil by laying down his life, thus subverting evil, rather than by triumphing through a superior deployment of the same violent force in which evil rejoices. For Lewis-Anthony, therefore, leadership must be seen as ultimately a heresy, a distortion of Christian truth about power and weakness and about what it means to follow Christ:

> Leadership is an alien virus ingested by the Christian host. It seems to be reasonable ... but is fatally flawed by its roots in violence, the will to power and destruction ... it is antithetical to the model, ministry and challenge of being a disciple of Jesus Christ.[18]

Those who critique leadership from a postmodern or a feminist perspective, in company with Lewis-Anthony, tend to have in their sights a form of leadership understood as the work of prominent individuals, and one that celebrates the contribution of the leader as instrumental agent rather than as a catalyst for shared work. We have already suggested that leadership is a far more complex and multi-dimensional enterprise within which the role of the leader is significantly focused on the animation and empowerment of others. It would be easy, on one level, then, to dismiss such arguments as inapplicable to our own model of leadership. However, because we countenance the possibility that, occasionally, individual leaders may be required to use power more directly, for example to challenge consensus where that consensus might lead to the mistreatment or neglect of others, we have to find appropriate grounds for the legitimacy of such uses of power and also take seriously our capacity to abuse even power that is entrusted to us for benevolent purposes.

In a searching critique of transformational theories of leadership,[19] Dennis Tourish highlights some of the dangers associated with a fixation upon visionary leaders with high levels of personal charisma. Despite the insistence from transformational writers that such theories of leadership are essentially moral in that they are focused on inspiring, as opposed to coercing, others, Tourish raises a number of important questions about such leadership. How does one guarantee that the goals proposed by a transformational leader actually represent the best interests of all concerned and are not simply a reflection of the self-interests of the designated leader?[20] How might one guard against the tendency of all-embracing visions and norms to prohibit critical discussion and constructive dissent?[21] When leaders see themselves as spiritual engineers, transforming the already existing values and beliefs of followers (as opposed to spiritual explorers, bringing hidden treasures to the surface), how might one enable others to think independently and critically for themselves?[22] In a sobering passage, Tourish draws a comparison between some of the defining traits of transformational leadership and some of the common hallmarks of cults, including an unhealthy devotion to a particular leader, the deployment of unethical coercive techniques of persuasion and control, and the removal of opportunity to express dissent. Tourish is at pains not to suggest that the practice of transformational leadership will automatically turn host organizations into cults, but rather argues that its defining traits 'have the potential to move organisations further along the cult continuum than is desirable'.[23]

How do we respond to these criticisms? Must any use of power to influence others inevitably be violent and abusive? Is there still a place for leadership?

Given the postmodern suspicion of power, the observations of one of postmodernity's most seminal thinkers make for fascinating reading in this respect. Michel Foucault[24] insists that power and authority are to be found everywhere and are unavoidable. We do not exist in a power vacuum, nor are human affairs free from the impact of hostile and destructive forces. One of the very reasons why leadership matters is that such hostile forces need to be challenged and subverted, and the damaging environments they create be replaced by ones more conducive to human flourishing. Power is required in order for this to be enabled. Taking up legitimate power as a leader is very different from using it abusively. Not to take up properly designated power may itself be a denial of responsibility and may result in more harmful consequences for those for whom we should have a concern.

In the light of Lewis-Anthony's assertion that leadership is predicated on an understanding of power that is heretical, what might we say about Jesus'

own use of power? It is certainly the case that the ground of Jesus' authority is not the kind of self-confidence and assurance typical of all-American
movie heroes, but rather the assurance of his own divine calling. Far from
being a heroic, independent agent, Jesus models perfect submission to the
will of his Father, insisting that he only does what he sees his Father doing,[25]
and that he has come to do the will of the one who sent him.[26] His strategy
for defusing a volatile situation, in which the life of a vulnerable woman is
threatened, and of exposing public hatred, is by asking penetrating questions
that hold up a mirror to the hypocrisy of her accusers.[27] His way of coun-
tering the self-focused jockeying for position among members of his most
intimate associates is to shame them by washing their feet, shocking them
by his modelling of a very different understanding of status and authority.
His way of overcoming the most hostile and destructive powers set against
God, and against those created as his image-bearers, is to lay down his
life in death, thereby disarming those hostile powers and triumphing over
them.[28] In doing so he very explicitly refuses the temptation to play those
powers at their own game through the deployment of a greater measure of
similar, violent force.[29]

However, for Jesus, submission and self-sacrifice do not appear to pre-
clude the exercise of appropriate authority and he is rarely, if ever, diffident
about using power.[30] He begins his public ministry with an affirmation that
God's Spirit has empowered him for good purposes, including the setting
free of those trapped in bondages of both spiritual and human origin.[31]
Those who witness his first acts comment on the new kind of authority he
demonstrates.[32] There is a sense of righteous anger about Jesus' pronounce-
ment of woes upon the self-righteous Pharisees who are dismissed as *foolish*
because of their neglect of God's will and their mistreatment of others.[33]
It is hard to find a word other than 'violent' to describe Jesus' actions in
purifying the Jerusalem Temple and opposing the abuses that were taking
place there.[34] Yet this is a power that Jesus uses entirely for the benefit of
others and never as a means to elevate himself in the eyes of others or seek
inappropriate adulation.[35] That he approves of its similar exercise by others
is clear from the instances when he entrusts to his companions power and
authority to engage in exactly the works with which he himself has been
involved.[36] It is especially striking that when faced with communities of
people who were distressed, dispirited and lacking oversight or proper care,
Jesus' compassionate response is both to suggest to his close followers that
they pray for God to provide additional leaders to meet this need, and then
to appoint a handful of those followers to fulfil this very role. Jesus' answer
to social need, very likely caused or exacerbated by corrupt and abusive
leadership, is to provide benevolent leaders. Indeed, we might say that it
was precisely because of his understanding of being under the authority of
another and because of his freedom from self-interest that Jesus was free to
act with power for the benefit of others and for the furtherance of God's
purposes.

We need to separate out in our thinking and practice the use of power for the benefit of others, which we embrace, and seeking to benefit from any privilege or status that may seem to be attached to such power. This we refuse. When, following the preferences of the New Testament writers, we favour leadership descriptors such as steward or servant, and when we see our leadership as being essentially catalytic of the contributions of others as opposed to being merely instrumental over others, we will be better placed to handle the power entrusted to us by virtue of position or calling and will have the capacity to lead in a manner that is neither abusive nor heretical. Those who will succeed in this are likely to be those who are able to lead from a place of security, and thus who do not look to power or position to compensate for areas of personal insecurity or incompleteness, and who, by virtue of a commitment to collaborative ways of leading, seek the counsel, feedback, challenge and wider contributions of diverse others.

## Leadership is elitist and results in the deskilling of followers

One of the most commonly expressed reservations to do with leadership arises from an unease to do with designating certain people as *leaders* and differentiating them from the mass of others who must inevitably be categorized as *followers*. The latter, it is assumed, are thus obliged to occupy a subordinate position, their role being simply that of submitting passively to the instruction, influence and direction of the leader. We have argued in an earlier chapter[37] for an understanding of leadership as consisting in part, at least, of a more equal relationship between leaders and followers (as opposed to being simply the agency of individual leaders), though we recognize that such a view is by no means always reflected in actual leadership practice.

In the world of business and commerce the growing gap between remuneration offered to senior executives and that enjoyed by the majority of the workforce[38] reveals the relative value and importance ascribed to the contributions of those occupying different places within the organization, and reinforces the sense of subordination and inferiority felt by those who are not leaders. In other contexts it may be the disparity in authority given exclusively to those holding certain offices or positions as opposed to other members of an organization that leads to a sense of disempowerment. In still others, it may be the experience of being excluded from opportunities to shape the trajectory of the organization, from offering contributions towards the discerning of future direction or from other activities in which one has an interest or concern. It seems pertinent in a book on Christian leadership to point out that the Christian Church is by no means immune from these tendencies. Even where leadership is dismissed as being a secular notion and not appropriate for a sacred context, leadership is usually found to be exercised by ordained or otherwise authorized ministers. No matter whether such ministers see themselves as set apart for the preaching of the word or as members of a sacramental priesthood in direct and unbroken succession with the first apostles, each runs the risk of reserving so much leadership activity to themselves that the fruit of their ministry is a disempowered and passive laity.[39] Whatever the context, the fundamental issue under scrutiny here is the tendency to celebrate the efficacy of individual action and the agency of the individual leader as of greater significance than that of the potential contribution of a wider group. The greater the focus, in leadership discourses, on powerful leader figures, possessed of the capacity to shape outcomes by dint of their own agency, the higher the likelihood of others in the process experiencing disempowerment.

At times, of course, there may be an element of collusion in this; some followers are pleased to abdicate personal responsibility for their own affairs to another and find reassurance in the idea of having a heroic figure working on their behalf. Gemmill and Oakley suggest that our desire for leadership can stem from the discomfort and fears experienced by those faced with uncertainty or ambiguity in any enterprise. The hope of leadership 'functions as a social defence whose central aim is to repress uncomfortable needs, emotions and wishes that emerge when people attempt to work together'.[40] The consequence of this over-idealizing of any leader is that followers thus deskill themselves in their own critical thinking, visions, inspirations and emotions, and bring upon themselves a passive dependence on leaders and their own disempowerment.[41] This experience of disempowerment is illustrated by a fascinating experiment in which a number of people were given mathematics problems to solve as individuals. They were then asked to perform a similar task in pairs, in which some were designated 'boss' while others were styled 'assistants'. Finally, a further set of problems were tackled by the group working once again as individuals. Those who had been designated 'boss' showed a marked improvement in their performance while the performance of those who had been given the title of assistant declined.[42]

Not every follower who experiences disempowerment necessarily does so as a result of their own personal acquiescence. Some find themselves in situations where their feeling of marginalization is due to the fact that people other than the leader are denied opportunity to participate in strategic work, and, more critically, is a consequence of the inevitable impact of a particular style of leadership on the well-being and development of others within the organization.

In the second volume of his outstanding *Undefended Leader*[43] trilogy, Simon Walker offers an analysis of the way in which followers are affected by the deployment of various leadership styles, each representing different uses of power (categorized by the author as strong or weak, front-stage or back-stage, expanding or consolidating). Arguing from Newton's Third Law of Motion, which insists that in the physical world every action has an equal and opposite reaction, Walker suggests that a loose analogy may be made with the world of social systems. The way in which social force is applied to one part of a system, insofar as that system is closed, will have direct consequences for other parts of the same system.[44] Applying this analogy to the work of leadership, Walker suggests that every deployment of power by a leader will tend to provoke a reaction among followers that is opposite in direction and character to the action that has provoked it. For the purposes of our current discussion, Walker's analysis would conclude that a heroic leader, acting in an essentially directive and instrumental fashion, will always tend to produce passive, servile and often diminished followers.

Walker points out that such instrumental leadership (categorized by him as commanding) may well be appropriate in a limited range of situations, usually in a crisis requiring firm and decisive action to reassure others and to rescue an otherwise hopeless situation. Indeed, he goes so far as to suggest that not to deploy such leadership in these situations would be an abdication of responsibility:

> The basic rule for when to use the Commanding strategy is this: when the consequence of not intervening would be dangerous if not catastrophic ... To allow the toddler to run into the path of a car for fear of intervening in a directive way would be absurd and appallingly perverse.[45]

The danger comes when this is the only style of leadership to which a leader ever resorts and when the whole of the business of leadership is viewed solely through this lens. The water is muddied by the fact that this form of leadership, focusing principally on the actions of the leader, is often the most visible part of the leadership process and may be seized upon by those in search of simple answers to complex leadership questions. It is also the case that because the impact of a single leader is usually especially evident when they succeed in turning around a crisis situation, leaders who emerge out of such contexts (Winston Churchill comes instantly to mind) are adopted as leadership paradigms by others for any and every situation and context. The autobiographies of those who have presided over significant turnarounds in the world of business, sport or politics tend to make for much racier reading than those of people whose leadership career might have been equally or even more effective but whose focus was on raising up and developing others across their organization rather than taking all the decisions for and on behalf of that organization. Given the prevalence in some quarters of this more instrumental understanding of leadership we understand why its critics equally tend to be suspicious of all forms of leadership, fearing the tendency of all leadership to degenerate to such a level.

Gemmill and Oakley conclude their article by advocating for an understanding of leadership exclusively as a social process hallmarked by the dynamic collaboration of individuals who, rather than surrendering authority to another, authorize each other for action and experimentation.[46] On this understanding, the role of the 'leader' in the leadership process becomes apparently redundant and certainly undesirable. What do we make of this? Our own exploration of leadership certainly affirms the idea of leadership being, at least in part, a social process, and our understanding of the Church as the body of Christ with every member contributing to its work underlines this conviction. We recognize too that such a process can be thwarted by an over-reliance upon individual leader figures. However, we agree with Western that it is often the case that the only way in which truly collaborative and dispersed leadership cultures can come into being is through the initial work of a strong leader who lays the appropriate foundations upon which such cultures can be established.[47] Leaders may well be required too for the continuing work of empowering and animating others, of being a catalyst for the release of their contribution. Far from disempowering followers, such a deployment of power will serve to produce active and engaged participants who share confidently in the work of the organization. The choice thus becomes for us not between the kind of charismatic leadership Gemmill and Oakley have within their sights and leaderless leadership. The choice is rather between leaders who empower and those who retain power for themselves.

## Theological reservations

In addition to the more general reservations about leadership we have thus far outlined, a number of further objections relate specifically to the appropriateness of leadership as a practice within the Church. Leadership, maintain some critics, is essentially a secular notion and thus has no place within the sacred space of God's Church. Indeed, an emphasis on leadership, it is suggested, will always end up subverting the true purposes of the Church and will be misleading at best and destructive at worst. The essentially secular nature of leadership is explained variously by different authors. The most common arguments tend to focus on:

- ends and means, and the stark difference in purpose between the Christian Church and those secular organizations out of which much leadership theory derives;
- the reservations expressed by biblical writers towards historic secular understandings of leadership and a conviction that a properly biblical understanding of holding office in the Church focuses more on ministry than on leadership, and particularly the ministry of God's word;
- the fact that while the modern world is fixated on leaders, the Christian Church has for centuries ordered itself under the oversight of those whom it styles bishops, priests and deacons, and that these terms carry within themselves a more fulsome and theologically rich understanding of the roles of those bearing responsibility within the Church.

What these views have in common is an understanding that the Christian Church has its own vocabulary and set of assumptions that govern what it means to hold responsibility in the Church. These assumptions are shaped by the ideas and values that are central to the Christian tradition. Contemporary leadership discourse, it is asserted, is shaped by alternative values and assumptions that are usually seen to be at odds with those of the Christian tradition. We will do our best to engage with each of these objections in turn, referencing in each case some of the most articulate exponents of these ideas.

## Secular leadership thinking emerges from a context with purposes entirely at odds with those of the Christian Church

The vast majority of all more recent writing and reflection on leadership theory and practice has emerged from the business sector and has been concerned to promote best practice in that sector. What is considered to be best practice in any organization is determined by the ends and purposes for which that organization exists. Given that business is essentially focussed on the maximization of productivity, profitability and growth, it is hardly surprising that good leadership in this sector is associated with the deployment of strategies towards the fulfilment of these goals in the most efficient ways possible. Herein lies the problem for a number of commentators. The underlying assumption that business goals are value-neutral and beyond question is itself a cause for concern,[48] resulting, as it does, in the eclipsing or suppression of other legitimate values and interests that might challenge or otherwise compete with the solitary focus on productivity. But even were it conceded that profitability and growth were legitimate ends on which business leadership ought to be focused, surely the purposes for which the Christian Church exists are different? Given this difference, should not Christian leadership be shaped around the fulfilment of these distinctive purposes? And, given the very different concerns of business and the Church, is not Christian leadership compromised and its purposes hindered when it subscribes to thinking from a context alien to its own? The importance of this question is flagged by the authors of the FAOC *Senior Church Leadership* report:

> The presence of language borrowed from secular sources is not itself proof that anything has gone wrong ... Nevertheless, the fact of this borrowing does pose, with considerable urgency, questions about what ways of thinking the church might inadvertently have borrowed when it took on this vocabulary, and whether in doing so it has bought into inappropriate patterns of behavior, relationship and organization. Has the appropriation of leadership language from secular sources been sufficiently critical?[49]

A number of different writers might answer this last question, posed by the report, in the negative.

For Willimon,[50] the Christian Church is defined by its existence as a counter-cultural community exercising a challenge against the prevailing values and outlook of the cultures in which it finds itself. As curators of such a community, Christian leaders are called to resist styles of leadership that are essentially an accommodation to the expectations and judgements of the world and its worship of efficiency.

> One of the challenges of the ordained ministry is to find those metaphors for ministry that allow us appropriately to embody the peculiar vocation of Christian leadership. Uncritical borrowing from the culture's images of leadership can be the death of specifically Christian leaders.[51]

It is not simply that the transformative work of the kingdom cannot be accomplished through styles of leadership that place their trust in instrumentalism, but the embrace of secular leadership praxis will inevitably draw leaders into mindsets that give no place to God and that diminish or erode faith and reduce the leader's capacity for real fruitfulness.

This thinking is developed further by Roxburgh and Romanuk through a reflection on the teleology of Christian leadership.[52] Taking as a starting point Aristotle's insistence on the nature of any entity being shaped by reflection on the end (*telos*) towards which that entity must move, the authors note that both in Scripture and in the earliest Christian tradition, the end of the Church was seen to be associated with God's work of forming a new humanity in Christ. Leadership in the Church is thus seen as being primarily concerned with forming people, of socializing them into this new community, of fostering within them an appetite for participating in God's work through the stimulation of their missional imagination, and thus of cooperating with God in the furtherance of God's purposes for his Church. The authors observe that contemporary leadership theory is not always quite so concerned with personal formation and tends to be more focused on the achievement of growth or productivity. To subscribe uncritically to such leadership practices may well distort the Church's understanding of itself and of its calling, drawing leaders into the pursuit of other goals and thus neglecting the primary work of the formation of others.

Roxburgh and Romanuk are right to draw attention to the impact of theory and practice upon leadership character and self-understanding. However, might the choice between drawing on secular wisdom or rejecting it out of hand be a little more nuanced than they suggest? Are there elements from the business leadership tradition that, far from undermining the achievement of the core goals of the Church, might serve to advance them? The business world may well, for example, promote collaboration in leadership as a means to greater productivity and may well to that end have devised strategies to enable the formation and positive functioning of teams and other types of collaborative working. Might the wisdom gleaned from these quarters not be embraced in order to facilitate the forms of collaboration and partnership that are central to participation in the work of God's kingdom? Given that the same threats face attempts in collaboration in any sphere and context, are we not foolish to overlook tried and tested strategies for overcoming common dysfunctional tendencies within groups of people and mitigating threats to constructive working? The transformational leadership literature emphasizes the importance, inter alia, of enabling all members of any organization to embrace a common vision and to play an appropriate role in the formation of that vision. One of the key responsibilities of the Christian leader is to enable the people for whom she is responsible to understand God's unchanging purposes, and to play a part in discerning and committing to the specific ways in which God is calling the Church to outwork those purposes in its own context in the present time. There is a good deal of wisdom that originates from various secular contexts, focusing on helpful ways of enabling others to share in the discernment process and to do with the role of the leader in communicating vision and enabling others to act upon it. Some of these strategies are enormously helpful for church leaders. As methods they are relatively value-neutral and their adoption does not inevitably compromise the overall aims and ends of those who subscribe to them. Indeed, not to adopt benign, tried and tested methodology may well be a less than responsible exercise of leadership, resulting in a less than satisfactory discharge of our leadership duties and failure to progress adequately in the aims set before us by God.

Ironically, the implicit leadership theories, to which many critics of secular discourse subscribe, face equal criticism from Roxburgh and Romanuk as being at odds with historic understandings of Christian leadership. The experience of living through the long period of Christendom resulted for the Church in a progressive move away from a focus on the formation of an alternative society and towards a concern for the maintenance of orthodoxy and orthopraxis. As the Church saw itself less as a movement and more as an institution, so the concerns and self-understanding of leaders shifted towards the maintenance of an existing order rather than the bringing into being of God's new reality. For those who are formed principally by the aims and values of the Christendom dispensation, the outlook of contemporary leadership discourse with its focus on change, development and forward movement is unsettling and unfamiliar. Without wishing to undermine the need to reflect critically on secular leadership theory or to minimize the extent to which the ends and aspirations integral to churches on the one hand and businesses on the other are genuinely different, we do need also to reflect critically on the actual grounds on which we base our assessment of secular leadership thinking. Does this criticism arise from reflection on biblical and patristic authorities, or is it rather motivated by a weddedness to a Christendom paradigm that may well itself be at odds with the end God has in mind for his Church? Are our objections genuinely theological, or are they cultural?

A word might also be offered here in relation to suspicion around ideas of growth or effectiveness. The mere fact that the business world is engaged in a single-minded pursuit of such goals and is constantly seeking to develop better methodologies to achieve its aims does not per se exclude them as matters of concern for Christian leaders. We are rightly suspicious of an instrumental approach that suggests that business methodologies alone can achieve kingdom goals. However, any reading of the New Testament does give the impression that growth is something that matters to God and that there is an expectation that his kingdom is something that should be both productive and expanding. Jesus' parables describing the nature of the kingdom[53] of God present it as something that is never static or small, while the expectation of the early Church was that both the kingdom would expand to the outermost limits of human habitation[54] and that numerical growth was to be seen as normal.[55] This growth was, on the one hand, impossible other than through the direct agency of God (it is he who 'adds to their number' in Acts 2, while in Mark 4.27 Jesus implies that the means of such growth is hidden from human understanding, coming about all by itself), and yet equally unlikely other than through faithful human partnership with God. The seed grows when the sower sows it; the gospel grows when people respond to God's summons to make it known to those who have not yet heard;[56] the vast crowd are fed when both a young boy offers the little he has as the basis for multiplication and as the disciples then obediently distribute this limited offering in obedience to the instruction of Jesus.[57] The adoption of sound strategies to facilitate the progress of God's work seems to be encouraged by Jesus in his parables to do with faithful stewardship of resources entrusted to us.[58] In the midst of pastoral and spiritual exhortation in the Pastoral epistles it is possible also to discern some wise strategic advice. We may sometimes need to be set free from misplaced confidence in our own abilities to effect those things that only God can bring about. However, it is equally likely that we need to be stirred into embracing strategies and practices that create an environment in which God is free to perform his works. To neglect this may result in our being regarded as lazy or faithless stewards.

## The Church does not fit happily within secular organizational paradigms

This view has been expounded with particular conviction by Martyn Percy.[59] Drawing on some of the early work of Philip Selznick,[60] Percy makes a contrast between organizations and institutions, and thus between the forms of leadership that are most suitable in each case. An organization is a utilitarian system of consciously coordinated activities designed to deliver on certain outcomes. In many ways, organizations are provisional and even expendable. Institutions, on the other hand, are defined by Selznick as organizations 'infused with value'. Their importance lies in their enduring significance as 'natural communities with historic roots that are embedded in the very fabric of society'.[61] An organization may well be self-serving, while an institution has a self-consciousness of serving wider social ends. Whereas an organization may well be useful for a limited length of time and never actually see the need to perpetuate itself, it is of the essence of an institution that it must always be concerned for its future and for the perpetuation of its values and ends. The Church, and specifically the Anglican Communion and the Church of England, is, for Percy, an institution. The distinction between the two matters, especially when one considers what form of leadership might be most appropriate for a church context. Percy's immediate concern is with a perceived obsession on the part of the Church with organizational leadership practices as a means to promote growth and expansion in a context of numerical decline.[62] He dubs such practices 'managerialism'. These for him are entirely inappropriate activities for an institution.

Insofar as the Church relies exclusively on such practices as the means to promote numerical growth, we share Percy's concern. One of our most basic assumptions throughout this book has been that any effectiveness in leadership, and any fruitfulness, is entirely due to the agency of the Holy Spirit and is as a consequence of our partnership with God. The authentic Church can never be grown simply through the exercise of independent human effort, no matter how informed by best business practice. However, the actual nature of the Church may be a little more complex and multi-faceted than Percy concedes. Selznick's understanding of the work of an institutional leader highlights a particular care and concern for the propagation of values, for the management of meaning through 'the elaboration of socially integrating myths',[63] and for enabling the continuation of the institution through the creation, telling and retelling of stories as a way of connecting the institution's past, present and future. All of this resonates strongly with many of the leadership responsibilities we have already articulated as being at the heart of Christian leadership. Where Percy's exegesis of Selznick may fall down, however, is in the absolute distinction he makes between organization and institution, a distinction that goes beyond Selznick. For Selznick, even though an institution possesses qualities absent from simple organizations, an institution still has organizational characteristics and qualities – it is an organization infused with value. Therefore, alongside her responsibility to manage meaning and to be the guardian of vision and values, the institutional leader must also take responsibility for the establishment and maintenance of systems that enable those visions and values to be propagated and acted upon. Perhaps the very reason why the contemporary Church senses the imperative to develop more structured and accountable systems for the oversight and management of its mission is that the absence of such systems has hindered the Church in the past in the performance of its God-given calling. A laissez-faire approach to organization, and a rather whimsical hope that faithful inattention to matters that we believe should not properly concern us, has left the Church ill-equipped to face the significant cultural and social challenges of our current age and left us passive in the face of significant numerical decline and the effective surrender of living witness in some of the most deprived areas of our nation. Deploying organizational insights garnered from other spheres may not alone solve the specific problems confronting the Church today. However, such insights and practices may well enable us to act in a more informed and thus more efficient way as we seek to safeguard the vital long-term future witness of the Church to God's healing presence in a broken world.

One key point to which Percy rightly draws attention in respect to our wider consideration of the nature of Christian, and especially church, leadership, is that of the impact of ecclesiology upon leadership. Given the contextual nature of leadership generally, in order to describe the precise contours and particular concerns of Christian leadership we need to understand the nature of the Church in which it is located and which it serves. We have already identified organizational and institutional dimensions to the Church and thus we suggest that Christian leadership will be concerned for both enabling the narration and propagation of the Christian faith and for the effective organization of the Christian community towards that end. However, the Church is far more than merely an institution or organization,[64] both of which terms imply a certain formality or fixedness. It is, among other things, an organic community, a living body, a sacramental sign and representation of God's dynamic kingdom. By virtue of its creation and sustenance and its inhabitation by God's Spirit, it carries within itself the imperative towards and capacity for continuous renewal as it seeks to express faithfully an unchanging truth in ever-changing contexts. Christian leadership is always concerned about strengthening the institution in its role as guardian and propagator of foundational truths and controlling narratives. However, it recognizes that these truths can only truly be safeguarded and propagated as they are brought to life afresh by being enfleshed in a dynamic community through the power of the Spirit. So leaders will also be concerned for the formation and sustenance of such communities and for the renewal of the Church in order to prevent the taming of the Christian faith by a drift towards institutionalism. In the light of this, Christian leaders will always inhabit something of a place of tension between conservation and creativity, between repetition and improvisation, maintaining proper continuity with the past while keeping their eyes fixed on God's anticipated future.

## The language of leadership is not the Church's language

Suspicion of leadership discourse may well be due to the fact that this language has not, at least until recently, been prominent in Christian circles. The Church has traditionally used alternative language of its own making to describe those who hold responsibility. Though some consequent reservations about leadership are clearly provoked by factors to do with theology or tradition, others appear to be more visceral, arising from a sense of unease with unfamiliar language and ideas, or a feeling that leadership represents something of an alien culture intruding and seeking to subvert the established culture of the Church.

Some ordained or otherwise authorized church ministers are more comfortable with the notion that they are ordained for ministry rather than leadership. They may well point to rich reflection on the role of those holding office in the Church offered by patristic writers, reformers and Puritans, Caroline divines or any number of more recent Anglican and Free Church authors, each drawing attention to the pastoral, teaching, representative and sacramental functions of ministers. Others, especially from a more Catholic tradition, will want to stress the currency of historic titles such as bishop, priest and deacon as appropriate and sufficient descriptors of the ministry and role to which they are called, and wonder what more recently coined words have to add to their self-understanding. Some from a variety of different traditions express an anxiety that leadership might be something of a cuckoo in the ministerial nest, seeking to displace the more distinctive, historic practices associated with authorized ministry. Paul Avis articulates these concerns:

> In ministerial training there is a heightened emphasis on leadership. Some of this material is sound and helpful. But all too often the idea of leadership that is deployed is an uncritical, naive one, drawn from the world of business and secular organisations ... The rhetoric of leadership has almost taken over Christian literature about ministry and mission. Notions of leadership derived from organisational or management studies threaten to displace ecclesiological reflection on Christian ministry. These disciplines have their uses and are not to be despised, but they can hardly replace theology.[65]

I have no wish to undermine such sincerely held convictions. However, I do wish to draw attention to a number of ways in which leadership might be exercised in a way that is congruent with a more traditional understanding of the role of the minister, and that may further shape the way in which such ministry or priesthood might be exercised.

We have already explored at some length[66] the presence of leadership motifs in the words used to describe those who held office in the early Church. Such leadership seems to have been significantly focused on the animation of the body of Christ, the equipping of all God's people for the work of mission and service. The calling of the minister or the priest can never be simply to provide spiritual services for the benefit of others in such a way that what is cultivated is a society of passive recipients (not to say an exhausted minister). The ministry of word and sacrament, of preaching and pastoral care, must always have in mind the release and growth of all God's people in the fulfilment of their own missional calling. It is simply an observable fact of ecclesiastical life that the more distinctive the role of the ordained or authorized leader and the greater the number of tasks that are reserved exclusively to him or her, the less animated is the wider Church and the more impoverished it becomes in terms of its ministry and mission.

Most of the more historic paradigms for ministry either originated or were significantly formed within the Christendom era. The primary focus for the Church generally in this long period was that of the correct formation of those whom it was assumed were already in the faith. Teaching, instruction, the administration of the sacraments and the right ordering of God's people, often in a manner shaped by the expectations of Christian rulers, were the principal factors that shaped the self-understanding of ministers charged with the task of preserving an inherited and established order and safeguarding it against error. It is a moot point as to whether this understanding of the ministerial task was sufficient even within the Christendom dispensation. What is certain is that it is not full enough to meet the challenges of mission and ministry in a post-Christendom era. Central though the tasks of teaching, nurture and the administration of the sacraments are, in an age in which society feels increasingly distant from an understanding of, let alone involvement with, the Christian faith, an age that for the Church seems to have far more in common with the first two Christian centuries than with the more recent past, the Church needs its leaders to have an enlarged understanding of their roles and responsibilities. Specifically, such an understanding needs to embrace the leadership practices and emphases we have outlined in previous chapters as the Church seeks to respond to the challenges of adaptive contexts and to engage in mission rather than merely the maintenance of an inherited order. We would go so far as to say that this is not simply a question of subscribing to a modern leadership fad, but reviving one of the earliest and most central elements of the Church's self-understanding, that of being apostolic. In Christendom, with its obsession with right order and the preservation of the past, the definition of apostolicity was easily reduced to maintaining the teaching handed down by the apostles and the continuance of a professional ministry who were able to trace their ordination back through an unbroken line to the first apostles. Might we suggest that apostolicity consists of far more, and may be more to do with engaging in the activities performed by the apostles (and especially those that arise from a sense of being commissioned and sent by the risen Christ to lead the Church to break new ground for the kingdom)? The task of leadership as we describe it in this book bears many similarities with the biblical and traditional understanding of the role of the apostle.

We may prefer words other than leader to describe those entrusted with responsibility in the Church. However, we suggest that no matter what title we give to such people, integral to a proper understanding of the calling of ordained or authorized ministers is an understanding of their call to exercise leadership. Our own familiar titles may well shed particular light on the precise nature of this calling and on the ways in which such leadership is to be exercised, drawing attention, for example, to the sacrificial and serving nature of such leadership, its concern for the careful nurture and oversight of others and its representative function. In this way the Christian tradition has much to offer the wider world in terms of a fuller understanding of what constitutes truly faithful and effective leadership.

Leadership may be an uncomfortable paradigm for some to inhabit, for any of the reasons we have outlined above. We hope that we may have made something of a case for the importance of embracing the role and responsibilities of leader. By way of a concluding remark we return to an idea hinted at in an earlier chapter. One of the most compelling reasons for embracing the idea of leadership and of exercising it in an intentional fashion is that if we fail to do so we may be found to be exercising an implicit leadership but in an unreflective, ill-considered and thus potentially dangerous fashion. Those who occupy positions of responsibility in churches or in any other organization inevitably exercise leadership and are followed by others. As Willimon, himself a critic of some leadership discourse observes:

> In visits to countless congregations, I have come to the rather frightening conclusion that pastors are the decisive element in the vitality of the church. To be sure, the pastor is not to assume all ministry in the church; the baptised are the chief ministers with Christ in the world. We lead by building a team, and we lead in concert. But having said all that, we must still say that the competence of the pastor is decisive. The pastor's mood and attitude sets the tone for the congregation, conveys hope and energy to the people, hurts and heals, binds and releases. Sometimes as a pastor, I wish it were not so, but what Jesus wants for the church must become incarnate in a pastor or it does not happen.[67]

The more we reflect on what we are doing, and the more we seek to bring this into conformity with the pattern of ministry and leadership we see modelled by Jesus, the safer we will be as leaders and the better able we will be to fulfil our calling.

## Leadership on the ground

Woodlands Church is well known in Bristol, though nearly always by its more informal name 'Woodies'. Established in 1995, as a plant from an independent church in the Henlees and Westbury area of the city, today the church numbers well over one thousand members. It is the central hub for the Woodlands Group of Churches (WGOC), a number of congregations, meeting on six different sites across the city, and is associated with a number of other churches who are part of the wider Woodies family. With a holistic understanding of mission as essentially partnering with God in the work of his kingdom, the church is widely involved with a range of ministries focused on social concern and evangelism. Their strong concern on leading people to faith may well be one principal reason behind their consistent growth throughout each year of their existence; for the last several years Woodies has seen more than 250 people per annum participate in their various Alpha courses.

Dave Mitchell led the team that planted Woodies and is still today the church's senior leader and senior associate leader of WGOC. Dave may well not fit into most people's stereotype of what a leader of a larger church looks like: he did tell me that it is not unusual for visitors to assume that he must be the youth worker, or some other team member, and find it hard to believe that he is actually the senior pastor. He is a profoundly gifted man with a developed capacity to discern God's direction, and a deep love for people and for enabling them to thrive. His love for God and his concern to help others encounter him is infectious, and a significant factor in Woodies' fruitfulness has been his capacity to model vision, values and purpose in such a way that they have become embraced by the wider community. However, those who want to ascribe success to the charismatic personality of a leader will find Dave Mitchell something of a challenge to this paradigm. He is, in truth, a very winsome person, but consistently draws attention away from himself, at times taking very deliberate steps to do so. Dave is adamant that what we are doing as leaders is far less important than who we are becoming as people. Leaders, he insists, should be concerned first about soul care before being concerned about anything else. Dave Mitchell is a wonderful illustration of the truth that effectiveness and consistency in leadership over a lengthy period of time is, perhaps more than anything else, the consequence of intentionality in cultivating godly character, no matter what the cost.

The son of a Methodist minister whose modelling of servant leadership left a profound impression on him from an early age, Dave grew up with a conviction that spiritual greatness looks like service. His years at university were a significant time of personal and ministerial formation. Realizing that God needed to be Lord of every area of his life, he found his own spiritual appetite growing and sought to feed it through devouring Scripture and other devotional writings. The Christian community, largely focused on a university Anglican chaplaincy, of which he had been part, and where he had increasingly been entrusted with leadership responsibilities, morphed, around the time of Dave's graduation, into an independent church, the Fellowship of Christ the King, with Dave invited to be an associate to the stipendiary leader. It was at this point that Dave took the first of a number of significant decisions to do with his own personal formation. Sensing a call to church leadership, and recognizing that in order to fulfil this calling effectively he would need to develop stronger people skills, on graduating from university Dave embarked on a course of training to become a registered mental health nurse, working with those having significant additional needs.

The Fellowship of Christ the King prospered and grew, especially after Dave and his wife Tina encountered John Wimber's ministry and began to see a deeper work of the Holy Spirit in the church. After seven years, and with Dave having more and more leadership responsibility, he began to feel uneasy that some church members seemed to be relying far too much on him and wanting to give him too much prominence. Aware of the seductive nature of popular acclaim and adulation, Dave decided that he needed to make sure that he was robust enough to resist the pressures that success tends to bring. He chose to step out of the limelight for a season and took a job with a Methodist charity, working among some of the most disadvantaged in a deprived area of Bristol. He describes the work in which he was involved – that of feeding the homeless, supporting those in chronic personal situations, at times cleaning up (literally) those in a mess – as a spiritual discipline. The work involved overseeing a small midweek, shopfront church in the community, and, freed from Sunday responsibilities, Dave and his family began to worship at Highgrove Church in North Bristol.

Rob Scott-Cook was the leader of Highgrove Church and today over-sees the WGOC. An apostolic leader with an ambition to see established a network of 100 missional churches reaching the whole of Bristol, one for each community in the city, Rob quickly began to entrust significant leadership responsibility to Dave. The relationship has been a fruitful one for many years, and is one that Dave particularly values as an opportunity for accountability, consultation and shared reflection. The two comple-ment each other well. Under Rob's oversight, Dave's particular gifts and insights were welcomed and he was given freedom increasingly to shape the culture of Highgrove. The experience of working with a senior leader who was simultaneously completely invested in the health and growth of a church yet so free from the need either for recognition or to control things, and who was so willing to release the contributions of others, profoundly shaped Dave Mitchell's own approach to leading with oth-ers. One of the hallmarks of his leadership style, and indeed of the wider Woodies culture, is that he is completely unconcerned about building a reputation for himself and chooses to see himself as one member of a larger team. Mindful of his particular strengths, Dave has a sound grasp of his need for the gifts of others to compensate for those areas, espe-cially to do with process and detail, where he is less competent. He is also a firm advocate of the need to be proactive in seeking out and enlisting others who will be prepared to disagree with and challenge him.

In due course, Dave and Tina were invited by Rob to lead a new church plant into the Westbury and Henlees area of Bristol. The idea was that Highgrove and Westbury/Henlees would be one church with two morning congregations and with a joint evening congregation meeting in a third venue. When, some few years later, the redundant Woodlands building became available, the evening service moved into this build-ing and Dave was asked to take a team from Westbury to start a new morning congregation, the genesis of the current Woodies church.

It was around the time of the Westbury plant that Dave and Tina were offered the opportunity to lease a large property that had formerly been a small school operating under the auspices of the George Muller Foundation. They and their young family, along with a group of others, moved into this rather run-down house and began to live as a struc-tured community. Over the years, this community has been home and, in some cases, a place of refuge and healing to a number of people, including many facing challenging personal situations. Today the cross-generational household of 22 people continues to practise the disciplines of community life including shared meals, a common purse and a regular pattern of common prayer and worship. This experience has, for more than two decades, been particularly formative for Dave, both in terms of his own personal growth (living in community, he suggests, is the best way of preventing you from placing yourself on a pedestal) and in his understanding of church leadership. Dave speaks of seeking to create a culture of 'non-possessive warmth' at the heart of the church, whereby people are embraced but never controlled, a family environment in which all people can flourish and develop a proper sensitivity towards those with whom they journey. Describing Woodies as a church with a wide front door and a wide back door, Dave has never felt proprietorial towards those entrusted to his pastoral care, but, while always keen that people develop and grow at Woodies, is very ready to give away good people to other churches and ministries for the sake of the growth of God's kingdom.

This focus on growing and developing others in leadership and minis-try has been one of the defining features of Dave's own ministry. Perhaps it is this intentionality in investing himself in the formation of others, allied to a generosity in enabling these growing leaders to bear fruit elsewhere, that has contributed so significantly to the fruitfulness of Woodies over the years. Dave and Tina have found the experience of community living to be extremely useful as a means of enabling the growth and develop-ment of other younger leaders. Over the years a number of such people have lived for a season in the community household, including Dave's current associate pastor (who first came to live with the Mitchells as a single, new Christian, and then had a further spell after his marriage and with a young family). Currently six of the household occupy positions of significant responsibility within the church, each overseeing key ministry areas, while a number of other former residents have gone on to become ordained ministers in other churches.

Perhaps the most significant lesson Dave has taken from living in com-munity, and learned to apply to the business of church leadership, is the need to be prepared to live with mess. He recalls, upon first moving into the community house, a sense of being overwhelmed by the scale of the task facing him in making a run-down, neglected former school into a place fit for habitation. This became something of a prophetic sign, as he felt God reminding him that in the same way the task of leading a church was too big for him and would never be tidy. The only way to manage the task was to rely on God and to be prepared to cope with a degree of mess. Perhaps it is the perspective that such insights bring that has enabled Dave to articulate and to bear the pain as well as the joys of leadership, as, over the years, some projects have failed, some people have disappointed and some relationships have faltered.

It requires a particular level of gifting to be fruitful in the way that Dave Mitchell has been fruitful. It requires exceptional character and an appetite for continuous personal growth for that fruitfulness to be sustained, and for the person achieving it to remain immune from its capacity to affect them adversely.

## Notes

1 Lewis-Anthony, J., 2013, *You are the Messiah, and I should Know*, London: Bloomsbury.

2 See Gemmill, G. and Oakley, J., 1992, 'Leadership: An Alienating Social Myth?', *Human Relations* 45(2).

3 Kellerman, B., 2004, *Leadership Warts and All*, Boston, MA: Harvard Business Review.

4 Nye, J. S., 2011, *The Future of Power*, Philadelphia, PA: PublicAffairs, p. 207.

5 Crouch, A., 2013, *Playing God: Redeeming the Gift of Power*, Downer's Grove, IL: InterVarsity Press, p. 13.

6 For example, Nye, J. S., 2010, 'Power and Leadership', in Nohria, N. and Khurana, R. (eds), 2010, *Handbook of Leadership Theory and Practice*, Boston, MA: Harvard Business Press, pp. 305–32.

7 For example, Carroll, S. J., 'Feminist Scholarship on Political Leadership', in Kellerman, B. (ed.), 1984, *Leadership: Multidisciplinary Perspectives*, Englewood Cliffs, NJ: Prentice-Hall.

8 Sinclair, A., 2014, 'A Feminist Case for Leadership', in Damousi, J., Rubinstein, K. and Tomsic, M. (eds), 2014, *Diversity in Leadership: Australian Women Past and Present*, Canberra: ANU Press, p. 18.

9 Gemmill and Oakley, 'Leadership: An Alienating Social Myth?', p. 124.

10 Ricoeur, P., 1990, *Oneself as Another*, Chicago, IL: University of Chicago Press.

11 Lewis-Anthony, *You are the Messiah*.

12 The influence of popular North American culture on leadership studies is also highlighted by Sinclair, 'A Feminist Case for Leadership', p. 20 : '[Because the US has dominated leadership research] aspects of an idealised American national character – individualism, self-reliance, competitiveness, assertiveness – have thus come to underpin much leadership theorising, development and training.'

13 Turner, F. J., 1893, 'The Significance of the Frontier in American History', in 1921, *The Frontier in American History*, p. 37.

14 Lewis-Anthony, *You are the Messiah*, p. 89.

15 Lewis-Anthony, *You are the Messiah*, p. 91.

16 Lewis-Anthony, *You are the Messiah*, p. 201.

17 Lewis-Anthony, *You are the Messiah*, p. 217.

18 Lewis-Anthony, *You are the Messiah*, p. 263.

19 Tourish, D., 2013, *The Dark Side of Transformational Leadership*, Hove: Routledge.

20 Tourish, *The Dark Side*, p. 21.

21 Tourish, *The Dark Side*, p. 57.

22 Tourish, *The Dark Side*, p. 65.

23 Tourish, *The Dark Side*, p. 31.

24 Foucault, M., 1980, *Power/Knowledge: Selected Interviews and Other Writings, 1972–77*, ed. C. Gordon, London: Harvester, quoted in Western, S., 2013, *Leadership: A Critical Text*, 2nd edn, London: Sage, p. 76.

25 John 5.19.

26 John 6.38.

27 John 8.1–11.

28 Colossians 2.15.

29 Luke 4.1–13. This appears to be the substance of the temptation Jesus endured in the wilderness.

30 Crouch, *Playing God*.

31 Luke 4.18–21.

32 Mark 1.27.

33 Luke 11.37–52.

34 John 2.13–17.

35 Philippians 2.6–8.

36 For example, Luke 9.1–2; 10.19.

37 See pp. 37ff.

38 A 2018 report by the Chartered Institute of Personnel and Development revealed that top executives typically earn more than 133 times the amount earned by the average worker in their companies (Makortoff, K., 2019, 'UK CEOs make more in first three days of 2019 than worker's annual salary', *The Guardian*, 4 January, www.theguardian.com/business/2019/jan/04/uk-ceos-make-more-in-first-three-days-of-2019-than-workers-annual-salary (accessed 25 November 2019)).

39 Greenwood, R., 2009, *Parish Priests: For the Sake of the Kingdom*, London: SPCK.

40 Gemmill and Oakley, 'Leadership: An Alienating Social Myth?', p. 114.

41 Gemmill and Oakley, 'Leadership: An Alienating Social Myth?', p. 120.

42 Langer, E. and Benevento, A., 1978, 'Self-induced Dependence', *Journal of Personality and Social Psychology* 36, pp. 886–93, quoted in Tourish, *The Dark Side*, p. 8.

43 Walker, S. P., 2007, *Leading with Nothing to Lose*, Carlisle: Piquant Editions.

44 Walker, *Leading with Nothing to Lose*, p. 40.

45 Walker, *Leading with Nothing to Lose*, p. 54.

46 Gemmill and Oakley, 'Leadership: An Alienating Social Myth?', p. 124.

47 Western, *Leadership*, p. 42.

48 Western, *Leadership*, pp. 7–8.

49 Faith and Order Commission of the Church of England (FAOC), 2015, *Senior Church Leadership*, Archbishops' Council, p. 37.

50 Willimon, W., 2015, *Pastor*, Nashville, TN: Abingdon Press, pp. 62, 71.

51 Willimon, *Pastor*, p. 55.

52 Roxburgh, A. and Romanuk, F., 2006, *The Missional Leader*, San Francisco, CA: Jossey-Bass, pp. 116–24.

53 For example, Mark 4.1–20, 30–32.

54 Acts 1.8.

55 Acts 2.41, 47.

56 This truth is forcefully expressed by the apostle Paul (Romans 10.14) when, in the midst of a long passage dealing with the sovereignty of God, he affirms the necessity of human action in preaching.

57 Matthew 14.13–21; John 6.1–13.

58 For example, Luke 19.11–27.

59 Percy, M., 2017, *The Future Shapes of Anglicanism*, Abingdon: Routledge, pp. 44ff.

60 Selznick, P., 1957, *Leadership in Administration: A Sociological Interpretation*, New York: Harper.

61 Percy, *The Future Shapes of Anglicanism*, p. 45.

62 Percy, *The Future Shapes of Anglicanism*, pp. 25–38.

63 Selznick, *Leadership in Administration*, p. 151.

64 Dulles, A., 2000, *Models of the Church*, 2nd rev. edn, New York: Bantam Doubleday Dell.

65 Avis, P., 2015, *Becoming a Bishop: A Theological Handbook of Episcopal Ministry*, London: Bloomsbury, p. 59.

66 See pp. 83–91 above.

67 Willimon, *Pastor*, p. 292.

# PART 2

# The Work of Leadership

# 6

# Leadership and Organizational Culture

*Culture is one of the most powerful and inspirational metaphors for organisation. By seeing organisations as cultures we can get a better or at least richer view of what goes on in organisations, of the thoughts, feelings, values and actions of people in everyday organisational life and in decision-making situations.*[1]

Throughout its 70-year history, the Daimler-Benz motor car company had developed a reputation for producing high-quality cars known both for their luxurious finish and precision engineering. With brands such as Mercedes in their stable, the company enjoyed immense success within Europe. Success at home had failed, however, to be replicated in the USA, one of the world's largest automotive markets. By the late 1990s only one in every hundred cars sold in the USA was manufactured by Daimler-Benz.

The Chrysler car company, on the other hand, a long-established US firm, had cornered almost 25 per cent of the same market and, in the mid-1990s, was regarded as the world's most profitable car manufacturer. Chrysler's reputation had been built on producing more economical cars for the popular market, and on high efficiency and low cost in both product design and in production methods. Despite this, given the over-saturation of the automotive market and a sense of vulnerability in the face of stronger competitors, Chrysler were experiencing significant anxiety as the millennium approached.

On 7 May 1998, the two respective CEOs announced a merger of the two companies and the formation of DaimlerChrysler AG.[2] The merger, which brought into being the world's third largest car manufacturing company, was seen by both parties as a merger of equals in which each might benefit from the strengths of the other. Each would now have access to previously untapped markets, and each could benefit from the different technologies and systems that contributed to the strength of the other. The aspiration of this new company was to become the world's leading car manufacturer.

With such similar aspirations, common vision, agreement about the immediate challenges with which the industry was currently faced, and given the strengths that each company enjoyed at the time, everything suggested that this would be a hugely successful move. However, the new company began to experience difficulties almost immediately. Tension at the highest levels led to the replacement of American, Chrysler senior executives by German,

Daimler-Benz counterparts. Within two years of the merger, the incompatibility between the philosophy and practices of the two companies so impacted the Chrysler brand especially that its share price fell by almost 60 per cent. Daimler suffered too as it was forced to pour large sums of money into its US partner in order to mitigate the consequences of its dramatic fall in income. It came as no surprise when, in 2007, the merger finally hit the buffers and Chrysler was sold off to Cerberus at a fraction of its former value. The marriage made in heaven ended in a painful annulment, inflicting serious and, in the case of Chrysler, almost fatal harm upon each partner.

The weight of opinion among those who have studied the merger and its aftermath is that, while there was a clear meeting of minds in terms of strategy, the differences in culture between the two companies were irreconcilable, and therein lay the single reason for the merger's failure. Hollmann et al. highlight the cultural differences generally between US and German companies, each shaped by prevailing national and social idiosyncrasies.[3] US culture values individualism and is essentially egalitarian and informal. By contrast, German culture values teamwork, respects hierarchies and is deferential. The Daimler-Benz approach to decision-making valued precision, careful and detailed planning, and wide consultation. This could not have been more different from the experimental, trial-and-error approach favoured by Chrysler. Had these differences in working practices been simply about different behavioural preferences, some synthesis between the two might have been possible. It seems, however, that they were rather symptoms of much more fundamental differences, described in the literature as cultural differences, sharp disagreements that go to the very root of the self-understanding of an organization and its members.

## Defining 'culture'

The language of culture has gained increasing currency in organizational discourse over the course of the last few decades. Although increasingly widely used, closer examination reveals some differences in terms of specific understandings and intentions in the application of the term to business and other organizations. Smircich points out that the concept is one borrowed from the world of anthropology,[4] a field in which equally there is no absolute consensus around the precise meaning of the term. Perhaps the way in which it has been readily embraced as an idea within the world of organizational theory indicates, above all, a growing awareness of the more subtle, less overt and non-rational dimensions of organizational experience and of the influence they exert on organizations. Our particular concern in this chapter is to understand the ways in which such dimensions impact upon leadership, acting as forces that either enable or hinder leadership actions and aspirations. We are also concerned to explore the relationship between leaders and culture, and specifically the capacity of leaders to shape and influence organizational culture.

The academic and management literature has essentially fallen into two camps in terms of its understanding of organizational culture. The more popular literature has tended to see culture as a property of an organization, something an organization *has*, which can vary both from organization to organization and within the history of an organization. Such an understanding arises from organizational theories that tend towards the instrumental and that often liken organizations to either machines or organic systems, structured around the accomplishment of particular tasks.[5] On this account, culture is one property among many belonging to an organization (whose other, related properties might include, inter alia, vision, strategy and structures), a property capable of being changed through the deliberate actions of leaders and others. More academic approaches prefer to see organizations as entities not to be compared with physical objects (such as machines) but rather with other social phenomena. Culture is thus seen as something that an organization *is*, a root metaphor to make sense of the whole experience of organizational life. One of the advantages of seeing culture in this more holistic way is that it lessens the likelihood of those aspects of culture not easily or directly seen as relevant to the immediate goals of the organization[6] being overlooked or ignored. Organizations that pride themselves on their cohesive and positive culture, as evidenced by productivity or other factors, may be oblivious to the blind spots they have when it comes to gender inclusivity, ecological concerns or other ethical issues. Thus, a church of my acquaintance, whose self-understanding (and publicity) emphasized its inclusivity, was challenged by its new vicar to reflect on the accuracy of this cultural statement. While its (theoretical) openness to embrace those from groups perceived to be minority groups in society was indubitable, why was it, he asked, that the declining church congregation was entirely unrepresentative of the wider, local community and composed exclusively of a small group of entirely like-minded people from identical social and intellectual backgrounds? What were the hidden factors that resulted in prospective new members from different backgrounds, or those who did not share the specific cultural assumptions and values of existing members, feeling unwelcome? Could it be that an overconfident focus on culture as a property had diverted attention away from a proper understanding of the cultural identity of the organization as a distinct entity?

Perhaps the most significant difference between the two approaches to culture lies in their consequences for understanding the nature of organizational leadership. If culture is seen as descriptive of the whole organization, then organizational leaders are inextricably part of that culture, as opposed to somehow being independent of it. This has significant consequences for how we understand the capacity of the leader to affect culture. Whereas popular literature often portrays the leader as possessing a unique capacity to act upon culture in a detached manner, the fact that the leader herself is actually entwined within the organization's culture exercises a limiting effect upon her capacity to think and act beyond the constraints imposed by that culture. An approach to cultural change and development will thus look rather different from, and may well be rather more nuanced than, some practitioners might lead us to understand.

What all approaches to understanding organizational culture have in common is a concern to explore non-rational qualities of organizations, those more subjective and visceral, usually taken-for-granted and implicit factors that exercise profound influence on the ways in which organizations function.

The Cambridge Dictionary describes culture as 'the way of life, especially the general customs and beliefs, of a particular group of people at a particular time'. Alvesson, in surveying a range of different writers, suggests that there is broad agreement around seeing culture as a 'shared and learned world of experiences, meanings, values and understandings which inform people and which are expressed, reproduced and communicated, often in symbolic forms'.[7] In common with many other writers, he sees the primary importance of culture as consisting in a shared sense of meaning for any group of people, providing a sense of security and stability and a rationale for actions and behaviours. Smircich observes that in this way culture operates in the organizational world in a strikingly similar way to the notion of paradigm as applied within scientific communities. Both describe integrated and complete ways of looking at the world, organized patterns of thought that give rise to a firm and settled understanding of what constitutes adequate knowledge and legitimate activity.

Schein suggests that culture evolves as a consequence of the human desire for meaning, stability and predictability.[8] All groups of people face the twin challenges of adaptation to their environment, alongside the need for internal integration, to enable basic functioning as well as coordinated growth and development. In any group, culture functions as a means to invest the group's experience with sense and order, and to remove the inevitable intimation of anxiety and uncertainty that is the consequence of disorder. Culture formation for Schein is thus always, by definition, a striving towards patterning and integration. Therein lies its peculiar power and influence. Because it has evolved primarily as a resource to provide meaning and stability, it is resolute in its resistance to challenge or change. Assumptions, beliefs or attitudes that run counter to the established culture are dismissed because to give them credence would be to call into question the adequacy of the existing culture and thus open the door to uncertainty. Schein offers a summary definition of culture as:

> A pattern of shared, basic assumptions learned by a group as it solved its problems of external adaptation and internal integration, which has worked well enough to be considered valid and, therefore, to be taught to new members as the correct way to perceive, think and feel in relation to those problems.[9]

While this definition offers helpful insights into aspects of culture formation it perhaps fails to take note of the extent to which culture functions at a more subconscious level.[10] Some social learning may well have the capacity to be articulated, explained and communicated by its proponents. However, one of the vital features of cultural learning is that it is often implicit, taken for granted, and operates at a level so far beyond consciousness that critical reflection upon it is virtually impossible. Group members are affected by these facets of culture irrespective of their own capacity to exegete or even articulate them. Schein recognizes:

> Cultural forces are powerful because they operate outside of our awareness. We need to understand them not only because of their power, but also because they help to explain many of our puzzling and frustrating experiences in social and organizational life ... If we do understand the dynamics of culture we will be less likely to be puzzled, irritated and anxious when we encounter the unfamiliar and seemingly irrational behaviour of people in organizations, and we will have a deeper understanding not only of why ... people can be so different but also why it is so hard to change them.[11]

Some have thus suggested that culture within an organization may be analogous to the personality of an individual,[12] something that has developed often imperceptibly, partly in response to events and influences, but which acts as an ordering influence itself and shapes and determines the nature of present and future actions.

In seeking to offer a definition of culture it should be noted that there is some disagreement as to the precise scope of the term. Schein, who subscribes to an understanding of culture that is fairly wide in scope, identifies what he describes as three levels of culture.[13]

Culture, for Schein, is usually first encountered through a group's artefacts. Schein includes, under this heading, phenomena such as shared language, myths and stories told about the group and its history, observable rituals and ceremonies, codes of conduct, and manners of addressing group members and leaders. Although these artefacts are very visible, their precise meaning is not always immediately obvious nor easy to decipher.

Less obvious are the espoused beliefs and values of an organization. While these may correlate with aspirational or stated values, Schein is clear that there may be a gap between such expressed values and the actual or accidental values that operate within the life of a group. Thus he notes that it is not uncommon for American organizations to posit teamwork as a stated value, while at the same time rewarding individual competitiveness. The aspirational value is trumped by an incongruent espoused value. Schein suggests that the real values of an organization are revealed in the remedies suggested by a representative of that organization as a means to address challenges or problems.

For Schein, these values arise out of the third, and most fundamental, level of culture, that of basic underlying assumptions to do with, among other things, the identity and role of the organization, about how far its individual members are to be regarded as trustworthy and how far their actions need to be regulated, and about who might be regarded as qualified to fill particular formal or informal roles. These assumptions are often so implicit and taken for granted that they are immune from exploration let alone challenge.

A church, or other faith-based organization, will usually articulate a system of core beliefs, often as a formal creed, but equally through its being expressed in the church's preaching, liturgy and other forms of prayer. Such publicly expressed beliefs may well appear to function rather in the manner of Schein's assumptions. However, buried deeper under the surface may well lie some more influential, controlling beliefs that may even conflict with and subvert the church's confessed beliefs. A church may profess faith in a God who is generous and who provides for the needs of his people. However, experience of decline and of shrinking resources may well have led them to the functional belief that God is actually sparing with his resources, and that he leaves us to fend for ourselves. The behaviour of church members towards one another and in their stewardship of resources becomes grudging and anything but generous, and stands in stark contrast to those beliefs that are publicly professed. One of the tasks of the Christian leader is to enable the group's members to discern what are the actual assumptions that shape behaviour, and to enable them to be challenged and reshaped in the light of biblical truth.

Alvesson and others prefer to define culture rather more narrowly and to confine its scope to the realm of meanings, assumptions and symbolism. Western insists that culture is not a material phenomenon, but rather is that which organizes material phenomena in our minds, enabling us to interpret and draw meaning from rituals and other artefacts.[14] Culture shapes the ways in which we experience and interiorize these phenomena. For such writers, Schein's artefacts are better described as social behaviours or structures rather than as culture per se. Perhaps this inclination to narrow the definition of culture arises from a realization that some behaviours and rituals are capable of a variety of different interpretations and may well signify different things according to the underlying assumptions of different host cultures. However, behaviours, rituals and other artefacts do have particular significance, both for understanding and reinforcing culture. Behaviours often have symbolic meaning and are frequently the most visible signposts pointing to less visible cultural realities. Notwithstanding their capacity to sustain different meanings or interpretations, it might be safe to describe them as *cultural indicators*. Furthermore, behaviours, rituals and other practices play a key part in reinforcing cultural values and systems of meaning. The rehearsal and repetition of such behaviours strengthens confidence in the culture to which they bear witness and deepens its hold on those who participate in it. By the same token, behaviours that challenge or call into question the underlying culture are resisted and dismissed as inappropriate.

The egalitarian style of the Chrysler motor company was a behaviour that expressed not simply a preference in terms of employee practice but flowed out of a whole body of assumptions and values that themselves reflected foundational, American, cultural beliefs about the nature of human identity. The potency of the discord between Chrysler and Daimler lay not in a clash of operating styles per se but rather in a clash of epistemologies, each rooted in lengthy cultural histories.

## The impact of culture

Perhaps the growing interest in exploring organizational culture as a distinct phenomenon is due to recognition of the extent of its influence and impact upon an organization. Positively, a clear culture enables effective and coherent action, giving a clear rationale for determining what actions might be regarded as appropriate, and providing impetus to perform those actions. One of the memorable moments from my final months in my former parish came in the course of a meeting in which I was asking the PCC to consider making an investment of human and financial resources for the benefit of a less well-resourced, neighbouring church. This would be moderately costly to us, would not directly benefit our own mission and ministry, but would be a significant fillip to the ministry of the other church. After introducing the idea, the short silence that followed was broken by one of the newer PCC members asking, 'But that's what we do, isn't it?' The subsequent nodding of heads from other PCC members suggested that there was wide agreement that this was indeed the kind of behaviour that was consistent with, and required by, our cultural values, and that would thus require little further discussion.

Hurst,[15] who also subscribes to the opinion that culture is a root metaphor for an organization, likens culture to the keel of a sailing vessel, that which keeps the vessel upright and stable in heavy weather and enables it to hold a forward course even when sailing against the prevailing wind. This is vital for the stability and progress of the vessel. However, Hurst observes, when the world changes, and when new destinations and directions are required, a heavy keel can create serious resistance to change.

The flip side of the capacity of culture to direct action is that a strong culture can constrain the behaviour of an organization unhelpfully.[16] Desirable or necessary innovation, for example in the face of changing context or environment, can be thwarted by a culture that has gained strength and acceptance over a lengthy period of time. In this instance, an organization is locked into established ways of acting, and departure from these ways is seen as threatening. This is a particular challenge for charities and other voluntary sector organizations as they face the need to transition from the start-up phase, often under the leadership of an entrepreneurial, visionary founder, to a development phase in which infrastructure is built to grow capacity and secure initial achievements. The emerging culture may well have been reinforced by the appointment of other leaders or managers recruited on the basis of their alignment with this particular culture. Pressure to continue to act in a manner consistent with past actions is created by appreciation of the security and sense of meaning that the culture has provided in the past, as well as by a sense of loyalty towards those who have been responsible for its creation. Culture thus exercises significant influence on the openness to change and innovation of an organization and its members.

Culture also impacts the way in which people are treated in an organization. It determines the level of opportunity afforded to various categories of people as well as conventions to do with how different groups of people are addressed. Culture determines how failure and conflict is handled, as well as how far trust is extended to different people within the organization.

Culture determines how decisions are made within groups and which people might contribute to the decision-making process. Schein points out that groups develop assumptions about which factors might be significant in making decisions, about how much information is required in order to make decisions, and the relative weight to be ascribed to different sources of information.[17] Groups sometimes display a stubborn resistance towards the acceptance of, even well-attested, empirical evidence as a factor in decision-making if it runs counter to established, cultural assumptions that have been cherished by the group.

Joseph Lister (1827–1912) is today widely regarded as the father of modern surgery. His pioneering work on the use of antiseptics to prevent wound infection during and after surgery revolutionized medical practice. However, his revolutionary new ideas, based on solid experimental evidence, were initially violently opposed by the majority of his contemporaries. In no small part this resistance was due to cultural factors, Lister's new doctrine both calling into question previously established medical wisdom and reputation and also requiring changes in practice that were seen as reducing the dignity and status of surgeons. The fact that otherwise rational people succumb to irrationality when it comes to embracing change and to making decisions is often due to factors that we might describe as cultural.

Although people join organizations for a whole host of reasons, it has been suggested that the single biggest determinant of whether they stay in or leave any organization is the strength and coherence of that organization's culture. Culture thus has the unique capacity either to galvanize or fragment its host organization.

## Leadership and culture

Given the extent of culture's influence on any group, it should be fairly clear that the stewardship of a holistic and helpful culture must be one of the primary concerns for any leader. Indeed, Schein suggests that the relationship between culture and leadership is so close that the two phenomena might be described as two sides of the same coin.[18] If all theorists are agreed that the leader's role as steward of culture is vital, there is a range of opinion as to how this stewardship might be exercised and what are the limits and possibilities of the leader's role in this area.

Culture for Schein is ultimately created, embedded, evolved and manipulated by leaders.[19] It is often the result of what a founder or other significant leader has imposed on a group and that has proved to be effective. Schein does acknowledge that cultures gain strength and stability the longer they last and the more widely they are embraced, gradually becoming more robust and resistant to the influence of leaders who might see fit to shape them. Indeed, mature cultures may well restrict leadership agency by specifying what kind of leadership might be acceptable for the group or organization. Nevertheless, Schein tends to give significant place to the capacity of leaders to create and shape culture in a broadly instrumental way. This confidence in the agency of leaders may well be fuelled by the fact that much of his work has been undertaken in commercial sectors where the influence of dynamic founders or other significant shapers is still experienced and celebrated. It is equally a conviction that resonates powerfully with US cultural assumptions to do with the power of the individual, the celebration of entrepreneurialism, and an essentially modernist approach to organizational paradigms. Western offers a metaphor for this approach to culture whereby an organization is likened to a greenhouse and culture to the plants contained within it.[20] Within this closed system, the leader controls variables such as light, heat and water to nurture and provide an appropriate culture, at the same time killing off unwanted pests and weeds.

It is perhaps the same cultural tropes, allied to assumptions about organizational paradigms borrowed from the commercial sector, that have led a number of writers from church contexts to describe the role of church leader as architect or creator of culture.[21] Culture is, on this account, reified and regarded as malleable in the hands of a visionary and powerful leader. One such author writes of the need for leaders to create new cultures and to destroy old, unhelpful ones, and to demand compliance with values, norms and behaviours associated with this new culture.[22] While we remain convinced that leaders can exercise exceptional influence in the shaping of culture, it seems important to understand properly how, in fact, this influence is exercised. A failure to do this may well lead to unexpected and destructive conflict, disappointment and frustration for leaders, and unnecessary harm to the organization and its members. Some church leaders have come unstuck by adopting the rather direct and overly optimistic approach to culture change commended by popular writers, not recognizing that such an approach may itself be the consequence of cultural assumptions and values that are not always immediately congruent with people who do not have affinity with US culture. How might we better understand the nature of the interaction between leaders and organizational culture?

Western draws attention to two important considerations to be borne in mind by leaders aspiring to be cultural influencers. First, organizations are not closed systems and organizational cultures are not entirely separate from wider cultural influences. The culture of churches has always been shaped by external, national, regional or other social influences, as well as by more internal cultural factors. The status of bishops in contemporary episcopal churches, and the role expected of them, owes at least as much to assumptions about the exercise of authority by secular officeholders within the later Roman Empire as it does to the teaching of the New Testament. How churches in the West understand what it means to be human, and what constitutes human thriving, is shaped today not exclusively by recourse to biblical insights but significantly by the hedonistic values of late modern culture. Failure to take account of the impact of these wider cultural forces will significantly restrict our capacity to affect organizational cultures.

Second, Western challenges the notion that leaders somehow stand outside of culture and survey it from some superior vantage point. Leaders themselves, according to Western, swim in the sea of culture and embody and are animated by that culture. Leaders do have the capacity to reshape the culture of a group or organization. This they do by carrying and expressing cultures that have shaped them and by reflecting the values and assumptions of that culture in such a way that this new culture becomes more meaningful and satisfying to others.

## Shaping culture

A strong impetus for culture change is usually precipitated by one or more of three particular factors: a growing realization that the prevailing culture is unhelpfully restricting the accomplishment of desired actions or goals; coming to terms with challenges from external forces or compelling fresh thinking, which the existing culture is unable to accommodate; a perception that the established culture is the cause of negative or destructive consequences for group members or other stakeholders. Many churches in recent years have had to come to terms with the deficiencies of 'pastoral' cultures, focused on the thriving of church members, formed in an era when a significantly larger proportion of the general populace attended church worship. Despite being theologically somewhat limited, the effectiveness of these cultures in meeting the needs of the faithful resulted in them remaining largely unchallenged in the years when a Christendom mindset still retained influence. The numerical decline in church attendance and the diminishing of Christian influence in public life has provoked a realization that churches need to engage in mission and recruitment if they are to survive. Some churches, often helped by insightful leadership, have recognized the need for change not simply in behaviours but in culture, and the importance of embracing a more missional culture in favour of the previous pastoral culture that generally served to restrain missional initiatives. These churches have generally fared better than others who have simply tried to bolt on additional, missional behaviours without addressing the more fundamental issues of a culture that gets in the way. Many reading this book may well find themselves in situations rather like this and having to deal with residual cultures that hold back meaningful, spiritual progress. How might we go about the business of culture change?

We want to suggest five broad strategies a leader might adopt to enable culture change within a church or any other group organization. Although these are presented sequentially, in reality they might better be seen as five overlapping spheres of action (Figure 2). Even when an organization is in the advanced stages of embracing a new culture, the leader will still be required to engage in the more foundational activities in this cycle as a way of strengthening and maintaining the emerging culture. None of these strategies are 'stand-alone' but each reinforces the others. As with so many different dimensions of Christian leadership, Jesus of Nazareth offers one of the clearest and most informative models of how these different strategies are to be deployed, and we will draw lessons, as we go along, from his own example in stimulating culture change.

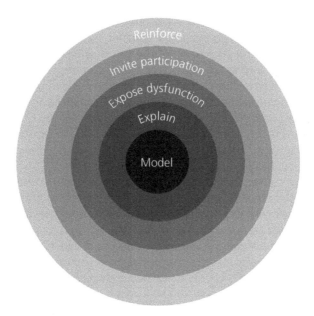

Figure 2. Strategies for shaping culture

## 1 Modelling

The central message of Jesus' ministry was that, in his arrival on earth, a new reality had dawned and that God's power and authority were now present in a fuller and more immediate way. The kingdom of God had drawn near in such a way that old cultural paradigms were no longer adequate for understanding and interpreting experience. Jesus' call to his listeners to repent (*metanoeite*)[23] is an invitation to change mindset and inhabit a more expansive culture. What grabs people's attention and alerts them to the presence of this new reality is not, in the first instance, simply Jesus' teaching but rather the way in which Jesus demonstrates or models the presence of God's kingdom. Sick people are healed, demonized people are set free, those who have been excluded from society are embraced and given new dignity,[24] and unjust power structures are challenged. Tenderness rather than judgement is extended to those who live with personal brokenness and, wherever Jesus is, the sense of God's presence becomes more immediate and apparent.[25]

Those who take a more instrumental view of the leader's role ascribe to the leader responsibility for creating or devising the culture that will be owned by the organization. Christian leadership is a far less original enterprise. Culture for the Christian leader is not something to be created but rather to be received. The kingdom of God is itself a culture, and the task of the Christian leader in any sphere is to commend and propagate this culture, which is designed for the flourishing of God's creation, by representing it accurately and modelling it clearly to others. Any departure from the norms of this culture will involve a lessening of the influence of God's kingdom and a frustration of his purposes. Jesus himself insists that he is not an original thinker when it comes to culture but that he seeks to perform the will of his Father[26] and act in accordance with the culture of heaven.[27]

For those involved in church leadership, or who are leading in an explicitly Christian organization, the requirement to enable an authentically kingdom-focused culture seems beyond question. But what about the Christian leader who finds herself in a context that might be seen as 'secular', such as a school or commercial enterprise, an office or a hospital? While recognizing that such a leader might be more constrained by other cultural and organizational factors, given that all of life matters to God and is thus, ultimately, sacred rather than merely secular, these too are spheres in which God longs to see the values and culture of his kingdom proliferate. The leader will very likely not have at her disposal some of the advantages possessed by her counterpart in a Christian organization (such as broad agreement on kingdom aims and concerns, on the appropriateness of prayer and partnership with God, on common experience of being shaped by shared theological convictions). Nevertheless, part of the leader's responsibility towards God and towards others is to do all within her power to see kingdom culture and values expressed in the economy of her organization. These values will include a respect for people and a concern for their growth and development, as opposed to seeing them merely as resources to be deployed for the achievement of organizational goals. The leader will be concerned for interests other than those of shareholders or directors, understanding that ecological, ethical and social dimensions of the organization's life are of concern to God. The leader will always be asking how her work might contribute to the progress of God's rule on earth and how she might enable others to contribute similarly.

The reflections of Western on the leader's role seem particularly apt for those who are Christian leaders:

> Leaders today must be cultural influencers and cultural transmitters ... Individual leaders do not so much lead culture change as the transformational literature claims, but are more likely to be cultural avatars acting on behalf of cultures that animate them as leaders. They become skilled transmitters of the cultures in which they swim.[28]

Our effectiveness in modelling this new culture will be largely affected by the degree to which we allow ourselves to be animated by it and the extent to which we are immersed in it. The most effective leaders of culture change may well not necessarily be those who have best mastered some of the hard skills of people management, but rather those who are most consecrated to God and most invested in the life and ways of his kingdom. Key areas in which we might most obviously model and live out the culture of God's kingdom will include:

- the ways in which we treat other people, especially those who are overlooked or marginalized by others;
- the behaviours we celebrate;
- the qualities we reward (generosity, faithfulness and endeavour rather than simply success or giftedness);
- the goals we pursue.

For those in church leadership, kingdom culture is propagated by the way in which we pray for and with others, stimulating faith and expectancy towards God. It is fostered by the stories we tell of God's activity and by our responsiveness to the present activity of God's Spirit. Whatever our context, it is worth observing that the opportunities for modelling something different are usually more available to a leader who is new in post than to one who has inhabited a role and its associated culture for some length of time. The longer a leader stays in a role the more difficult it is to question existing cultural values and to resist their capacity to conform that leader to their powerful norms.

## 2 Explaining

Although representative actions communicate powerfully in and of them-selves, further explanation is required to shed fuller light on the cultural values that underlie them. Jesus spends a significant amount of time during the course of his earthly ministry teaching about God's kingdom to the crowds, to those whom he is training to share his ministry, and in discourse with his opponents. Sometimes he is to be found teaching in a systematic way, painting pictures of the kingdom and offering a wider framework of interpretation against which his actions might be better understood.[29] On other occasions this teaching follows as a consequence of his symbolic actions and by the need to provide answers to the questions raised by those actions. Many of Jesus' works flouted accepted cultural norms of behaviour and subverted some of the tenaciously held assumptions about what it meant to live faithfully as the people of God. They provoked a range of responses among those who witnessed them, from bewilderment and wonder,[30] through curiosity and a desire to understand their significance more fully,[31] to downright anger and resistance.[32]

We too will need to shed light on the culture we are seeking to commend through teaching and commentary. In the New Testament there is a close relationship between the exercise of church leadership and the ministry of teaching. One of the ways in which the culture of a church is shaped is through the faithful and consistent exposition of the Scriptures. The task of the leader is to teach in such a way that the community grows in its under-standing of the nature of God's kingdom and members are equipped to shape their lives in conformity to the norms and attitudes of that kingdom. This will involve highlighting the specific ways in which the culture of the kingdom conflicts with that of the present age and encouraging people to live confidently as citizens of a kingdom that is not of this world.[33] Preach-ing and other public teaching should regularly cover such topics as the unfolding drama of God's story, kingdom ethics, both personal and social, the ministry of Jesus, and the experience of the first Christian community as they sought to live out their lives as an outpost of heaven on earth. Opportunity should be given for church members to wrestle with thorny issues to do with belief and practice that arise due to their experience of the clash of cultures. Indeed, it is often only as people engage dialogically in this way that previous cultural assumptions can be released and new ones embraced. As Schein observes, 'Learning and change cannot be imposed on people. Their involvement and participation is needed in diagnosing what is going on, figuring out what to do, and in the actual process of learning and change.'[34]

## 3 Exposing dysfunction

Because culture operates at such a deep level, its deficiencies typically remain unexamined. It often takes an outsider to raise questions that expose the dysfunctional aspects of that culture and that lead its proponents to reconsider its suitability. Although at times Jesus confronts the failings of first-century Jewish culture in a direct manner,[35] more frequently, and especially when dealing with those who might be more open to change than were his most bitter opponents, Jesus does this indirectly by inviting reflection upon that culture. He asks the congregation in a synagogue whether or not cultural understandings of the Sabbath were in accord with God's intention that this be a day for restoration and recovery, or whether they actually subverted the very purposes for which the Sabbath had been instituted.[36] The well-known parable of the good Samaritan[37] invites an expert in the Jewish law to consider whether or not the true intent of the law is being reflected in contemporary culture, or whether cultural values prevent God's law being fulfilled in the corporate life of his people. Leaders enable others to recognize dysfunctional elements within existing culture, often by allowing them to feel discomfort with the status quo.

One of the first things I did with the PCC in my first incumbency was to lead them in an away-day that we entitled 'Is my church worth joining?' This was a church that had faced some very significant relational and reputational challenges in recent months, and that had experienced decline in numbers attending worship and in morale. Like most churches they had an aspiration to grow, and especially to draw in more younger people (the best represented age group was those over the age of 65). It would have been relatively easy for me to point out some of the deficiencies in culture that were probably the most significant reasons for lack of growth and for the church's inability to retain newcomers and enquirers. Simply confronting these deficiencies would very likely have led to defensiveness and increased resistance to contemplate change. What we chose to do instead was to invite reflection on some biblical passages that set out something of the purpose and calling of the Church. The PCC members compiled a list of cultural attributes and behaviours associated with the Church that they had uncovered in the biblical texts. They were then asked to score our own church according to how well these features were expressed in its life. This exercise served both to reveal areas of dysfunction or deficiency and to provide a starting point for discerning what steps might be taken in order to overcome them. The changes that eventually flowed from this process were uncomfortable, at least initially, for many, and disorientating because they were in conflict with a culture that had offered meaning and stability to church members for a considerable period of time. They were embraced because to do so seemed less difficult than living with the realization that the prevailing culture was dysfunctional and its previously hidden deficiencies were now open and acknowledged. Alvesson offers a helpful insight into the realities of the process of culture change:

> The leader is involved in the negotiation rather than the imposition of new or revised orientations on people. Cultural change then tends to be gradual, partial and an outcome of social processes in which a group of subordinates have as much if not more to say than the leader.[38]

One further point to note is that the deficiencies in the prevailing culture were largely addressed by taking advantage of some of the positives within that same culture. Unearthing hidden or submerged values, such as neglected aspects of biblical teaching, provided the impetus for culture change. The resulting change was emergent rather than instant, co-discerned rather than imposed, and thus resilient rather than transient (when, nine years later, the church was faced with the prospect of recruiting a new vicar, they were quite insistent that they would not contemplate any candidate who was not in accord with the new culture that had now become established within the church).

## 4 Inviting participation

Because culture is a visceral rather than purely rational phenomenon, described by Western as 'the way things *feel* round here',[39] culture change is achieved at least as much by people experiencing what the new culture feels like as being intellectually persuaded of its worth. Leaders are there-fore concerned to give members of their organization every opportunity to inhabit the new culture and share in it.

Jesus' invitation to his followers to follow him and to be with him was an invitation to see at first hand what life in God's kingdom felt and looked like. As these followers began to participate with him in his works of power, witnessing food being multiplied as they distributed it in accordance with his instructions,[40] and the sick healed as they prayed in his name,[41] and as they experienced a new closeness to God in prayer,[42] so they began to inhabit the new cultural reality of God's kingdom. In the same way, leaders will find opportunities for church or other group members to participate in the emerging culture and thus test its validity.

As we sought to commend a more authentically kingdom culture in my first incumbency church, we deployed a number of strategies to this end. We looked for opportunities to take church members along to other churches or events that might enlarge their own spiritual experience and understanding, whether celebration evenings or day conferences in other local churches or, in due course, weeks spent camping at New Wine summer conferences. As people began to take tentative steps forward in spiritual growth, I looked for appropriate opportunities to encourage them alongside me in ministry or in other ways in which they might be drawn to rely more intentionally on God and his provision. Most significantly, from the first few weeks of our time in the church, we began a weekly meeting in our home (which we called 'Open to God') as an opportunity, outside of the rather formal Sunday worship, for people to encounter God in informal worship and through studying the Bible, and where people could learn to pray for one another and grow in expectancy towards God. The dozen or so who came to the first meeting (some never came back!) grew over the course of three years to a group of over 40 people, most of whom became very influential in reshaping the culture of the wider church family.

## 5 Reinforcing

Because culture is not static or fixed and is vulnerable to being undermined, the wise leader will be concerned not just for its creation but also for its maintenance and strengthening. We have already referenced the role of behaviours and practices as those things that, when rehearsed consistently, reinforce and embed culture. Leaders are thus called to encourage positive behaviours and discourage and criticize behaviours that subvert kingdom culture. Culturally appropriate behaviours can be identified and celebrated in the stories we tell and in the opportunities we provide to others.

Culture is further reinforced by the structures we form to enable the church or other group to perform its work and fulfil its responsibilities.[43] The structures we adopt speak volumes about what we believe to be of most importance, what we hope to achieve and also about who is qualified to share in different activities and be trusted with different levels of responsibility. Although a leader will have prime responsibility for the shaping of organizational structures, once again organizational architecture is something best undertaken as a collaborative exercise, engaging others who are beginning to inhabit the emerging culture. Those who share in the creation of effective structures will also tend to share the responsibility of protecting and sustaining those structures.

Leaders, concludes Western, cannot change cultures by themselves, nor can they manipulate culture at will.[44] They can, however, work with others to create open spaces that will allow new and healthier cultures to emerge. This may well be one of the most important aspects of the leader's role.

## Leadership on the ground

When the Warrington Clinical Commissioning Group (WCCG) won the 2012 Health Service Journal national award for 'Best Commissioning Organisation', more than a few eyebrows may have been raised in surprise. The gaining of this award reflected an astonishing turnaround in the fortunes of health-care commissioning in the town.

The WCCG came into being in April 2011, as a consequence of a major NHS reorganization, inheriting responsibilities for commissioning health-care services from a predecessor Primary Care Trust that had been faced with very significant difficulties. As a 'new town', Warrington's population was ageing faster than the national average, with associated increased demands upon the health service. The local economic situation meant that the town enjoyed none of the additional funding enjoyed by areas of deprivation, and, in consequence, the PCT had major financial challenges. These were compounded by the organizational challenge of an unusually high turnover of chief executives and finance directors.

The expectation upon the new CCG was to modernize the services it commissioned, gain increasing efficiencies and provide new cutting edge technologies, while incorporating a £25 million savings requirement into its £239 million budget, in addition to the delivery of all primary general practice, dentistry and pharmacy.

In order to deliver its objectives the CCG had to work with multiple partners: the independent small businesses, general practices that were its constituent members, the local district hospital, the local council, MPs, local ward councillors, Community Trust (which had been an integral part of the predecessor PCT that had been 'let go'), Mental Health Trusts and third-sector organizations. In addition it had to work in partnership with neighbouring CCGs (all of whom were better funded), to commission specialist services across a wider footprint. Finally, its most important relationship needed to be with the people of Warrington, who could be viewed both as patients and public in differing contexts. The scale of the task facing Sarah Baker, the newly appointed CEO, was not insignificant.

Having trained initially as a GP, Sarah's previous leadership experience was as a director of various health-care organizations, of a large social enterprise, and in private-sector management consultancy. An ordained Anglican minister, she had for a number of years also been involved in the establishment and leadership of a Fresh Expression church plant in the community where she lived. Her experiences, both good and bad, in these various different contexts led her to appreciate the crucial influence of culture in any organization. She saw her primary task to be ensuring, from the very beginning, that the culture was right and conducive to organizational health. With that in mind, she set out to design an organization where hierarchy was less important than outcome, where everyone was valued for their contribution, and where everyone was focused on the key delivery of improved health outcomes for the people of Warrington.

In the run-up to the establishment, Sarah visited each and every one of the general practices that made up the new organization to understand their gripes and concerns with the predecessor organization and understand their ideas for how things might be better. She reflected back what she had heard in an iterative process, so that by the end of the series of visits she had a good feel for how things could be different. She also invested time having 'coffee' with the CEOs of the other organizations in the health and social-care system, trying to develop relationships that had more depth and substance than just a business focus, so that she knew the people she would be working with, not just their job titles.

The next step was to bring together those who would have responsibility for leading the strategic direction of the organization and for overseeing its implementation. This included the CCG board (a mixture of GPs and lay people) with a currently practising GP as chair, an executive team and a wider senior team. Considerable time was invested in discussing vision and values.

Sarah explains:

> The vision we articulated was 'Excellence for Warrington'. On the face of it this might seem vague and non-specific but it affected the gut, the heart, and immediately chimed with those who think big picture. We went on to flesh out what this might mean in practice, sharing the thinking with other stakeholders across the town, in whole-system events. Everyone could understand that wherever their position in the system, whatever their role, whatever their speciality, they could all aim for excellence. This work allowed those who prefer detail and specifics also to begin to own the vision. Our mantra became 'Good enough is the enemy of excellence'.

We also considered our key values: excellence, valuing patients and partners, accountability, partnerships in everything, honesty and integrity, open and transparent. We further unpacked these values and described in detail how this would impact upon our behaviours, both positively and negatively. We intentionally explored how we could practically espouse these values, recognizing that they should be lived out in everything we did. This led to work with partners across the health and social care system to develop a memorandum of understanding that described the principles and values that would guide our interactions, explicitly described expected behaviours and how we would hold each other mutually accountable. We similarly worked to hold each other mutually accountable for attitudes and behaviours within the board and senior team.

We invested significant time and effort into branding to try to visually reflect our vision and values. We ensured all communications were consistent, with branding, colour, font and style so that wherever in the organization it came from the receiver would be able to know immediately it was from the CCG and hopefully associate it with the vision and values. We also looked to describe our service proposals and changes in pictures and diagrams in addition to words to ensure effective communication across all learning styles and personality types.

Recognizing the value and impact of story, we developed 'scripts' so that anyone in the organization could tell the story of who we were and what we were trying to achieve, and specific stories for each service change focused on the needs and impact on individual patients.

We paid great attention to the language we used, trying always to respect 'the other' and see their perspective in order that we might concentrate on areas of agreement and intentionally 'park' difficult areas for later focused shared attention and problem-solving.

We also carefully considered the working environment. We moved to open plan, with quiet work pods for concentrated work time, sofas, stand-up work counters and a glazed refreshment area that allowed for communal coffee, lunches and working meetings. There were two 'private offices' for use by the CEO and Chair, for visitors and confidential meetings, otherwise everyone, board and executive, worked in the team environment. We used colour to provide a vibrant and relaxed environment and incorporated our vision and values in the decor. We also had 'creative' spaces for innovation. Key value-related statements were displayed throughout the building. We posted up the infographics for our major service changes and quotes from patient experiences so that at all times our key purpose was visible to everyone. Finally, we posted performance metrics of our progress against key targets so that everyone in the organisation could see how we were doing.

Underpinning all of this was a significant investment in personal and organizational development to ensure that all members of staff could catch the vision, espouse the values and live them out.

Sarah adds:

This job for me was the culmination of years of leadership experience and personal learning. I had got many things wrong in the past but in this I actually think we did a great job, and the feedback we got from other partners, the wider NHS and staff members would reflect this. My only regret is that I had to retire through ill health just as we got to the next stage of bedding in and establishing our practice.

Sarah Baker is an insightful leader who understands that effective work is always the product of fruitful collaboration, and yet who also recognizes the vital catalytic role of the individual leader without whose contribution those of others will not be realized. She understood the importance of developing a vision and a shared narrative, to which everyone at every level within the organization could relate, and which enabled every single person to appreciate that their own contribution made a difference to the organization's results, specifically, improving the quality of care for the people of Warrington. Furthermore, Sarah understood the importance of whole-system thinking, which meant encouraging change not merely in her own organization but also within the partners with whom they did business. Perhaps one of the reasons for the remarkable success of the WCCG lies in Sarah's capacity to deploy herself well as a leader of others. She recognized that her role as leader was to identify others with skills and capacities and then to empower them to perform well. She understood the need for the leader to be the one who asks critical questions and encourages reflection. She also understood that such reflection had to begin with the leader herself:

I learned that the most important person to change was me! Being open to feedback and constantly reflecting on my own behaviour and that of the team, acknowledging the gap that would always exist between our own espoused behaviours and our actual practice.

Perhaps the comment that offers the most telling insight into Sarah's leadership was a final comment she offered: 'Leadership is about being prepared to let go, and being willing for others to get the credit for work you have done.'

## Questions to aid reflection

1  What has been your experience of cultures that have exercised either a positive or restrictive influence within an organization?

2  What stands out for you from the strategies and practices that Sarah deployed in order to enable change to come about? Can you think of particular ways in which you might helpfully adopt some of her practices for the benefit of your own organization?

3  What, in your experience, are some of the particular factors that equip a leader to be an effective catalyst for change?

## Notes

1 Alvesson, M., 2013, *Understanding Organizational Culture*, 2nd edn, London: Sage, p. 16.

2 Fuller analysis and reflection on this initiative and its aftermath are offered by Hollmann, J., Carpes, A. de M. and Beuron, T. A., 2010, *The DaimlerChrysler Merger – A Cultural Mismatch?* www.spell.org.br/documentos/download/5150 (accessed 25 November 2019).

3 Hollman et al., *The DaimlerChrysler Merger*, p. 437.

4 Smircich, L., 1983, 'Concepts of Culture and Organisational Analysis', *Administrative Science Quarterly*, 28, pp. 339–58.

5 Smircich, 'Concepts of Culture and Organisational Analysis'.

6 Alvesson, *Understanding Organisational Culture*.

7 Alvesson, *Understanding Organisational Culture*, p. 4.

8 Schein, E., 2010, *Organizational Culture and Leadership*, 4th edn, New York: Wiley, p. 16.

9 Schein, *Organizational Culture*, p. 18.

10 Alvesson, *Understanding Organizational Culture*, p. 39.

11 Schein, *Organizational Culture*, p. 7.

12 This is an image favoured by Chand, S., 2010, *Cracking Your Church's Culture Code*, San Francisco, CA: Jossey-Bass.

13 Schein, *Organizational Culture*, pp. 23–33.

14 Western, S., 2013, *Leadership: A Critical Text*, 2nd edn, London: Sage, p. 109.

15 Hurst, D. K., 2012, *The New Ecology of Leadership*, Chichester: Columbia University Press, p. 164.

16 Alvesson, *Understanding Organizational Culture*.

17 Schein, *Organizational Culture*, p. 123.

18 Schein, *Organizational Culture*, p. 3.

19 Schein, *Organizational Culture*, p. 3.

20 Western, *Leadership*, p. 108.

21 For example, Timmis, S., 2012, *Gospel-centred Leadership*, Epsom: The Good Book Company; Lewis, R. and Cordeiro, W., 2005, *Culture Shift*, San Francisco, CA: Jossey-Bass.

22 Chand, *Cracking Your Church's Culture Code*, pp. 113–28.

23 Mark 1.15.

24 Mark 1.21–45.

25 John 3.2.

26 John 5.19.

27 John 6.38.

28 Western, *Leadership*, p. 116.

29 The sermon on the mount (Matt. 5—7) is an explicit description of the culture of God's kingdom, while more cryptic teaching on the same theme is contained in a number of Jesus' parables of the kingdom (e.g. Matt. 13.24–52).

30 Mark 1.27.

31 John 3.1ff.

32 Mark 3.1–6; Mark 12.13ff.

33 John 18.36.

34 Schein, *Organizational Culture*, p. 383.

35 For example, Luke 11.37–52.

36 Mark 3.4.

37 Luke 10.30–37.

38 Alvesson, *Understanding Organizational Culture*, p. 113.

39 Western, *Leadership*, p. 109.

40 John 6.1ff.

41 Luke 9.6.

42 Luke 11.1.

43 The place of appropriate, functional structures is addressed more fully in Chapter 8 below.

44 Western, *Leadership*, p. 118.

# 7

# Animating the Body: Growing and Developing Others[1]

*How often do organisations forget that there is no such thing as instant leadership? Growing leaders is like growing fruit trees. Others may one day have the benefit of your trees but maybe you will also benefit from other unknown owners of other orchards. The best organisations take pride in the fact that they grow more leaders than they need; they are net exporters of leaders.*[2]

In 1968 the Christian international development charity Tearfund was formed, largely in response to the growing humanitarian and refugee crisis in the wake of a spate of wars and natural disasters. Its work of providing aid to those caught up in the most extreme crisis situations still continues to this day. However, within a very short time after its foundation, Tearfund began to focus not simply on providing short-term relief but on longer-term development programmes, recognizing that extreme poverty might best be tackled by addressing some of the causes of that poverty. Campaigning on the global stage around issues such as fair trade, overseas debt, modern slavery and climate change became a priority, as did the provision of agricultural materials and expertise in order to enable some of the most disadvantaged in the world to engage in farming and other projects through which their lives might be developed. Although these strategies were clearly making a significant difference in lifting people out of poverty, their effect-iveness relied upon the continual supply of resources from the developed world to the developing, something that inevitably limited their potential to effect change on the scale required. In addition, those working on the ground were concerned at the ways in which even such positive strategies still tended to have the effect of creating a level of dependence upon external providers and a passivity on the part of recipients of such assistance. It was around the turn of the millennium that Tearfund came across a whole new approach to community development that promised to deliver sustainable and long-term change on an unimaginable scale, an approach that has now become the backbone of their work in around 50 countries throughout the world.

Church and Community Mobilisation Programme (CCMP) is an asset-based approach to development, focusing primarily not on what is lacking in local communities but, more significantly, on what resources (however limited) are to hand and able to be deployed for the purposes of development. The programme is focused very much on enabling local church members, through engagement with a series of carefully constructed Bible studies drawing attention to God's purpose for his creation and his desire to work in partnership with his people, to experience a change in mindset whereby they begin to see themselves as dynamic participants in God's work of stewardship rather than merely passive dependants upon the largesse of others. This new mindset enables them to take stock of what resources and capabilities they 'have in their hands' and to work collaboratively with each other and with the wider community in discerning ways of deploying these resources in order to meet specific needs that they themselves have identified as being most urgent. The impact of these initiatives is nothing short of miraculous and becomes very apparent when comparisons are made between communities that have begun to engage in CCMP and other neighbouring communities thus far untouched by it. Neglected land has been turned over to cultivation, wells have been dug at the initiative of the community, malarial swamps have been turned into fish farms, schools and clinics have been established and funded out of the profits from community enterprises, and dignity and hope have been restored to some of the poorest and most abandoned people on earth.

CCMP still requires a modest level of external funding to resource it. However, this funding is invested purely in the training of local facilitators who then themselves become catalysts for churches and communities to adopt CCMP. Not only is development much more extensive, but its longer-term future is far more secure, being identified as the fruit of 'our own' labours as opposed to being somehow the product of the provision of others. And having learned the effectiveness of this strategy at first hand, those who have benefited most become the greatest evangelists for it, enabling other communities to embrace it.

The tension between seeing our role as concerned with the provision of services for others and seeing it as equipping and enabling others to be fruitful themselves is one that is faced by those in positions of responsibility in many different contexts. It is a tension felt keenly by most church leaders. Rather like those working in international development, the level of need we encounter on so many different fronts is way beyond our capacity to meet. The resources we have at our own disposal, whether in terms of time, energy or headspace, are woefully inadequate even to make the slightest impression upon the situations and crises that clamour for our attention.

The missional challenge in the communities we serve as local church leaders is immense. The task of communicating faith to an increasingly unchurched and post-Christian culture requires far more imagination and engagement than we were prepared for. Even though we may see some fruit from our labours we feel that at best we are scratching the surface: there is always far more to do and more people to reach. We are profoundly aware that there are whole areas of our communities and different groups of people, organizations and other spheres with which we have very little, if any, involvement. Even if we had twice the amount of time and three times the levels of energy we fear that we would still make little impression.

It may be that the communities we are called to serve contain dispro-portionate levels of social need. I well remember my own experience of overseeing the establishing of a new church plant in a relatively unchurched and seriously deprived community. A high proportion of those whom we encountered through the various ministries and projects we initiated were young adults who had left the care system as teenagers, had significant mental health issues, were single parents, and had never enjoyed any real nurture or stability in life. There was no end to the support required, nor to the crises with which we were asked to deal. Disciple-making was at least as much about enabling growth in personal and social skills as it was about encouraging growth in faith and obedience to Christ. Exhausting though it was for all involved, even harder to bear was the knowledge that we had only touched the tip of the iceberg on that estate. Goodness only knew how the work might be grown.

For those of us who are ordained or otherwise authorized ministers, the matter is exacerbated by the fact that there is a certain level of expectation, either of our own making or put upon us by others, that it is our job to perform the tasks of ministry, all of them, and that not to at least attempt to do so is somehow a dereliction of our responsibilities and calling. We may not have great hopes of making much of a difference, but we feel under pressure to invest our limited resources towards tackling the mounting number of tasks that clamour for our attention. The training we received was still largely styled in such a way as to equip us to be pastor to a single congregation, perhaps with an additional daughter church, a challenging task anyway, but surely within our capabilities. However, the fact that at the time of writing 71 per cent of all Anglican churches (and 93 per cent in rural areas) are now grouped in multi-parish benefices means that we are more than likely to find ourselves as vicar of anywhere between four to eight churches, and even more in some places. An impossible task just became even more difficult!

The Church's response to this has often been to bewail its lack of resources (usually defined in terms of numbers of available clergy), cross its fingers in hope that the resource situation might one day improve, and in the mean-time simply spread itself even more thinly and try to maintain business as usual. Hardly surprising then that levels of impact diminish while levels of need continue to increase, and that the culture of dependence upon religious professionals to provide for spiritual need is never addressed. Not only is ministry within the Church impoverished, and church members disempow-ered, but one of the most pressing responsibilities of the local church is almost completely overlooked, that of equipping all God's people for the work of mission and ministry in their own particular life place, whether work, community or third space.

Perhaps the contemporary challenge in terms of resources might serve to propel the Church back towards a more historic understanding of the role of the ordained minister as being that of oversight exercised in such a way that the whole body of Christ is mobilized for mission and ministry. As Robin Greenwood reflects:

> whether paid a stipend or not, parish priests (within teams of many kinds) should not regard as their primary role the provision of ministry to others. Rather, precisely through the celebration of the sacraments, preaching and pastoral care they are to stimulate, interweave and support God's calling of all.[3]

We find ourselves in a very similar place to that occupied by those with a concern for international development and asking similar questions. Might there be a better and more productive way of investing our limited resources in such a way that God's aims for us might be fulfilled, in our case, that mission be enabled and ministry be undertaken?[4]

Our strong conviction is that at the heart of our calling, and at the centre of God's purpose in appointing some to leadership in his Church, is a focus on what we have described previously as animating the whole body of Christ. Central to this calling is the work of equipping all God's people for ministry and service, thus enabling the whole Christian community to fulfil their God-given potential and to assume their divinely appointed vocation. And, counter-intuitive though it might be, given the pressure upon us to perform tasks of ministry, we are convinced that responsible leaders need to turn away from some of these tasks in order to make time for this greatest priority. Not only does growing others take some of the heat off us, but it might just turn out that some of those in whom we invest prove to be better at performing aspects of the task than we are. It will certainly be the case that many of them will have access to spheres of influence, whether in workplaces, social groups or other contexts, that will remain closed to us.

There are a number of compelling and related reasons why we believe this to be such an imperative, some practical and some theological.

## Theological considerations

### 1 The universal experience of receiving the Spirit

A number of the later Old Testament prophets[5] signal the coming of a future age in which all believers will share an experience of receiving God's Spirit in a way that, previously, has been the province of a select few. This will be a distinctly different dispensation from that which has thus far prevailed and in which ministry has been confined exclusively to certain categories of people (for example, judges, prophets, kings and priests), singled out and anointed by God for special tasks. In this coming age all God's people, irrespective of age, gender or background, will enjoy the privileges of knowing the Lord,[6] hearing from him and speaking on his behalf.[7] The anointed individual upon whom others must rely is replaced by an anointed community in which each has a role to play. Although, as we will see below, in this New Covenant era the Spirit's work includes the calling and equipping of some to exercise particular leadership roles, such leadership is far more to do with the business of enabling all God's people to fulfil their own vocation and ministry than it is to do the work of ministry for the benefit of or in the place of others.

It is remarkable how easily the Christian Church, throughout its history, has neglected such a vital truth, and one central to its own identity, and allowed itself to drift back into models of leadership and ministry that are far more characteristic of the Old Covenant era than the New. Indeed, it is striking how often, in seeking biblical foundations for leadership and ministry, we resort to Old Testament patterns and models. Little wonder that we find ourselves with depleted resources when we restrict the scope of those whom we deem qualified for ministry, restrictions that God himself lifted many generations ago. If we are to keep in step with the Spirit then we will be keen to recognize and affirm his calling and empowering of all who belong to Christ.

## 2 The Church as the body of Christ

What is promised and outlined in these prophetic texts becomes the experience of the post-Pentecost Church and is articulated more fully by the apostle Paul.[8] Not only does the Spirit indwell every believer but by so doing forms the whole company of believers into a mutually dependent *body* with Christ as the head. Under his direction, each and every member has a vital and indispensable role to play, without which the body itself is impoverished and its ministry to the world compromised. The apostle Paul could not have imagined a local church in which any member did not have a clear sense of their own vocation to share in God's mission and ministry in both congregational life and in the wider world, and in which proper attention was not paid to envisioning and equipping them to fulfil this vocation. One of the most striking things about the growth of the Christian faith in the earliest centuries of its existence, and at other times of significant expansion and growth,[9] was that this came about largely through the witness and influence of ordinary church members.[10]

### 3 Recognizing the purpose for which leadership is given

The expectation that all God's people will be involved in the work of ministry is made explicit in a further passage.[11] What is equally significant for us here, given that perhaps the greatest impediment to the releasing of all God's people in this way is the tendency to see ministry as the preserve of clergy and other leaders, is the clear exposition of the true purposes for which leadership roles are given to the church.[12] Apostles and others exist to 'equip the saints for the work of ministry'. Thus those occupying leadership roles in the Church might best see themselves as curators, enabling the body to do its appointed work through the resourcing of every limb and joint.[13] As Howard Snyder observes:

> The chief priority of pastoral leadership is discipling people for the Kingdom ... [E]ssentially, the pastor's first priority is so to invest himself or herself in a few other persons that they also become disciples and ministers of Jesus Christ. It is so to give oneself to others and to the work of discipling that the New Testament norm of plural leadership becomes a reality in the local congregation. In other words, it is to bring the ministry of all God's people to functioning practical reality.[14]

This understanding resonates profoundly with our own earlier, suggested definition of leadership that draws attention to the role of leader in enabling the whole body to be inspired and mobilized towards the accomplishment of shared goals, and away from any idea of the leader doing the work of the body on behalf of that body.[15]

### 4 The practice of the New Testament Church

Further light is shed on the commitment of biblical leaders to develop others by references made by the apostle Paul to his own practice and his commendation of such practice to his own protégés. Not only is his stated goal 'to present every person complete in Christ',[16] and not only does he encourage the development of wider ministry in the local church,[17] but it is clear that he saw his own ministry journeys as opportunities for the development of others whom he invited to accompany him. Several of those who perhaps were first given a taste of leadership while accompanying Paul[18] ended up sharing in the leadership of some of the churches we subsequently hear of in the later New Testament documents. In this, Paul is, of course, simply following the example set by his own master, Jesus.

## Practical considerations

### 1 Growing capacity

We are not the only ones ever to have been outfaced by the demands of ministry and the needs of others. Jesus himself was more than familiar with such an experience.[19] For him, the obvious solution is to increase the workforce. This he does both by exhorting his associates to ask God to raise up other workers and then by sharing his own responsibilities with a group of others, seeking to extend his own ministry by reproducing it in the lives of this wider group. Taking a leaf out of Jesus' book makes good sense not simply as a means of taking the pressure off ourselves and generating resources to sustain existing ministry. As we grow the workforce and release the missional imagination of others, so we broaden the scope of the ministries in which we are able to engage. Our own horizons as church leaders are restricted. Others may well see the potential for harvest in contexts of which we are quite unaware. Many of the mission and ministry initiatives that were birthed during the second half of my time as vicar of my last parish came about as a result of growing the range of those to whom leadership was entrusted, and encouraging these people to share in the process of discerning what new areas of mission and ministry God might be seeking to bring into being. Left to my own devices it would very likely never have occurred to me to give time and attention to the establishment of any of these remarkably fruitful avenues of ministry.

As well as growing capacity on a local level, leadership development is vital if we are to fulfil our responsibility to raise up leadership and ministry for the benefit of the wider Church. The more leaders we raise up, the more we will have to give away, and the better placed the wider Church will be not simply to maintain existing ministry but equally to plant new churches and develop new missional initiatives. Leaders do not grow on trees. They are nurtured and grown from within the life and ministry of thriving churches. Local churches need to be seen as seedbeds in which emerging leaders are raised and grown. As Walter Wright observes:

> Leadership should be empowering. It is the process of giving power away, not collecting it. It is moving the power to influence into the hands of the people we are leading so that they can pursue the mission. Like God's leadership, it is a relationship that cares enough to walk patiently with people towards a shared purpose.[20]

## 2 Compensating for our limitations

Even the most competent leaders have areas of weakness and even the most insightful are restricted by significant blind spots and blinkers. As Deborah Ancona notes:

> Rarely will a single person be skilled in all areas. That's why it's critical that leaders find others who can offset their limitations and complement their strengths. Those who don't will not only bear the burden of leadership alone but will find themselves at the helm of an unbalanced ship.[21]

It is not unusual for leaders who are either particularly visionary or most adept at being catalysts for the formation of vision to be far less competent when it comes to enabling vision to be translated into action. It is rare for 'big picture' leaders to excel at small detail and to have the inclination, let alone the skills, to devise processes whereby ideas can come to fruition. Excitement in followers at the communication of fresh vision can easily turn to cynicism and disillusionment if such vision never moves beyond the aspirational stage and is never translated into reality. The key to overcoming such potential limitations is not to try and learn new skills ourselves but rather to draw alongside us others with complementary gifts and skills.

## 3 Ensuring continuity

It is striking how many churches live a kind of hand-to-mouth existence when it comes to resourcing areas of ministry responsibility. The only time we pay attention to recruiting and resourcing new leaders is when faced with the crisis that follows the retirement of an existing leader. What follows is often a series of increasingly urgent pleas for someone, anyone, to step up and take on this vital role. Even if someone can be recruited fairly quickly, such a change in overall leadership can be very disruptive for others involved in this ministry area and for the ministry itself. This is in sharp contrast to the practice of those leaders whose stories feature as case studies in this book. One of the notable aspects of their leadership is the way in which almost all of them were concerned about succession planning, and for the health of their churches or organizations beyond the span of their own incumbency. While there are times when any ministry needs to be overhauled and refreshed in terms of approach, by and large most ministries thrive under stable leadership and when a major hiatus in oversight can be avoided. Continuity in purpose and practice is infinitely preferable to discontinuity. The best way to facilitate such continuity, whether in the overall leadership of a church or in the leadership of a specific area of ministry, is to encourage the development of shared leadership at every level of a church. All those who are leading any ministry area should be encouraged to identify and to begin to develop a co-leader who would be able to take on responsibility should the main leader have to step back for whatever reason, and who may well, in due course, succeed that leader as overall leader.[22] It was precisely to counter the possibility of facing such a hiatus that, early on in my time in my last parish, we resolved to create a leadership development culture in the church through raising as widely as possible the expectation that all Christians might exercise leadership influence at some level, and offering training and formation in leadership for significant numbers of people each year. Our express aim was to grow more leaders than we might ever need; this proved to be a remarkably effective strategy. As Baroness Lydia Dunn reflects, 'A good leader is one who leaves behind them women and men who possess the conviction and the will to carry on without them.'[23]

### 4 Only leaders can raise up other leaders

Leadership development is a priority for leaders, partly because we are the only ones who are able to give permission to others to share leadership responsibility, but also because of the nature of the process by which leaders are formed. Essentially, such formation is relational in its nature, a form of apprenticeship in which a person learns from observing and being coached by someone who is a little further ahead on the way being travelled. It is only those who have learned a skill who are able to pass such a skill on to others in hope that those others might even outstrip their teachers in capacity to exercise such skills. Those who understand the work and character of leadership are best placed to nurture others for similar work.

## Stumbling blocks

Given the persuasive rationale, both theological and practical, for seeing leadership as inevitably focused on the equipping of others, why, we might ask, is this task of growing others so frequently neglected? What are the specific things that work to divert our attention away from giving time and energy to wider leadership development? A few common reasons spring to mind.

### 1 The tyranny of the urgent

Not only is leadership development time-consuming, its benefits are rarely immediately evident in the short term. Given the volume of short-term and urgent demands upon our time, our tendency all too often is to put the idea of leadership development on the back burner until we have a little more time to spare. Henri Nouwen reflects on the controlling attitudes of what he describes as the 'compulsive minister':

We simply go along with the many musts and oughts that have been handed on to us, and we live with them as if they were authentic translations of the Gospel of our Lord ... Thus we are busy people just like all other busy people, rewarded with the rewards which are awarded to busy people![24]

The trouble is that that illusory day when urgent demands upon us are all fulfilled never comes around. As we have seen, the most effective way of hastening its coming is to raise up a few others who might be equipped to take on some urgent tasks themselves in due course. What is required is a mindset shift, whereby we cease to see leadership development as an optional extra but rather as our core business.

## 2 Submitting to inappropriate expectations

Most leaders find themselves to some extent driven not simply by a dispassionate reflection upon what might be most strategic or authentic to the exercise of leadership but by particular expectations to do with their role, whether those they impose upon themselves or those imposed upon them explicitly or implicitly by others. We feel the need to justify our appointment, or our stipend, or to prove our worth in some way, and our desire to demonstrate our willingness to work hard tips over into a driven-ness to fill every minute and to take on as many tasks as possible. We fear that the delegation of tasks to others might be interpreted as laziness on our behalf and we feel a level of guilt at asking others to do things that have been traditionally understood to be the province of the clergy or of other appointed leaders. Perhaps the best antidote to this is to spend time reflecting on what expectations God might have for us as those whom he has called and appointed to leadership.

We might note in passing the ways in which such expectations upon clergy can be fuelled by particular theologies of priesthood and ministry.[25] Pickard explores the relationship between the priesthood of the ordained and that of the whole people of God. Those theologies that mark out the former as effectively belonging to a different caste tend to result, he suggests, in the diminution of the ministry of the wider Church and the narrowing of the ranks of those from whom leadership is expected. Building on the work of Greenwood, he posits the notion of the two priesthoods as being inter-animative, affirming our own assertion that, whatever status we ascribe to the ministry of the ordained, a key function of such ordained ministry will be to foster and grow the ministry and leadership of all God's people.

It is so vital that the priest takes delight in drawing out the understanding, the skills, the commitment and the hope of every church member.

The ministry of blessing is about praising, encouraging, and expecting the growth in ministry of the whole of the body of the church.[26]

## 3 The need to be needed

Not unrelated to this is a reluctance to suffer a diminishing of our own position and status. Howard Snyder insists that 'Clergy, like all professionals, very quickly take on the mentality of a closed club and have sensitive antennae for picking up any threats to their clerical status and privileges.'[27]

To be truthful, one of the most potent disincentives to encouraging the emergence and growth of others is the fear that such protégés might outstrip us, or that we will look less good in comparison to them. Perhaps we need to reflect more on the example of Jesus who seemed to take great delight at the prospect of those whom he had raised up not only replicating his own ministry but doing greater things than he had done![28] Ralph Waldo Emerson once sagely observed that, 'There is no limit to what a person can achieve if they do not mind who gets the credit.'

## 4 The complexity of people

Working with other people is a lot more complex and challenging than working with inanimate structures and systems, which is why we often find it a whole lot easier to tinker with things that do not answer back to us and are more willing to accede to our preferences and desires. Because the task of shaping and developing others is at times laborious, can be frustrating and disheartening and is a task whose outcome can never be wholly guaranteed, it is tempting to invest our energies on tasks that have more measurable outcomes. One of the things I find myself reflecting on, after more than 30 years spent in church leadership, is that no matter how hard we work to devise effective strategies, launch new initiatives and perfect systems, we can never guarantee the longevity or fruitfulness of such efforts. We may have led churches or ministries faithfully and seen fruit from our labours, but we have no control over how those churches will fare beyond our own incumbency. However, the investment we make in other people and the effort we expend in growing others in ministry and leadership has every chance of being far more impactful over the longer term. This is an investment that might well keep on producing a return. No wonder the apostle Paul sees the real fruit of his own ministry as being those whom he has seen raised up and whom he describes as 'our letter, written in our hearts, known and read by all people'.[29]

## 5 *Shortage of potential leaders*

We may well subscribe in theory to all that has been suggested thus far. However, our enthusiasm for raising up others evaporates and turns to despair when we begin to consider the actual people we have available to us. It might be that we have very few people at all in the various congregations for which we have oversight. Those whom we do have may be predominantly elderly and lacking in energy; they may be time poor because of the demands of work or other existing commitments; or they may not obviously display many of the qualities we would see as being the bare minimum for those who should be entrusted with leadership. Or it may be that the context in which we find ourselves leading is one in which social conditions and other factors tend to rob most people of any sense that they could take on any level of responsibility. The chaotic nature of peoples' lives, their lack of basic life skills and their own sense of disempowerment all work to convince both them and us that any participation in leadership would be way beyond their capability.

In most situations, the biggest problem facing those with a concern for developing others is not about having an embarrassment of riches. Most of us will find ourselves having to work with unlikely or, in some ways, unpromising people. Jesus himself, in selecting his closest band of apprentices, seems to have ended up with a number who were profoundly flawed and who might well have been regarded by others as poor choices not worth considering. Many of those who have become primary catalysts and community transformation facilitators within the CCMP programmes have not been those who would necessarily have been regarded previously as possessing great leadership potential. We may well have to shed the habits of looking at others through the world's eyes rather than God's and tending to see leadership potential as being evidenced by the possession of those qualities that the world identifies as being prerequisites for the exercise of leadership. While we may rightly be wary of those who do not understand the importance of such qualities as love for others, a servant heart and a willingness to learn, we should not overlook people simply because they do not yet display the skills we might expect of accomplished leaders. Because we understand competence in Christian leadership to be significantly the result of the work of God's Spirit we should not be disheartened at the apparent thinness of the resources we have available to us. We need to hold fast to a conviction that God is himself committed to growing and developing all those who belong to him, that his gifts are bestowed without exception on all who have received his Spirit, and that although the task of developing leaders may be much lengthier and more complex in some contexts than in others, this should not deter us from committing to it.

# Three priorities for leaders

Equipping and releasing others in ministry and leadership has to be an intentional business: it does not happen automatically nor without the direct action of leaders. Leaders who want to take seriously the business of equipping others will need to attend to three important disciplines if they are to see this come about.

## 1 Establish a development culture

Perhaps the first step to take in terms of seeing others equipped and released in ministry is that of working to establish an environment in which people are not only encouraged to develop and grow but one in which this is seen as normal and, indeed, expected. This may well involve us in working to change and supplant rival and conflicting expectations, which, left unchecked and unchallenged, will serve to prevent the accomplishment of the very aims to which we aspire. This process of culture change brings us into the territory we explored in our previous chapter and will involve us in the various processes of modelling, teaching and reinforcing a culture that is favourable to the growth and development of all God's people.

There are a number of practical ways in which we can model what it is to live according to such a culture. These might include leading ourselves, not so much on the basis of any formal position or office we might hold but rather on the basis of our experience of having received God's Spirit. It will certainly include being honest about our own weaknesses and short-comings and demonstrating an openness to receive the ministry of others, and encouraging others to do the same.

Second, modelling must be accompanied by an explanation of this rather different culture that we are seeking to establish. In one church I served, the five statements that summarized our core values as a church (and that were hopefully an accurate expression of key kingdom values) were represented on five small banners mounted on the wall that faced (and thus were hope-fully read by) every worshipper as they left the church building each week.[30] From time to time I would invite the whole congregation to join with me in rehearsing them out loud together. This repetition and reinforcement is vital if such values are to become ingrained in to the very fabric of the church and its people.

Having begun both to model and illustrate this culture, our third step will be to enable people to experience it and participate in it. This is best done by creating opportunities for people to serve in safely defined ways. Having created an expectation that all God's people are somehow involved in ser-vice, in my last parish we went on to devise a leadership training course for existing and emerging leaders to which we invited, over the course of a number of years, the vast majority of the church membership.[31] This further reinforced the notion that involvement in ministry and leadership was normal for all followers of Christ.

## 2 Cultivate a vision for 'whole-life discipleship'

When, in the past, the Church has concerned itself with growing the ministry of the laity, it has all too often appeared to see this as little more than a strategy for plugging the gaps left, for example, by falling clergy numbers. The ministry of the Church is seen as that which is performed by clergy and other accredited ministers, the ranks of whom might be swelled by enlisting others. Our conviction is that the mission and ministry of the Church is far wider in scope than that envisaged by so narrow an imaginary, and that the mobilization of God's people for ministry and leadership requires the casting of a more fulsome vision. A recent report by the Archbishop's Council of the Church of England[32] asks the searching question of the wider Church:

> Will we determine to empower, liberate and disciple the 98% of the Church of England who are not ordained and therefore set them free for fruitful, faithful mission and ministry, influence, leadership and, most importantly, vibrant relationship with Jesus in all of life? And will we do so not only in church-based ministry on a Sunday but in work and school, in gym and shop, in field and factory, Monday to Saturday?

Whole-life discipleship[33] implies that the sphere in which discipleship is worked out is not primarily the ecclesial nor that of our own personal spirituality, but rather the public spaces in which we spend the majority of our time. The task of the local church is to envision and resource its members for missional ministry in the places in which they interface with the world. It is to give a vision for whole-life discipleship.

There are a number of practical ways in which this might be fostered. Those of us who teach and preach need to pay particular attention to the manner in which our teaching is applied in practical ways. It will be important for us to try hard to imagine ourselves inside the shoes of those whose discipleship is worked out in the workplace, in the local sports club, at the school gate or in voluntary organizations. Our aim must be to make connections between these contexts and the biblical texts as we seek to enable people to live life faithfully and engage missionally in the light of Scripture.

In my last church, taking a lead from LICC,[34] we developed practices designed both to celebrate the ministry of those involved in 'ordinary' life places and to give such people a sense of being commissioned by the wider Church for their ministry. It was not unusual when we gathered together for worship on Sunday mornings for us to interview a member of the congregation, inquiring as to what they would be doing 'this time tomorrow' (TTT), that is, in the middle of Monday morning. This gave them opportunity to describe their own unique missional context, its opportunities and challenges, and also gave opportunity for the local congregation to pray specifically for them and for anyone else involved in similar contexts. Another exercise like this was often undertaken by midweek small groups. Such practices have many benefits. Church members have a sense of being commissioned for mission and ministry, are set free from the pressure of seeing ministry as being narrowly confined to those activities that are focused on the local church and its appointed officers, and, most significantly for our present purposes, the expectation is raised that all God's people are engaged in God's ministry no matter what their own unique life setting might be. Enabling people to see their whole life in such an intentional fashion is one of the key steps we can take in order to cultivate a vision for engagement with ministry and leadership, and an appetite for being resourced for such ministry.

## 3 Devise a strategy for leadership development

As we have suggested throughout this chapter, leaders are not formed by accident. Unless we are intentional about the formation and development of others and unless we approach this business in a studied fashion we are unlikely to make much progress. We noted earlier the way in which Jesus himself in his own ministry deliberately prioritized the raising up and development of others. Our suggestion is that those who wish to follow his example might do well to replicate the leadership development process he himself adopts. Of all the evangelists, Luke gives us the fullest description of this process. We have identified eight distinct stages to it.

### (a) Casting the net wide

After Jesus has begun his public ministry at Nazareth we find him preaching to a large group of people on the shores of Galilee.[35] In an attempt to avoid the press of the crowd, Jesus prevails upon some local fishermen to allow him to use their boat as a floating pulpit. Their attention is grabbed in a dramatic fashion when, having failed to catch any fish during the previous night, the favourable time for fishing, in response to Jesus' invitation they cast their nets out once again and pull in a completely unexpected (fish are not usually caught in the middle of the day) and astonishingly large haul of fish. Their astonishment is doubled when Jesus goes on to invite them to follow him effectively as his apprentices in the business of catching people for God's kingdom. A number of elements of this narrative might inform our own practice.

First, Jesus' criteria for identifying potential leaders are subtly different from those we sometimes deploy ourselves. This is an important point for us to grasp as we can tend to have a somewhat restricted view of who might qualify as a candidate for leadership development. Peter, who is Jesus' choice here, would certainly have been a surprise selection by the standards of his own day. It was not unusual for itinerant rabbis (and Jesus seems to fit into such a category) to invite promising young people to join their band with a view, ultimately, to sharing in similar ministry themselves. Such candidates were selected from the highest academic achievers who would have progressed through the local religious education system. The fact that Peter has a career as a fisherman is the clearest indication that he has long ago left the education system and is obviously not the kind of material of which future rabbis are made. One of the little ironies of this narrative is that while there is a large crowd of people pursuing Jesus and keen to hang on his every word, the spiritual 'enthusiasts', Peter is not one of this crowd; we find him sitting by the shore, preparing his nets for the next night's fishing, and no doubt more than a little grumpy at having nothing to show for the labours of the previous, fruitless night. Peter is a practical man who, for all manner of reasons, has never remotely contemplated the possibility of holding any level of spiritual responsibility. His reaction to the miraculous catch of fish and his recognition that he is in the presence of true holiness is to urge Jesus to move on; the gist of his response is to suggest that if Jesus really knew the kind of man Peter was, he wouldn't be wasting his time with him.

What becomes clear is that Jesus is not primarily interested in academic prowess, nor necessarily with a particular familiarity with the rituals of the religious community. What we might imagine draws him to Peter is Peter's willingness to obey (as evidenced by his readiness to throw out his nets, despite his many reservations, at the request of Jesus) and his humility. We must be careful not to overlook potential candidates for leadership simply because they do not fit with particular human paradigms we might have constructed, often to do with academic ability or conformity to particular spiritual practices. Humility, a willingness to obey Christ and a teachable spirit may well be the most vital qualities to watch out for in a potential leader. These are discerned as we extend a wide invitation to as many as possible to follow Christ and as we give extensive opportunities to as many as possible to become involved in his ministry.

We should note that Jesus' invitation to Peter is, in the first place, an invitation to follow him. We do well to remember that leadership always arises out of followership and that the most effective leaders never lose their appetite for growing in their capacity to imitate Christ. Indeed, if we want to grow leaders we need to invest time and energy to make sure that the focus of our church is on developing and growing disciples.

### (b) Giving a vision of what they might become

The invitation extended by Jesus to Peter is simultaneously one to follow but also, in the process, an invitation to do things one could never hope to accomplish without God's agency. Jesus does not invite Peter to use his existing fishing skills now with a human catch in mind. Rather, he invites him to follow with the promise that he, Jesus, will now cause or enable him to catch people for God. Perhaps it is this vision, of becoming something he could never otherwise hope to be, that inflames Peter's heart and spurs him on to embrace Jesus' invitation to follow.

Christian ministry and leadership will always fundamentally be concerned with enabling others to hear and receive God's invitation and with helping others to enter God's kingdom. Our task as those who recruit others for this ministry is to excite them with the prospect of what God might do with them and how God might work in their lives to enlarge them. Many of us find ourselves today in leadership roles because, at a formative stage in our past, God used someone to sow into us a vision of how we might be used by God and of what he might cause us to become through the agency of his Spirit. One of the most helpful contributions we can make towards the spiritual growth of others is to raise their expectations of how God might use them and to help them appreciate the potential that God sees in them (even if they don't see it themselves!).

### (c) Praying for wisdom in selecting those in whom to invest

Some time later, after Jesus has collected a sizeable band of followers, we find him spending an entire night alone in prayer, asking the Father to show him those among the wider band in whom he might especially invest.[36] This, of course, leads to him choosing 12 whom he designates apostles.

Without neglecting the wider group of disciples, much of Jesus' attention from this time on will be devoted to the formation of this smaller group of 12 and at times to the more intensive formation of a smaller 'inner' group of three. Neil Cole helpfully outlines the different 'circles' of influence, all with different levels of demand and opportunities for impact, occupied both by Jesus and also by local church leaders today.[37] On the one hand, Jesus ministered to the multitudes, for whom he fulfilled the role of visionary teacher, and to the band of disciples for whom he was shepherd. We too find ourselves ministering to the larger crowd (perhaps those in our parish or community who expect us to fulfil a particular public or pastoral role) and to the congregation with all its demands. Cole suggests that ministry to these larger groupings of people is especially demanding in terms of allocation of time, but the more 'scattergun' nature of our involvement with such people means that ministry in these spheres has limited impact. By comparison, Jesus' ministry to the Twelve, for whom he is discipler, and to the three for whom he is mentor, has far more impact yet is far less demanding in terms of time spent. We may get fewer accolades for time spent with the few, but investment in these people might just be the most significant thing we do. For Cole, this begs the question as to why we often neglect more intensive investment in a few, preferring to focus on the ministry to the 'crowds' with its lesser impact. Perhaps, like Jesus, we need to give time over, now and again, to ask God to show the people in whom we should be investing particular time and attention. Each of us should be able to identify a small group, possibly those who are currently exercising particular ministry oversight or responsibility, whom we regard as our special responsibility for shaping and growing in leadership, and one or two people whom we are mentoring or coaching in a more direct way. Not to do so may well be to deny to others the possibility of benefiting from the wisdom and experience that God has stored up within us and that he longs to release through us to others.

### (d) Sharing our life with them

Jesus' invitation to his prospective disciples is to accompany him, to share time and space with him. The developing of others is by no means simply a matter of 'instruction', an impersonal process of training. Rather, it is a relational activity, a form of apprenticeship accomplished through the opening up of our lives to others.

I suspect that the most influential people in our own lives have not simply been those who have passed on to us helpful information, but rather those whose lives have made an impact on us. We tend to remember best not those of our schoolteachers who were simply good at opening up a particular subject to us but those who took an interest in us and invited us to step into their world. We learn most from those leaders who do not simply instruct us about how to perform some ministry task but who invite us to journey with them and whose lifestyle stimulates in us a desire to be like them. Jesus invites his own followers to accompany him on his travels around the villages and towns of Galilee and Judea, and to share in the intimate details of his life and ministry. They are deeply affected by the ways in which Jesus responds and reacts to people in all manner of situations, especially the grace he extends even to his opponents. They learn from him what it is to trust God in situations of need and vulnerability and see modelled the very character that Jesus himself has described and espoused in his teaching. We might also suggest that the seeds of their own future commitment to growing others in ministry and leadership are sown here in their experience of being welcomed into this sphere of intimacy with Jesus.

Few of us will have open to us the opportunity to invite people to join us on itinerant ministry journeys, but effective formation will always contain with it an element of sharing life (that is, more than merely engaging in shared ministry tasks) with those whom we are seeking to develop and grow. This may be as simple as the giving and receiving of hospitality, but may equally involve the very intentional identification of activities with which we would be involved anyway but which might become opportunities for sharing time with others.

## (e) Modelling leadership and ministry

Bewildering though it often is for them, from the moment they respond to Jesus' invitation to discipleship, the Twelve or, at times, the three, are witnesses to all the moments of ministry with which Jesus himself is engaged. This learning experience first expands their own expectations as to what God might be concerned with, but also begins to shape their understanding as to how one engages in such ministry.

At some stage during my career as a local church leader, the realization dawned upon me that, with the exception of some ministry that was inevitably confidential in nature, there were very few ministry activities that could not be shared with others, and that most of these activities could profitably be used as training and learning opportunities with others. The best way of raising up people to share in different aspects of pastoral ministry is to begin to take such emerging ministers along with us when we visit, for example, those who are bereaved or who have other pastoral needs. The best way to shape those who may be sensing a call to a teaching or preaching ministry might be to 'tag preach' with them. This involves sharing with them in the process of preparing a sermon, explaining each stage of your own method of preparation, and then preaching together (if you preach the opening and concluding parts of the sermon and your apprentice some part of what lies between, even if their contribution flops badly, the sermon can always be rescued and brought to a good conclusion).[38] The call of God to particular ministries often originates in, or is significantly furthered by, an experience of witnessing particular ministry and having one's heart stirred by the prospect of doing this oneself.

## (f) Giving opportunities to 'have a go'

Perhaps the watershed moments in Jesus' process of forming others are those described in Luke 9 and 10 when Jesus sends out first the Twelve and then 70 'others', to engage in the kind of ministry that they have seen him performing in their time with him. This is not Jesus handing over or delegating full responsibility for the ministry that has previously been his, but rather inviting his apprentices to undertake something that, though stretching for them, is limited in time and scale.

Discerning God's call to ministry can be perplexing both for those who are exploring such a call and for those who are 'talent spotting'. Discernment often occurs most naturally in the context of engagement in ministry, as opposed to in some more abstract sense. It is as people try out that a sense is gained of their 'fit' with a particular ministry. Having the opportunity to dip a toe into a particular sphere of ministry without the pressure to commit to this for the long term is a vital part of the discernment process. So as leaders, we need to find ways of creating opportunities for short-term 'tasters' in different ministry areas. For example, as well as inviting people to commit to a month's involvement in some ongoing area of ministry, there may well be specific short-term projects that provide the ideal opportunity to observe people and reflect with them about their own calling. These might include a children's holiday club, a summer 'holiday at home' venture for the elderly, or a community visitation project. Inviting people to get involved with such projects gives us an opportunity to observe their gifts and skills, their character and their ability to work collaboratively. It should also give us further insight as to how we might contemplate involving them in more long-term ministry and leadership in the future.

### (g) Reflecting with them

Having completed the tasks set them, the disciples are invited to withdraw with Jesus in order to reflect on all that has happened. Indeed, reflection on ministry, both theirs and his, seems to be a central feature of the training methods of Jesus. Perhaps the greatest contribution we can make to the formation of others is to enable them to reflect insightfully on their own performance in ministry, helping them to build on their strengths and to grow in areas where they are weak. We will always want to encourage where possible, but we must never fight shy of tackling underdeveloped areas of practice and, especially, of character, which, left unaddressed, will have the potential to undermine anyone's effectiveness in ministry. My life-long enjoyment of playing cricket has been significantly enhanced by the various people who, at different stages of my career, have taken the time to enable me to hone my skills and iron out flaws in my technique. If we appreciate the contribution of those who coach us in sport or in other activities, how much more vital is the similar contribution made by those who might help us grow in effectiveness in ministry and leadership. If we as leaders fail to make this investment in our own apprentices then we are denying them the opportunity to grow and very likely condemning them to repeat errors such that bad practice becomes ingrained in them.

### (h) Releasing them

The final stage of Jesus' leadership development was to release those whom he had spent three years growing and developing. The final instructions he gives to them are in preparation for life and ministry when he will no longer be physically present with his followers.[39]

Our goal in growing and equipping others must never be to raise up people who will either always remain within our shadow or continue to be dependent in some way upon us. A good parent does not have children in order for them to remain as infants but rather works to prepare them for independent and fruitful adulthood. Our aspirations as leaders must always be to grow others who will not only thrive without us but, hopefully, in all ways outstrip us in effectiveness. To this end we will always strive to focus peoples' attention on God, rather than on ourselves, as their helper and place of sustenance; we will stimulate proper kingdom ambition and imagination within them, enabling them to dream big dreams; and, most importantly, we will entrust to them significant responsibility.

## The nature of our legacy

Ultimately, the true quality of our leadership and ministry, in any church or other context, is defined by what happens after we move on from that place, and by what we leave behind us. Do we want to be remembered as a highly competent practitioner whose indispensability is highlighted by the way in which our church has struggled to cope without us and by the way in which things have stalled since we moved on? Or do we, rather, want to be remembered as one who, through careful investment in others, developed a church with a wide-ranging commitment to shared ministry and leadership, where ministry is able to be sustained for the long term and where the vision for leadership development is owned widely? If we are to be faithful to the leadership paradigm modelled by Jesus and commended by him, then we will strive to avoid a leadership style that simply cultivates dependence upon ourselves and give ourselves wholeheartedly to the equipping of all God's people for works of service and for the building up of the body and towards its effective functioning.

---

### Leadership on the ground

When Angus Bell took up his new role as Consultant Psychiatrist in the Tees, Esk and Wear Valleys Mental Health Trust in August 1994, morale in the service for which he was now responsible was extremely low. The team he inherited had for some time suffered from the absence of regular or consistent leadership, with a series of locums taking temporary charge. Lacking coordinated vision and with poor functionality, confidence in the service's capacity to heal those suffering from psychiatric illness was at rock bottom, with local GPs being profoundly reluctant to refer patients. Staff found themselves spending time and energy providing services to a small number of patients with less severe conditions, who were being maintained in the service rather than improved and discharged. Angus found himself wondering where all the more seriously ill people were

---

and why his service appeared not to be treating them. He also found himself reflecting on the obvious lack of courage within the organization to reflect on effectiveness, to innovate, to close down activities that were clearly no longer fruitful and to be led by a vision that was therapeutic, shaped by patient needs as opposed to institutional habits.

## Skills development

Angus realized that his priority was to enable his team to recapture a sense of vision for its work and for each individual member to rediscover a sense of joy and fulfilment in the work in which they were engaged. To this end, his very first action was to initiate a series of one-to-one meetings with each team member. As well as introducing himself, and explaining his own initial vision of leading a service that existed to treat the most unwell people, and getting them better as fast as possible, his goal was to assess the capabilities of his new team. Although he realized that some people would either be resistant to or incapable of change and would inevitably have to move on, his intention was to develop and grow as many of his staff as possible. Shaped by a firm conviction that Jesus' longing for all people that they experience life in all its fulness should extend to their experience of the workplace, Angus believed that people were most likely to be fulfilled by working in areas to which they felt most strongly called, and that people were most likely to excel in those very areas. As well as inviting them to comment on how they felt the team was functioning and on where they saw their own future, Angus asked them where their own particular passions lay in terms of mental health provision, and about how happy they were in their current work.

It became clear that, in the absence of leadership, his team had become a group of generalists in which everyone was involved in everything, and in which most things were done badly. Responding to team members' description of their own passions, Angus began to encourage specialization among team members. Responsibility for overseeing specific service provision was devolved to those who had a particular interest in that area along with opportunities to develop skills. Early examples of this were of an occupational therapist with a concern for those with eating disorders, who was offered additional training in order to develop a new service; and an ineffective member of staff, obstructing change, turned out to be frustrated with their role, but had significant and neglected talents in engaging patients on an individual level. That person was given the opportunity to retrain as a cognitive behavioural therapist, a role at which they began to excel. Staff morale and effectiveness began to rise dramatically as passion and a sense of vocation was rekindled, as staff experienced personal and professional investment, and as people began to spend more time and energy in areas of medicine for which they had a particular concern. Existing group activities that were seen as ineffectual or that did not fit with the mission of the team to make seriously ill people better were stopped. This freed up resources to establish in their place new specialist services with one-to-one provision that were more appropriate, highly valued and beneficial. All this was done without extra money or staff.

Within three months the referral rate to the service had increased tenfold as GP confidence grew rapidly. By the end of Angus's first year, his team were energized, motivated and took a pride in their work, those (25–33 per cent of the original team) who felt unable to embrace the new regime had moved on, and the team was now in a position to revisit their vision and set new targets.

## A vision for patient well-being

In the light of the overarching vision of enabling ill people to become well and to stay well, the team set targets of lowering the admission rate to hospital and of reducing the length of time patients spent in hospital. To achieve this they recognized that they needed to be able to react faster on behalf of those experiencing the onset of psychiatric conditions and to offer greater support at home. So resources began to be diverted away from maintaining expensive hospital wards and reallocated towards the establishment of new mobile-home treatment teams. These were not only more local and more flexible in terms of capacity to offer immediate care, but quickly proved to be far more effective. Faster and more flexible approaches were adopted towards decision-making around in-patient treatment with responsibility for such decisions delegated out to responsible staff other than the consultant, within the parameters of agreed patient treatment plans.

## Strategic thinking

Good practice, especially when it brings positive therapeutic and financial results, is often noticed, and those responsible for it given additional responsibility. Within a reasonably short time, Angus Bell found himself as Senior Clinical Director for adult psychiatric services across the whole of the trust, with responsibility for mental health provision for more than 2 million people. This required considerable strategic initiative at a time of immense financial challenge for the health service; growing demand for services was coupled with dramatic reductions in funding. Angus saw this challenge as an opportunity for innovation and improvement. Convinced by one of the tenets of lean thinking, that an organization's best and most rapid innovation emerges from times of greatest crisis, Angus set about excising waste from the system, identifying others within the organization who might be skilful in enabling strategic allocation of resources, and, above all, continuing to seek improvements in the level of care offered.

The consultant's weekly ward round, during which all patients are seen and decisions taken about changes in treatments and whether patients are ready for discharge, is a long-established hospital tradition and regarded in many ways as sacrosanct. It is one of the pivots around which other features of patient care revolve. For Angus Bell it was indicative of a system that was conceived for the benefit of the service provider rather than the service recipient, and actually hindered good decision-making on behalf of patients. So in 2000 he abolished weekly ward rounds and replaced them with a more flexible and responsive system. The time-consuming and at times theatrical weekly round gave way to a daily review in which nursing staff briefed consultants verbally on each patient. Critical decisions could now be taken on a daily, as opposed to weekly, basis. This had a number of dramatic consequences. Hospital stays were now significantly shortened as patients were discharged when ready rather than at the convenience of the consultant. The average hospital stay was now 18 days as opposed to the previous average of 40 days. Patients were much more content and far less frustrated by a perceived lack of attention from consultants. Incidents of violence or aggressive behaviour towards staff dropped by 90 per cent. The service became much more efficient and, significantly, much more cost effective, resulting in huge savings of money.

## Reflective leadership

Perhaps one of the most significant reasons behind the success Angus enjoyed during his senior career was his commitment to reflect hard on his own leadership. Recognition that he was good at strategic innovation and at engaging others positively, at recognizing the skills of others and enabling them to be deployed appropriately, and awareness of his own limitations around the detail of the delivery process, enabled Angus to deploy himself to the greatest benefit to the service. Continually finding himself in the position of being offered more responsibility, he felt that the key question that would determine whether to take on such responsibility was whether or not he had both the skills and the resilience to sustain the work in question. His deep personal faith convinced him that any success he experienced was purely through the operation of God's grace, but equally gave him a proper confidence in God always to provide the resources to sustain him in whatever roles or works he was called to undertake. Angus's own calling to be a psychiatrist first and foremost, and his passion to see sick people made well, evidenced by his commitment even when occupying a very senior management position to continue with his own patient caseload, meant that concern for patient well-being shaped the decisions he made and the strategies he introduced.

When Angus Bell talks about leadership and the most vital qualities for a leader to display, he talks above all about compassion, both for those who benefit from the service provided or enabled by the leader and also for those who serve alongside the leader. A leader is required to reflect on the effects of his working practices, the systems he constructs, on those who work with him, always asking whether or not colleagues feel cared for, and whether or not opportunities to express such care are deliberately designed into working practices. Perhaps it is this concern to reflect proper compassion that enabled Angus on retirement not only to hand on a service that was one of the most efficient and cost-effective in the country but also a workforce that was so energized, equipped and fulfilled.

## Questions to aid reflection

1 Why do you think it is often harder to stop existing practices than to start new ones?

2 Angus believed that people were most likely to perform best and be most fulfilled when operating in the areas to which they had the strongest calling. What steps might you take in your own context to enable others to serve more fully in the light of their vocation and gifting?

3 How far do you agree that an organization's best and most rapid innovation emerges from times of greatest crisis? What might threaten the possibility of this taking place?

4 What might compassion look like in a leader, and how is it being expressed in your own leadership?

## Notes

1 Some of the ideas articulated in this chapter first found expression in Parkinson, I., 2015, *Reignite: Seeing God Rekindle Life and Purpose in Your Church*, Oxford: Monarch, ch. 6.

2 Adair, J., 2005, *How to Grow Leaders*, London: Kogan Page, p. 79.

3 Greenwood, R., 1995, *Transforming Priesthood*, London: SPCK, p. xii.

4 Almost a century ago, Roland Allen, a USPG mission partner, reflected similarly upon his experience working with the Anglican Church in China, lamenting the attitudes and methods that resulted in a dependence upon overseas leadership and patronage, the consequent disempowerment of local Christians and the restriction of access for them to appropriate leadership positions, and thus of limitations in church growth. His writings seem especially pertinent to our own contemporary context and remarkably prophetic. See Allen, R., 2011, *Missionary Methods: St Paul's or Ours*, Mansfield Centre, CT: Martino Publishing; Allen, R., 2006, *The Spontaneous Expansion of the Church – and the Causes which Hinder It*, Cambridge: Lutterworth Press.

5 For example, Jeremiah 31.31–34; Ezekiel 36.26–27; Joel 2.28–29.

6 Jeremiah 31.34.

7 Joel 2.28.

8 For example, 1 Corinthians 12ff.; Romans 12.4ff.

9 The emergence and growth of the Pentecostal churches in Latin America, and the rapid expansion of the Chinese church in the late twentieth century, eviscerated of leaders and other resources, are clear examples of this.

10 This is well documented by Stark, R., 1997, *The Rise of Christianity*, New York: HarperCollins.

11 Ephesians 4.7–12.

12 I am fully aware that scholarly opinion is divided in terms of the proper interpretation of Ephesians 4.12 and specifically concerning the relationship of the first two prepositional phrases in this verse. Lincoln (1990) is one of a number of recent commentators arguing for a distinction between the two. On this reading, God's gift of certain ministries (or offices) to the Church constitute God's equipping of his Church, are given so that works of service may be undertaken (by the recipients of such gifts), and are God's way of building up his Church. My own conviction, both on linguistic grounds and because it has greater resonance with the argument of the whole paragraph, is that the reading favoured by Barth (1974), Bruce (1961) and Caird (1976) among others, in which the second prepositional phrase is seen as related to the first, is preferable. On this reading, which is assumed in the argument above, the equipping of all God's people for works of service (which is of a piece with the universal receiving of grace referenced in verse 7) is accomplished through, and is a function of, the exercise of the ministries given by God to the Church.

13 Ephesians 4.16.

14 Snyder, H., 1983, *Liberating the Church*, Downers Grove, IL: InterVarsity Press, 1983, p. 248.

15 See p. 99 above.

16 Colossians 1.28.

17 For example, 2 Timothy 2.2.

18 For example, Timothy, Epaphroditus, Prisca and Aquila.

19 See Matthew 9.36–38.

20 Wright, W. C., 2000, *Relational Leadership*, Carlisle, Paternoster Press, p. 135.

21 Ancona, D., Malone, T. W., Orlikowski, W. J. and Senge, P., 2007, 'In Praise of the Incomplete Leader', *Harvard Business Review*, February 2007.

22 For a fuller treatment of issues to do with planning and effecting succession in leadership, see Parkinson, I., 2017, *Enabling Succession*, Cambridge: Grove Books.

23 It may be that this quote should actually be credited to the American journalist Walter Lippmann, who phrased it: 'The final test of a leader is that he leaves behind him in other men the conviction and the will to carry on.' Although this is frequently quoted, no one seems to be able to point to an original location/reference.

24 Nouwen, H., 1981, *The Way of the Heart*, New York: Seabury Press, p. 22.

25 Time and space prevent us from exploring this in any depth. Those wishing to do so are referred to the excellent overview of Anglican theologies of priesthood provided, for example, by Pickard, S., 2009, *Theological Foundations for Collaborative Ministry*, Farnham: Ashgate; Greenwood, *Transforming Priesthood*; and to the wider implications of different theologies upon our understanding of leadership, in Volf, M., 1998, *After Our Likeness: The Church as the Image of the Trinity*, Grand Rapids, MI: Eerdmans.

26 Greenwood, *Transforming Priesthood*, p. 170.

27 Snyder, H., 1980, *The Radical Wesley*, Downers Grove, IL: InterVarsity Press, p. 156.

28 John 14.12.

29 2 Corinthians 3.2.

30 The first of these value statements was, ironically, 'All Involved', signifying

that ministry and leadership was the province of the whole Church and not confined to selected officers.

31 *Growing Leaders* (CPAS) is an excellent off-the-peg resource for the development of leaders in a local church context. Further details of this course, and of other related resources, can be found at www.cpas.org.uk/church-resources.

32 'Setting God's People Free', GS 2056 (2017), p. 1.

33 This descriptive phrase was originally coined by the London Institute of Contemporary Christianity (LICC).

34 See especially Greene, M., 2014, *Fruitfulness on the Frontline*, Nottingham, InterVarsity Press.

35 Luke 5.1–11.

36 Luke 6.12–16.

37 Cole, N., *Organic Leadership*, 2009, Grand Rapids, MI: Baker, p. 161.

38 This became my favoured method of introducing people to preaching ministry and was a strategy I employed with special delight with one or two members of our youth group who were beginning to sense a call to this ministry.

39 Luke 24.44ff.; Acts 1.3–8.

# 8

# Fostering Collaboration

*Today's leaders must be skilled in bringing people together in order to pool knowledge and skills. They must struggle to create the right 'chemistry' of human relations, so that those they lead spark ideas in one another, urging each other forward in ministry and outreach.*[1]

*I am a strong believer in team leadership since I know from experience that a team has more hands than I do and more wisdom as they see things from a variety of perspectives.*[2]

In 2016, Leicester City won the English football Premier League title for the first time in their 132-year history. This was a memorable achievement for all manner of reasons. In being crowned champions, Leicester gained membership of a very select group; over the previous 25 years this competition had been won by only five other teams, one of whom had won it on one occasion, the others multiple times. Every expectation was that one of this elite group of four teams would, yet again, win the title in 2016. This expectation was not unreasonable, given that each of these teams contained within its ranks a number of the world's leading players, and that each club had invested between six to eight times the amount of money in purchasing those players than Leicester City had in assembling its own squad. Indeed, during the course of the season, on the occasions when Leicester City played against other leading teams, it was not unusual for the substitutes on the opposition's bench to carry a higher total price tag than that of the entire Leicester first team. By contrast, the Leicester squad comprised a small number of low-budget purchases and a collection of players who had effectively been dispensed with by other clubs as surplus to requirements. Furthermore, Leicester were judged by many to be somewhat fortunate to be playing in the top flight of English football at all. For most of the previous season they had been at serious risk of being relegated into the second tier, and only a late-season rally had secured their Premier League status. Little wonder that the bookmakers rated their chances of winning the Premier League as minimal and, at the beginning of the 2015–16 season, offered odds of 5,000–1 against their ending up as champions. A former Leicester City player, now a leading TV football pundit, even when at the mid-point of the season Leicester found themselves at the top of the table, insisted that their chances of winning the trophy were so remote that, were they to do so, he would present his weekly television programme wearing only his underpants. This rash threat came back to haunt him when Leicester were eventually crowned as champions.

The endurance test that is the Premier League campaign, and the hegemony of a small group of previous winners, bears witness to the fact that no team can win this prestigious title by good fortune alone. To what, then, might Leicester's success be attributed? A number of themes seem to be common in the accounts written by various pundits and analysts in response to this question. In the absence of the kind of elite stars possessed by some other clubs, Leicester sought to play a style of football that was not a less accomplished version of the brand played by others but rather a distinctive one that suited the particular strengths and capabilities of their own squad. Players tended to be aware of their own limitations, but also many felt that, having been discarded by other clubs, they had something to prove. There was within the squad a hunger to succeed and a recognition that the only way to achieve such success was through team effort. Facilitated by a manager who understood how to inspire and motivate effectively, to direct when appropriate, but also to invite contributions from players and to make everyone feel that their insights were valued, this was a team that became collectively very much more than the sum of its individual parts. In an environment in which often all the focus is on the individual skills of exceptional stars, Leicester's story offers a remarkable illustration of what can be achieved through genuine teamwork and a thoroughgoing commitment to the disciplines of collaboration.

In our last chapter we began to consider some sound reasons for extending the range of those who might be involved in leadership and ministry. One of the central responsibilities of leadership, we suggested, is that of identifying and nurturing the gifts of others in this way. However, this is really one half of a broader responsibility, which might be described as fostering effective collaboration.[3] Lawrence helpfully defines collaboration in the following way:

> Recognising that we seek to join in with what God is doing, and that leadership is best exercised with others, collaboration is the action of working interdependently with others in a mutual, caring and complementary way, towards a shared, kingdom-honouring goal.[4]

Leaders are required not only to develop others in their respective vocations but equally to provide systems and structures in order to harness the efforts of those others and to enable everyone to work in a constructive way with one another.

We have already drawn attention to some of the key theological motifs that fix collaboration as essential to any understanding of Christian leadership. Our creation in the image of a God who is Trinity, a relationship of three persons who each somehow find their own fullness not in their distinctiveness as persons but rather in their mode of togetherness,[5] reminds us that the work that this God entrusts to us can never be contemplated as an essentially solitary activity. Indeed, none of us has the wherewithal within ourselves alone to accomplish the tasks that God asks of his Church; each of us not only needs the complementary ministries of others to complete what is lacking in us but equally must recognize that it is only through our collaboration with others and through the operation of grace through those others that our own work is truly enabled.

> The ministries of the ecclesia are called to recognise and call attention to the trace of God's energetic and holy order. As the ministries of the church serve this implicit divine order they enable the church to realise itself as the embodiment and witness to the reality of God in the world. But the ministries cannot do this if they are not properly coordinated as instantiations of God's own ordering, i.e., intrinsically related in a 'mode of togetherness' such that they raise each other to the fulness of the ministry of each.[6]

The relational metaphors used by the apostle Paul to describe the economy of the Church, especially that of the body, remind us that the nature of the whole of Christian experience is essentially corporate not individual. Our relationships with others tend to be the arena in which our Christian discipleship is worked out,[7] and each member of the Church seems to have a responsibility for the welfare and growth of other Christian sisters and brothers.[8] The different members of the Church, irrespective of their unique function or sense of self-importance, can never perform the whole work of the body independently of others. Thus the body of Christ needs to be so ordered and animated that its different members enable one another to participate fully in God's ministry both to the Church and to the world. In the natural world, human and other bodies whose limbs and organs do not operate in a coordinated and collaborative manner are regarded as sick and dysfunctional. When a local church departs from this norm, it too must be seen as in some way in need of healing and restoration.

The practice of Jesus and of those who followed him bears witness to these assumptions. Jesus never sees himself as operating alone in his own earthly ministry but rather in relationship with the other persons of the Trinity. His ministry is seen as being instigated by the Spirit of God[9] and conducted under the direction of and in partnership with the Father.[10] The earliest records of Jesus entrusting responsibility to others describe him as sending those others out not singly but in pairs. The earliest Christian communities appear to have groups of people sharing oversight together, and those responsible for establishing these new communities leave behind them teams of leaders to continue what they have started. Whatever else we might say about leadership in the New Testament we must certainly say that it was always plural and instinctively collaborative, a quality that for Pickard arises out of the nature of the gospel to which the Church bears witness in its common life.[11]

In the wider leadership literature, a shift from an exclusive focus on the work of individual leaders to an acknowledgement of leadership as a more widely dispersed phenomenon within groups and organizations has led to increased concern to understand and advocate for effective collaboration. Keith Grint sees the ability to facilitate such collaboration as the distinguishing mark of a truly effective leader:

> holding together the diversity of talents necessary for organisational success is what distinguishes a successful from an unsuccessful leader: leaders don't need to be perfect but, on the contrary, they do have to recognise that the limits of their knowledge and power will ultimately doom them to failure unless they rely upon their subordinate leaders and followers to compensate for their own ignorance and impotence ... In effect, leadership is the property and consequence of a community rather than the property and consequence of an individual leader.[12]

Grint, along with a number of other writers, highlights the danger of more monarchical approaches to leadership. In particular, leaders who resist collaboration, and the organizations which they lead, are always going to be restricted by the leader's own personal limitations in capacity, expertise, understanding and insight. Not only does this inevitably hold back the progress of the organization but it is equally a source of immense frustration for others involved in the organization who are denied opportunity to make potentially helpful contributions, leading to them becoming demoralized and disaffected. A collaborative approach enables organizations to transcend some of the limitations of the leader and also brings with it a number of other positive benefits for the organization and its members. What might these be specifically in the context of a local church?

## Benefits of collaborative working

### 1 Efficiency

Collaborative leadership tends to be smarter, more informed and more adaptive than monarchical leadership. When more people are involved in the leadership process then more information is available to those responsible for decision-making and the group is better placed to be able to resist the pressures of individual bias or prejudice. In an age when churches are faced with challenges previously unknown and for which existing strategies are inadequate, those who will be able to pursue God's mission faithfully are those who are able to find adaptive solutions to these new challenges. This sense of having to sing the Lord's song in a strange land is compounded by the rate at which members of our communities experience social change, by the physical changes to the structure and make-up of local communities and by the way in which church leadership is changing with fewer stipendiary resources spread ever more thinly. The wisdom to find intelligent solutions to these challenges may well be found in a group of people, but will rarely be found in a solitary individual. This will in part be due to the fact that groups of people working together are much more likely to experience bursts of creativity than those who work alone and who feel increasingly overwhelmed by the mounting impact of pressing challenges.

## 2 Confidence

Collaborative leadership tends to inspire greater confidence in the wider community. Those who lead in company with others inevitably have to submit themselves to more obvious accountability for their decisions and opinions, and are less able to conceal improper or unworthy motives or prejudices when leading in community. Followers will by and large regard decisions made by a group of reputable people as being more reliable than those made by a single leader, especially where such a decision might itself be challenging or innovative. Perhaps the biggest single challenge facing the earliest Christian community was to do with the status of converts from non-Jewish backgrounds. Opinion was sharply divided as to whether these converts needed to submit to the requirements of Jewish ritual law (including that of circumcision for male converts) or whether such requirements were rendered obsolete by the atoning death of Jesus Christ. It appears likely that the fledgling Church was in danger of splitting into factions over this issue around prominent leaders each espousing differing viewpoints based on passionately held conviction. The issue was resolved at a conference of those leaders and other concerned parties, the first council of the Christian Church.[13] The opinion of the council is commended to the wider Church in a letter that affirms that the decision reflects what 'seemed good to us, having become of one mind'.[14] Although similar disputes rumbled on at times in certain quarters, and are addressed in some of Paul's letters, nevertheless, in the short term this collaborative decision seems to have won over even those for whom the new polity now advocated would have been previously unthinkable. Decisions to launch new ministries or to bring to a close existing projects, decisions to invest significant financial or other resources in particular ways, or to change patterns of public worship or other significant and familiar structures are all more likely to gain approval when they are the fruit of collaborative decision-making rather than simply the brainchild (no matter how inspired) of a single leader.

## 3 Community

Collaborative leadership is a far more satisfying experience for those involved in leadership (despite the inevitable challenges and frustrations at times of having to work with those from whom we are temperamentally different). As those created in the image of a relational God, we too are designed to work communally. Encountering genuine synergy in an effective team is one of the most richly satisfying experiences. For pastors and other stipendiary ministers, the experience of working collaboratively is a glorious antidote to the loneliness that so many clergy and others seem to experience as a consequence of bearing responsibility alone. And while a sense of responsibility is still very much present, the knowledge that a decision has been taken in conjunction with others diminishes the weight of that responsibility that so often exerts a crushing pressure on those who have to live with the consequences of decisions made alone.

## 4 Coordination

Churches, like any other organization, especially those in which responsibility is largely undertaken by unpaid people in somewhat informal roles, are prone to the kind of atomization whereby those holding responsibility tend to operate largely independently of other office holders and all too often without any proper supervision. I still recall coming across one church where the leaders of the Sunday children's ministry put padlocks on the equipment storage cupboards in the church hall to ensure that those involved in midweek toddler groups and other ministries to children were not able to use their own precious equipment and resources. When the midweek group leaders responded in kind it bore eloquent witness to the fact that neither group saw themselves as in any way working collaboratively in the same mission field, but rather somehow in competition. Little wonder that the fruitfulness of each was significantly compromised. Many clergy and other authorized ministers working across groups of churches find one of their greatest challenges to be the unwillingness on the part of such churches to pool resources and operate in a collaborative way. Indeed, it is sadly all too often the case that such churches see themselves as rivals for a share of resources, especially the time and energy of the clergy or other leaders, rather than as partners in mission and ministry.

Whether on the local church or multi-parish benefice level, fruitfulness depends upon individual leaders and office holders being willing to sacrifice narrow self-interest for the sake of the good of the larger body, to cultivate a wider vision that enables them to understand what is the unique role and contribution of their own area of responsibility and how it relates to and enhances other areas of ministry and responsibility, and to work collaboratively with others rather than in isolation. Fostering such a mindset change and creating structures that enable such collaborative working may well be principal responsibilities of a leader in this all-too-common situation.[15]

## Forms of collaborative working

Collaboration is something of an umbrella term to describe a variety of modes of working jointly with others. What each has in common is, among other things, a commitment to a shared purpose or vision, a willingness to work in an interdependent as opposed to independent fashion, and a willingness to devolve responsibility, power and authority away from the centre and towards others occupying different places within the organization.[16] We are going to examine three distinct modes, each reflecting different degrees of collaboration. Each mode has its proper place in the life of a church or other organization. Leaders need to understand the appropriate place in which each might be deployed and develop the necessary skills in order for each to be practised most effectively.

### 1 *Supervision*

Supervision may be described as a formal relationship in which support, accountability and partnership is offered by a church leader, or other authorized person, to another who themselves hold responsibility for some ministry area within the church. Although most usually practised as a one-to-one relationship, it may be appropriate to offer group supervision to a number of people involved in the same area of ministry, for example, those involved in preaching, leading small groups or any group of people involved in leading similar but distinct areas of ministry.

Supervision has a number of benefits for the individual leader, for his ministry area and for the church or organization as a whole. By committing to meet regularly to discuss his area of ministry, personal concerns and other related matters, the church leader is showing interest in and concern for the ministry leader and for his work. This communicates to the ministry leader a sense that what he does has value and significance in the overall scheme of things. It serves as a powerful antidote to the sense of isolation that so many people feel, a feeling that can easily spill over into resentment that my work is not valued and the sense that I have to champion the cause of my ministry area aggressively because no one else will. A commitment on the part of the supervisor to invite reflection from the other on the ministry area and his own leadership of it, coupled with constructive feedback where appropriate, enables the ministry leader to develop and grow as well as revealing potential areas for personal development and the opportunity to recommend helpful resources and training opportunities. By asking informed questions about particular challenges and difficulties currently being experienced, the supervisor not only enables the other to feel that these, sometimes apparently overwhelming, challenges are being shared and their burden thus lightened, but may also enable better solutions to be found to them. Proper supervision enables those holding responsibility to see far more clearly where their own area of service fit into the whole life and mission of the church. It also serves to stimulate within them a renewed sense of vision and a rekindled vocation to this responsibility entrusted to them by God. It also gives the supervisor a much more informed understanding of the strengths, weaknesses, challenges and resourcing needs of this area of ministry, information that will enable her to lead across the whole organization in a much more intelligent way.

The ministry area in question benefits from having a suitably resourced and energized leader. Key disciplines that may have run the risk of being neglected, such as recruiting other workers, discerning fresh vision for the ministry in the light of changing circumstances and planning for succession in leadership, are now given attention as a result of having been raised and discussed in supervision meetings. The church benefits as a result of its various ministries becoming far more coordinated, leading to clarity in missional focus and a more intelligent approach to deploying resources.

Given the benefits that result, where time and energy are invested by church leaders in overseeing other workers and towards their flourishing and personal growth, it is astonishing that supervision of this sort is such a low priority for so many church leaders. Whether this is due to a lack of time and the pressure of other more urgent tasks, or whether it is overlooked because church leaders simply do not see its value or see it as something that gets in the way of them performing their own (implicitly more important) work, its neglect is ultimately a failure to appreciate the imperative to work collaboratively as opposed to monarchically. It is certainly the case that many church leaders may not have had good practice in supervision modelled to them and thus may feel underqualified to engage in supervising others. Skills in supervision are not difficult to learn, and helpful resources to set people going along this path are readily available.[17] Applying oneself to invest in others will pay enormous dividends.

## 2 Working groups

The term 'working groups' is not commonly used in churches, or indeed in other organizations, but is one we find convenient to categorize a number of different ways in which people work collaboratively, and that may actually be the most helpful description of many forms of collaborative work undertaken in local churches. The term was popularized by Katzenbach and Smith,[18] who use it to distinguish between teams (of which more later) and other significant forms of collaboration. Perhaps the most fundamental difference between the two is that while teams are concerned primarily with the accomplishment of shared work, a working group's performance is a function of what its members do as individuals: 'The members interact primarily to share information, best practices, or perspectives, and to make decisions to help each individual perform within his or her area of responsibility.'[19] Working groups provide a context in which mutual accountability can be provided for the faithful performance of one's own areas of responsibility. A good working group results in a greater sense of synergy between the various members and the varied areas of involvement that they represent.

There are a number of different contexts in the life of a local church in which working groups might be appropriate. The mission and ministry of any church will gain significant momentum if such a group is formed to bring together on a regular basis those with responsibility for overseeing different spheres of the church's ministry. Some churches will have a person designated to oversee ministry to children, and a smaller number might have a similar person to oversee ministry among young people. Yet another might have responsibility for prayer ministry or for pastoral care or for a community outreach project that is central to the life and mission of the church. The church may have a worship group or a choir with a recognized leader. It is well worth a church leader listing all those within the church who have some oversight responsibility for each of the different ministries in which the church engages. Those on the list can then be gathered on a regular (at least half-termly) basis at a mutually convenient time. A typical meeting will include some inspirational input from the leader, whether reiterating an aspect of the core vision or values of the church or offering some wider leadership or biblical wisdom, with opportunity then for the group to respond to the material. On each occasion when the group meets, one or two members will give a brief report on the progress of their own particular area of responsibility, sharing joys and challenges and other news. After questions from the rest of the group, time is given to pray for those who have given reports in the light of what has been said. Other members of the group are now given much briefer opportunity to raise matters of concern or flag up issues that might impinge upon other ministry areas or the relationship between different groups. The remainder of the time will be given over to forward planning, the allocation of tasks and responsibilities to do with future projects, and to prayer for one another.

In a multi-parish benefice a more collaborative approach to mission and ministry might be fostered by forming a working group composed of one or two people from each of the parishes in the group, who are exercising particular oversight or who have been entrusted with responsibility for ministry within each of those different parishes.

The real value of working groups such as these is twofold. On the one hand, they resource those who hold responsibility. In an encouraging environment, in which such individuals are both affirmed and held accountable for their work by others, and in which sometimes they are helped by others to find solutions to some of their most pressing challenges, people begin to see more clearly how their own responsibility fits into the wider picture. On the other hand, as the life of a church or group of churches becomes more complex and varied, the regular meetings of such working groups enables the overall leader to ensure that the vision and values of the church are maintained and that there is a consistency to the diverse work undertaken by a growing number of people.

## 3 Teams

Although 'team' is a word frequently used to describe all manner of different collections of people, only a small number of collaborative groups properly qualify to be described as teams. Perhaps the key distinction between teams and other working groups lies in their respective purposes: whereas working groups exist to enhance the effectiveness of the work projects of individuals (for the common good), teams are concerned with collective projects and with shared work. Team leadership is thus somewhat different from that exercised in working groups. The effectiveness of the latter depends to an extent upon the presence of a clearly focused leader who directs and over-sees the group, drawing out and coordinating the contributions of others. Team leadership is a far more fluid entity. The purpose for which the team exists, the goals it seeks to achieve and the values that govern its way of operating may well provide the real leadership that animates the team. Although there may be one person who carries overall responsibility for ensuring that the team holds fast to its purpose and values, in an effective team a sense of mutual accountability means that the whole team takes some responsibility for this, and the shared nature of its work means that leadership may well be more like a baton that passes effortlessly between members as the moment requires. Katzenbach and Smith give a definition of team, which we offer here in a version slightly amended to make more sense of our own concern for distinctively Christian leadership:

> A team is a small number of people with complementary skills who are committed to a common purpose, clear goals and an agreed approach, for which they hold themselves mutually accountable, *in order better to serve the purposes of God's kingdom.*[20]

### A small number

Teams by definition are small, ideally composed of between four to eight people, and for a very good reason. Research into the effectiveness of teams[21] suggests that the essence of a thriving team is the productive interaction between team members, often described as team communication. The greater the number of people on the team the lower the probability that such interaction might take place. In a team of five people there are effectively

20 channels of communication between the different team members, as each person speaks to and listens to four others. When another person is added to the team the number of communication channels increases to 30. Add two further members to this team and the number of communication channels now stands at 56. The larger the team, the greater the likelihood of the contribution of one or more team members being overlooked, of particular people dominating, and of the potential for real collaboration to be diminished. Frustration and resentment build among those who feel excluded from team discussion, 'back-channel' discussions take place outside team meetings between the disenfranchised, and the work of the team is frustrated. Pentland suggests that productive teams have several defining characteristics to do with the ways in which they communicate.[22] Everyone on the team talks and listens in roughly equal measure; members connect directly with one another, not just with a team leader; team members are actively engaged when communicating with others and see it as their responsibility to engage others. Patrick Lencioni observes that when teams comprise more than eight or nine people then members tend to advocate a lot more than they inquire.[23] This is due to the fact that people become less confident that they will have opportunity to contribute to discussions so use their rather more scarce floor time to announce their position or to make a point. Healthy interaction becomes less likely, members begin to compete rather than collaborate, and the synergy that is at the heart of genuine teams is lost.

### Complementary skills

One of the greatest temptations to which those responsible for forming teams are prone is that of selecting team members who are 'just like me'.[24] Certainly the more homogenous a team is in its make-up, the less likely it is to experience disagreement among its members. The leader prides herself on the harmonious nature of the team's interactions and on the way in which consensus is usually reached on all decisions that the team is required to make. Indeed, so precious is the sense of unity that the team experiences, and so different from the leader's previous painful experience of teams whose members fought with each other, that she is resolved never to admit anyone to membership of this team who might in any way threaten its equilibrium. This superficial sense of health and functionality is usually a sign of a largely ineffectual team. Irving Janis's[25] research into factors precipitating events in US foreign policy, subsequently judged to be disastrous, led him to propose the idea of *groupthink* as a description of rationalized conformity, an insistence on group cohesion as the highest value in a group, the maintenance of which justified the exclusion from consideration of opinions or strategies that challenged the group's existing values or assumptions. Groupthink is the likely consequence for any team or other form of group that elevates conformity or unity as its highest value and seeks to maintain this no matter what the cost. It is also the consequence for teams that, formed in the image of the leader, are comprised of members who feel, or who are made to feel, that disagreement with that leader's preferences constitutes disloyalty or resistance to the team's goals. The research conducted by Eisenhardt et al. suggests that where conformity is enforced, teams make not only less informed, and therefore poor, decisions but also take far more time to make those decisions.[26] Team relationships tend to become superficial, team members apathetic and withdrawn, key issues are overlooked and limiting assumptions remain unchallenged. The wise leader will steadfastly resist the temptation to form or cajole teams towards sterile uniformity, whether in terms of personality or opinion, and will actively look to create diversity in the make-up of teams in pursuit of better outcomes.

The awkward truth is that effective teams are always composed of people who reflect difference in terms of skills and abilities, experience and perspectives, and very likely temperament. Not only that, but the wise team leader, far from seeking to minimize or suppress such differences, will actually seek to utilize them as a catalyst for creativity and team synergy. Moreover, she will always be reflecting on critical gaps in team make-up and seeking to bring into the team others whose skills or outlook might effectively plug those gaps.

One of the principal challenges, especially for those engaged in church leadership or in other voluntary sector contexts, is the availability of suitable people possessing necessary skills, and the reality of having to work with those whom we either inherit or who are available to us. To those who are disheartened at the poverty of skills or experiences currently available to them, what follows might seem hopelessly idealistic and unrealistic. In describing some of the requirements for an ideal team our intention is not to demoralize further those who are frustrated with their current lot but rather to suggest a standard to which we might all aspire and towards which we might work. In a book on Christian leadership it is worth reflecting once again on the almost certain truth that the team that Jesus formed around himself was, at least initially, lacking in many key skills and attributes (although certainly diverse in background). It was three years, and a whole series of formative events, before this group of people was remotely able to function in the manner required for the leadership task entrusted to them in the period beyond the earthly ministry of Jesus. Rather than giving up in despair, wise leaders, drawing on some of the insights from our previous chapter, will set themselves the goal of growing people who might ultimately function well as team members, even if this process takes some time to accomplish.

Ideal teams will contain members who are different in their concerns. We have found it helpful to conceive of leadership in terms of three related and equally important concerns. A team needs to act in a balanced way to fulfil the requirements of each of these concerns. Most leaders will instinctively prioritize one, perhaps understand a second, but often have a blind spot when it comes to the third. Some leaders are primarily concerned with *purpose*. They are energized by the big picture, they love to imagine future possibilities, and are excited by the new thing. When it comes to forming vision they are a huge asset to the team: they ensure that the team never gets stuck in minutiae, that it is always alert to the new opportunities that God might be setting before it. Others are similarly energized by *process*. Their particular concern is for getting things done. They love nothing more, after a good visioning process, to sit down and work out a road map that will enable the vision to come to fruition, allocating tasks and responsibilities and holding the whole team accountable for what has been decided. A third group of leaders have at the forefront of their minds *people*, whether within the wider organization or those whom the organization exists to serve. They always tend to be concerned primarily not about where the community is going or how it will get there, but about how it will enable others to come along with it and what needs to be done in order to secure the involvement of others.

Given the diverse nature of these three concerns, tensions can easily arise between those who espouse them. Those who are focused on purpose can become frustrated at what they see as resistance from process-obsessed people asking hard questions about the mechanics of how the team will achieve its aspirations. This latter group can easily become equally frustrated with the dreamers who have so many bright ideas, few of which ever seem to be properly fulfilled before the team is asked to consider something entirely new. All the while, the people-focused leaders are alarmed at the potential fallout from the schemes dreamed up by the other groups, which appear to take no cognisance of the need to communicate effectively and engage those who might for all manner of reasons be resistant to these new ideas. Effective teams are those that enable the distinctive contributions of all three different groups.

Some of the most significant work on the importance of diversity and complementarity in team roles has been undertaken by Meredith Belbin.[27] Belbin's research into those factors that enabled success or failure in teams led him to posit the need for nine different roles (see Figure 3) to be fulfilled among team members.[28]

Belbin, too, picked up on the idea that teams must pay attention to three related concerns, which he identified as thinking, action and people. Under each of these broad headings he posited three distinct roles, the combination of which enabled a team to perform its work effectively.[29] Healthy teams will contain not only those with the ability to think in innovative and creative ways and those with the capacity to research existing practice and resources from other contexts, but also those with skills in forming strategy and ensuring that agreed work is appropriately completed. Some on the team will provide specialist knowledge vital for the task in hand, while others are required to coordinate the work of the whole team, or to make

Figure 3. Belbin Team Roles

Reproduced by kind permission of Belbin (www.belbin.com)

sure that the team stays on task, and still others enable the team to gel and facilitate good working relationships between team members.

Belbin's work has proved to be immensely helpful in enabling teams in all manner of different contexts, including churches, to explore their own strengths and deficiencies, and to recognize which skills and aptitudes are missing from the team and need to be added in order to enable the team to function more productively. When a team engages together with some of the psychometric tests linked to Belbin's work, not only does this enable team members to appreciate one another's contributions and roles more fully, but it also enables much fuller collaboration as team members grow in their understanding of how their own contribution meshes with and is enhanced by that of other team members with different gifts and skills.

One further fascinating feature of Belbin's account of team roles is his description, for each role, of what he terms allowable weaknesses. Recognizing that there is a shadow side to every strength, which manifests in tendencies that may be irritating to others, Belbin acknowledges that, though these tendencies are indeed at one level weaknesses or faults, they may need to be tolerated as being simply the concomitants to the strengths they shadow. So those who are free-thinking innovators (plants) often seem to be irritatingly unconcerned with detail, and have a tendency to work independently of others. This, for Belbin, may well be inevitable for those who are gifted with a soaring imagination, and to insist that they change behaviour in the sphere of their allowable weaknesses may well be to constrain their creative capacity unhelpfully. Teams that give time to working on the respective roles of their members may come to understand better why particular members tend to behave in different ways and may thus be better equipped to extend grace and tolerance to one another around these particular allowable weaknesses.

### Commitment to a common purpose

Hartwig and Bird describe purpose as the invisible driver of any team.[30] When teams are made up of a very diverse range of people, often the only thing that enables such a disparate group to work collaboratively and transcend differences is the existence of a compelling purpose that makes the work of a team seem worthwhile. An individual who is gripped by a desire to see a particular work accomplished, and yet who understands that such work cannot come about solely through her own individual effort but only as a consequence of the collaborative effort of a team, will always be prepared to prioritize collaborative endeavour over personal or individual work projects. Without such a sense of purpose, teams will tend to fragment as fault lines are exposed between the concerns of individuals, team members become disengaged, and time and energy is wasted on inconsequential matters.

A frequent mistake is to assume that the essential foundation for effective teamwork is strong interpersonal relationships. A number of teams and their leaders work on the presumption that before any meaningful work can be done by a team an enormous amount of time and energy needs to be invested in team building, and in particular on creating a strong relational base for the team. While fractured relationships among team members may well significantly undermine the viability of a team, and while teams whose members get along well may move more fluently than those whose interpersonal relationships are difficult, the most critical component in building a team is the owning of a clear, common, compelling task. Indeed, a misplaced focus on team building may be indicative of a common team dysfunction, that of seeing team as an end in itself rather than a means to an end. An over-concern for good team relationships and dynamics may well subvert the purpose of the team, which is to achieve an external task. The real priority for an effective team is not primarily to get along[31] but rather to get aligned. Such alignment comes about through engagement with the team's purpose, and thus one of the key responsibilities of a team leader is to facilitate such alignment by reminding the team of its core purpose and preventing the team from drifting in terms of its focus.

It is also worth noting that it is the purpose for which the team exists, the task for which it is responsible, rather than any other factor (for example, the length of time someone has served in a particular capacity), that should determine how the team is made up. Populating a team with people who are not primarily focused on the purpose for which the team exists will always undermine that purpose and compromise a team's effectiveness.

### Mutual accountability

One of the defining features of effective teams is that commitment to the common purpose, and to agreed values, modes of operation and other expectations are shared to such an extent that the whole team, as opposed to the team leader alone, shares responsibility for reinforcing and upholding them. Because the team is highly committed to achieving the purposes for which it exists, it will have in place clear structures to facilitate decision-making and procedures that enable the monitoring of agreed actions and desired outcomes, monitoring that is seen as the joint work of all team members. The team leader thus is concerned not so much to control what happens but rather to maintain an environment in which creative inter-action might flourish. If such a leader is ever called to be directive, this will not be in a way whereby she directs the individual work of a team member (unlike the leader of a working group), but rather as a means of focusing the corporate efforts of the team in order to facilitate true collaboration.

## Collaboration and conflict[32]

The joy of working collaboratively is that it usually produces better and more considered results. The challenge of such work is that it often involves working with people who are different – from me and from one another – and conflict will inevitably occur between those who are brought together.

The very possibility of conflict arising between team members is profoundly alarming for many. Indeed, and perhaps this is particularly the case in church contexts, there are a good number of people who assume that any significant level of disagreement between people must inevitably be destructive and wrong, and should thus be guarded against at all costs. This may be, in part at least, a consequence of painful previous experience of personal conflict; it may well stem from a conviction that all conflict is ultimately threatening to or damaging of personal relationships and undermines the unity of the church. A compromise must be found between competing viewpoints in order for peace to be maintained. Such a viewpoint neither understands the complex nature of conflict and its diverse categories nor the vital function it plays in enabling good decisions to be made.

Lederach[33] helpfully distinguishes between three different categories of conflict.

- *Affective conflict* is conflict that is more personality focused, as opposed to ideological or philosophical, and is focused on personal prejudices or preferences. It may well be triggered by character flaws in the protagonists, is nearly always destructive and thus is rightly to be avoided, arrested or resolved. Because constructive forms of conflict can display many similar external hallmarks or features to affective conflict, some find it hard to distinguish between the two and thus categorize all conflict as harmful.

- *Procedural conflict* includes disagreements about factors such as meeting dates and times, the ways in which tasks are assigned, how groups are organized and so on. It is primarily to do with methodology and practical details rather than more fundamental issues. Lederach points out that while conflict of this type can easily be resolved, it has the tendency to be used as a smokescreen for not attending to more substantive issues.

- *Substantive conflict* is conflict around ideas, issues, goals and priorities. Not only is this form of conflict productive, in that it gives collaborators opportunity to consider a range of alternative ideas and scrutinize proposals in the light of a wider body of informed opinion, but it is also, therefore, desirable. As Senge points out:

> Contrary to popular myth, great teams are not characterised by an absence of conflict. The free flow of conflicting ideas is critical for

creative thinking, for discovering new solutions no one individual would have come to on his own ... On the other hand, in mediocre teams either there is an appearance of no conflict on the surface, or there is rigid polarisation. [The former] ... fears the team being torn apart by irreconcilable differences [in the latter] ... everyone knows where everyone else stands and there is little movement.[34]

Lencioni insists that allowing conflict to surface actually saves time for a team.[35] When it is pushed below the surface or ignored, teams find themselves revisiting issues time and time again without resolution. Many will have had personal experience of elders' boards, PCCs or other teams who have endlessly gone round and round the houses debating a particular issue, while the board chair avoids bringing the issue to a concluding decision out of fear of conflict from those who might be opposed, holding out a forlorn hope of unanimity arising for one side or the other. Furthermore, in an environment in which conflict is suppressed, there is a risk that communication becomes less than clear and even dishonest. Fearful of presenting bald facts or opinions that would be interpreted as conflicting with what might be construed as the orthodox line, team members look to find other, more acceptable, though perhaps underhand or covert, ways of advocating for their own position. This is clearly profoundly destructive of any effective team dynamic. When substantive conflict is avoided in this way, protagonists are far more likely to descend into affective forms of conflict as they increasingly identify opposing viewpoints with those who champion them and, unable to challenge those opinions appropriately, begin to challenge those who hold them, either openly or in conversation with other kindred spirits. So vital a part does Lencioni see substantive conflict playing in good decision-making that he insists that, when there is any likelihood of such conflict being suppressed, one team member needs to take on the role of *conflict miner*, one who extracts buried disagreements within the team and sheds the light of day on them.[36] The need for such a person is diminished when the team leader cultivates a team environment in which substantive or ideological conflict is seen as normal. One way to enable this is to establish the habit that whenever a new proposal, paper or similar is brought to the team, it is presented as a conversation starter or first draft to stimulate further thinking, rather than a complete, or almost complete, plan simply to be confirmed. When a team leader is able to present her own ideas in such a fashion, even explicitly inviting competing or alternative opinions, the team begins to regard such an exchange of ideas as normal and unthreatening. It begins to understand the possibility of engaging in robust ideological conflict without this ever degenerating into personal or affective conflict.

One of the consequences of avoiding conflict, according to Lencioni, is that in its absence team members are reluctant to commit to even agreed actions. This may be because they do not have confidence in the decision made and are aware of unspoken opinions and unarticulated evidence, pushed to one side through fear of conflict, which might call the decision into question. Robust ideological conflict serves to promote commitment to action and enables wider ownership of decisions.

## The role of the team leader

Throughout this chapter we have stressed the shared nature of leadership. This being the case, we might well then ask is there a distinctive role for the team (or other group) leader to fulfil? Given our reservations expressed earlier about the possibility of leaderless organizations, our answer to this must be unequivocally affirmative. However, the nature of such leadership will be shaped by the particular requirements of the collaborative functions of teams. Essentially, team leaders avoid the temptation to do the work of teams on behalf of the team, or to act in so instrumental a fashion that the proper scope of the team's work is somehow limited. Rather, they see themselves as cultivators and guardians of an environment in which effective collaborative working is genuinely enabled. MacMillan identifies five different assumptions that form the mindset of an effective team leader:[37]

1 They appreciate the collective brilliance of a team, understanding that the best teams think together. Thus they will always seek to release the corporate imagination of the team and not allow it to be diminished by powerful individuals.
2 They believe in the power of diversity. They are unafraid of difference but seek to channel it productively and will actively seek to cultivate diversity within the make-up of teams.
3 They understand their own leadership to be a role from which to serve rather than a position to be served. They recognize that this service consists in empowering the whole team and each member of it to play its proper part.
4 They see power as something to be released and shared rather than something to hold and control. Their greatest satisfaction is in releasing the creative energy in everyone, and they are not threatened by initiatives of which they are not the author.
5 They understand that teams exist to fulfil tasks, not vice versa. They will always hold before the team the need to pay attention to the work in hand.

With these in mind, we might summarize the role of the team leader under the following titles:

• *Steward.* The leader's role is to cultivate the team, to facilitate its health and vitality, to be the primary (though not sole) guardian of its vision, values and accepted ways of working, and to hold before it its responsibility to fulfil a particular purpose or task.

- *Facilitator*. The leader is there not to accomplish the work of the team, but rather to enable the team to function well together towards the accomplishment of those tasks. The leader is responsible above all to ensure that the tasks are achieved through the coordination of the efforts of the whole team.
- *Coach*. The leader takes responsibility for team development, introducing the whole team and individual members to resources that will enable their own personal development and growth in team practices.
- *Example*. The team will usually take its lead in terms of practice and behaviour from the team leader. Thus it is vital that the team leader sets a positive example, especially in such areas as inviting criticism of ideas, listening to others, showing respect and encouraging contributions. A leader who is in the habit of putting down others or speaking about others behind their backs legitimates such behaviours and invites others to share in them.

There is a reasonably well-known African proverb that suggests that if you want to go fast you should go alone. However, if you want to go far, then you must go together. Collaborative ways of working may well, in the short term at least, slow us down, and it is for this reason that some are reluctant to embark upon them. However, it is for exactly the same reason that so many fail to travel far and end up frustrated both by the amount of work that remains for them to do and for the apparent lack of fruit to show from the work they have undertaken.

## Leadership on the ground

Trinity College Bristol has been training candidates for ordained ministry in the Church of England for almost half a century. Like all similar institutions, its financial viability rests on its capacity to continue to attract healthy numbers of students and to offer training that is seen to be suitable for the demands of mission and ministry in a rapidly changing context. When Emma Ineson was appointed as Principal of the college in 2014 she was under no illusions as to the extent of the challenge facing her.

For a variety of reasons, the college had recently been through a tricky patch. Student numbers had dipped alarmingly, and confidence in Trinity's ability to be a significant evangelical training institution serving the mission of the Church had taken a knock, both within the college community and in the wider Church. Emma understood her major task to be that of restoring proper confidence and increasing student recruitment.

In many ways Emma came as a classic 'outsider-insider'. Having trained for ordained ministry herself at Trinity and, some years later, having spent seven years as a member of the teaching faculty, Emma had a deep understanding of and love for the college, and a good working knowledge of its systems and structures. She knew, and was known by, other staff members, and enjoyed significant trust capital with them. All this meant that, upon taking up her appointment, she could hit the ground running. However, having spent the previous year away from the college and serving in a different role within the Diocese of Bristol, Emma had developed some critical distance from the college and brought a much needed fresh perspective to the issues confronting it. Her sense of apprehension at the size of the task, and at the realization that she had not held so significant a leadership responsibility in any previous role, was tempered by a strong sense of call from God to this position.

## First steps

Emma's first action was to conduct a series of interviews with key people from within the college. She asked them for their own perceptions about the college and about the most pressing issues and challenges facing it. She invited comments about possible responses by asking, 'What would you do first, if you were in my position?' Not only did this give Emma wider insight into some of the issues facing the institution, but also enabled her to establish deeper relationships with key stakeholders. Informed by these conversations, and recognizing the need for a properly informed focus and ordering for the life and mission of the college, Emma set in motion a vision-setting process. A series of focus groups were established among different strategic groupings within the college, including students, staff, faculty, student spouses and trustees. As the responses of the different groups were collated, a clear sense emerged of a college that longed to be forward facing, somewhat audacious and adventurous, and that was summed up in a vision strapline, 'Live like the kingdom is near', which caught the imagination of the existing community and seemed to raise wider interest in the college. Alongside the vision-discernment process, the college employed someone on a short-term contract to lead a major rebranding exercise. This was informed both by the vision process and also by a desire to appeal specifically to a younger constituency of students.

## Strategic actions

Central to the long-term financial viability of the college was the recruitment of students. All other activities had to be focused on this key goal. Emma referred to this goal at every meeting and wrote it at the top of every one of her regular reports to trustees.

Various decisions were made to support the achievement of this goal. Investment was made in the creation of two new roles, a publicity officer and a tutor to develop recruitment among younger ordinands. In the short term this was going to be a stretch financially for the college, but was seen as of strategic importance in the achieving of key goals. The recruitment officer was moved into the same office as the publicity officer, and both were moved into the office next door to Emma's own office, in order to facilitate a sense of synergy between the different roles, enabling good communication and ensuring that all were kept quickly informed of all relevant developments. A new weekly, *School of Leadership*, was instituted in partnership with CPAS as a way of addressing some of the specific needs of leadership training for a younger set of students. Each of these decisions quickly began to pay dividends in terms of student recruitment.

## Deployment of self

One of the most strategic decisions Emma had to take concerned the use of her own limited time. One thing she chose to do was to interview personally every prospective Trinity student so that she could speak with them about the college's vision and begin to get to know them a little before they arrived at college. She sees this as being a vital move, both in terms of encouraging people to choose to study at Trinity and as a way of cementing the vision and enabling people to own it from the earliest stages of their involvement with the college.

Emma also realized that an important part of her own role was that of representing the college to the wider Church and increasing its profile. To this end she accepted all manner of invitations to speak about Trinity in different contexts and places, and offered to sit on various Anglican committees and other bodies, including the Church of England's General Synod. Recognizing the importance of building relationships with those responsible for directing ordinands towards particular training pathways, she very purposefully spent time with bishops and others, becoming an unashamed evangelist for Trinity and for the particular training it offered. All of this meant that Emma had to decline to be involved in other worthwhile initiatives that would have diverted her from the priorities she had agreed for herself with other senior colleagues, and also meant that she did less teaching than she (and possibly some of her colleagues) would have liked.

It is perhaps a mark of Emma's undefended[38] style of leadership that she was always keen to discern how Trinity was perceived by the wider Church and to gain an accurate picture of how the college was truly performing. Interviewees who chose not to study at Trinity were surveyed and invited to offer comments on what they perceived to be strengths and weaknesses of the college. The perspective of others was vitally important as Trinity continued to shape itself to be of most use to the contemporary Church.

## Leadership structures

Emma is an instinctively collaborative leader, who is always ready to give credit for organizational success to those others with whom she works closely, and who recognizes that any leadership team is strengthened by enlisting the contributions of everyone. It was very important for her to establish a collaborative style of leadership from the start of her time as Principal. Taking her lead from Jesus' practice of sharing responsibility with different groups of people (the three, the Twelve, and the 120), Emma identified different groups with whom to share leadership at different levels. Students had, at times in the college's past, been seen principally as recipients of the college's services. Now Emma sought to establish a culture where their views were respected and valued. Students were encouraged to participate in the leadership process, and Emma prioritized meeting weekly with the student president of the college. Emma reorganized the senior management team to be a smaller, more effective unit, and she and the college's Executive Director, Andrew Lucas, intentionally shared senior leadership. Emma identifies one key breakthrough point in the life of the college as coming when that team took the decision to meet to pray together early every Friday morning.

Indeed, one of the striking features of the life of Trinity is the commitment of different groups (senior leadership, faculty and others) to pray together and thus consciously to understand their responsibilities to be spiritual as well as practical.

This collaborative approach extended to the provision of teaching (team teaching was encouraged) and to drawing on the experience of those outside the immediate college staff (all training was made contextual so that every student had the benefit of receiving training from a local vicar as well as from academic theologians).

The fruit of Emma's leadership was seen within months of her starting in her new role with an encouraging increase in admissions for the new academic year. Within two years, numbers of students choosing to study at Trinity were rising exponentially, and by the start of Emma's third full academic year as Principal, Trinity, with well over twice the number of students she had inherited, was now very comfortably the largest residential Anglican theological college.

## Incarnational leadership

On one level, it would not be immediately obvious to a visitor to Trinity, during Emma Ineson's tenure, which member of the college community was actually the Principal. However, the visitor who stayed any length of time would quickly discern that, although leadership was widely dispersed and the whole community energized by a clear and widely shared vision and values, Emma clearly understands the particular representative role of the senior leader. Not only does that leader have the primary responsibility for modelling and championing vision and values, but the leader also needs to emit a sense of positivity and enthusiasm, giving others confidence that vision can be accomplished. For Emma, this modelling extended beyond her public role. It was important to her that she conducted herself, in the unseen areas of her life and ministry, in a way that was consistent with the culture she was seeking to propagate throughout the college. Perhaps no one knew (until now!) that Emma used to go regularly and clean, tidy and hoover the college chapel, for her an important, representative (and very useful) act of service.

Emma was utterly committed to seeing Trinity thrive, and gave herself unreservedly towards that end. Her effectiveness in seeing her goals achieved was in part due to the application with which she approached the task facing her, but at least as much because her own sense of identity and worth was not in that success but rather in her relationship with Jesus Christ. Emma insists that it is important for any leader to think about the person who will ultimately succeed you. If your own leadership has been all about you and your own charisma, then it will be difficult for your successor to match up to you. However, if your focus has been on establishing a healthy organization, set on the values of Christ, then the next person can very easily take that on.

Perhaps it was this conviction that enabled Emma to facilitate the kind of fruitfulness that was not only apparent during her own five-year tenure as Principal but that has continued beyond her incumbency.

## Questions to aid reflection

1 Which are the groups or individuals within your own organization whose contributions and insights might be most in danger of being overlooked or ignored?

2 How intentional are you in terms of setting priorities? What criteria do you use to determine how you might allocate your time and which activities you will undertake?

3 To what extent would you say that there is integration between the public and private spheres of your life? What steps might you take in order to foster greater integration?

4 Are there other specific ways in which your own leadership performance might be enhanced by the adoption of some of the specific disciplines modelled by Emma?

## Notes

1 Gibbs, E., 2005, *Leadership Next*, Leicester: InterVarsity Press, p. 93.

2 Wright, W. C., 2000, *Relational Leadership*, Carlisle: Paternoster Press, p. 50.

3 Our English word is derived from the fusion of two Latin words, *con* and *laborare*, the literal translation of which might be 'working with' or 'working together'.

4 Lawrence, J., 2020, *Leading Well with Others*, Cambridge: Grove Books.

5 Pickard, S., 2009, *Theological Foundations for Collaborative Ministry*, Farnham: Ashgate, p. 144.

6 Pickard, *Theological Foundations for Collaborative Ministry*, p. 143.

7 This is why the New Testament writers in their ethical exhortation have so much to say on matters of relationships and family life, and why instruction on matters to do with the inner life is often given with an eye on the public consequences of inner attitudes and practices.

8 This includes the responsibility to encourage each other and build one another up (1 Thess. 5.11), to stimulate one another to love and good deeds (Heb. 10.24) and to confess sins to one another (James 5.16).

9 Luke 4.18; Matthew 12.28.

10 John 5.19; 12.45; 14.10–11.

11 Pickard, *Theological Foundations for Collaborative Ministry*, p. 232.

12 Grint, K., 2005, *Leadership: Limits and Possibilities*, Basingstoke: Palgrave Macmillan, p. 37.

13 Acts 15.

14 Acts 15.25.

15 The Church of England's formation criteria for those involved in ordained ministry make explicit the need for such ministers to demonstrate competence both in the creation and oversight of collaborative leadership structures and also in the effective supervision of those holding positions of responsibility.

16 Nash, S., Pimlott, J. and Nash, P., 2008, *Skills for Collaborative Ministry*, London: SPCK, p. 3.

17 Three such excellent resources are Nash, S. et al., *Skills for Collaborative Ministry*; Hawkins, P. and Shohet, R., 2012, *Supervision in the Helping Professions*, 4th edn, Maidenhead: Open University Press; Prior, S., 2017, *Effective Line Management in Ministry*, Cambridge: Grove Books.

18 Katzenbach, J. R. and Smith, D. K., 1993, *The Wisdom of Teams*, Boston, MA: Harvard Business School Press.

19 Katzenbach and Smith, *The Wisdom of Teams*, p. 91.

20 Katzenbach and Smith, *The Wisdom of Teams*, p. 45; emphasis added.

21 For example, Pentland, A., 2012, *The New Science of Building Great Teams*, Boston, MA: Harvard Business Review.

22 Pentland, *The New Science of Building Great Teams*.

23 In Hartwig, R. T. and Bird, W., 2015, *Teams that Thrive*, Downers Grove, IL: InterVarsity Press, p. 125.

24 Sample, S. B., 2002, *The Contrarian's Guide to Leadership*, San Francisco, CA: Jossey-Bass, p. 125.

25 Janis, I. L., 1982, *Groupthink: Psychological Studies of Policy Decisions and Fiascoes*, Boston, MA: Houghton Mifflin.

26 Eisenhardt, K. M., Kahwajy, J. L. and Bourgeois, L. J., 1997, 'How Management Teams can have a Good Fight', *Harvard Business Review*, July 1997.

27 Full information about Belbin's theories and a number of resources for exploring and applying them further can be obtained at www.belbin.com/about/belbin-team-roles/.

28 It is worth noting that Belbin did not suggest that teams should therefore be composed of at least nine different people; different team members may fulfil more than one role on a team. Nor is it the case that someone will inevitably fulfil the same role on any team of which they are a member. Team roles are sometimes deter-

mined more by context and the needs of the team, and people may fulfil different roles on different teams.

29 See Figure 3.

30 Hartwig and Bird, *Teams that Thrive*.

31 MacMillan, P., 2001, *The Performance Factor*, Nashville, TN: Broadman and Holman, p. 59.

32 For those wishing to explore in much greater depth appropriate strategies for embracing and navigating conflict, especially in local church situations, the Christian charity Bridge Builders offers a whole range of resources at www.bb ministries.org.uk.

33 Lederach, J. P., 2003, *The Little Book of Conflict Transformation*, Intercourse, PA: GoodBooks.

34 Senge, P., 2006, *The Fifth Discipline: The Art and Practice of the Learning Organisation*, rev. edn, London: Random House, p. 232.

35 Lencioni, P., 2002, *The Five Dysfunctions of a Team*, San Francisco, CA: Jossey-Bass.

36 Lencioni, *The Five Dysfunctions of a Team*, p. 204.

37 MacMillan, *The Performance Factor*, p. 98.

38 Walker, S. P., 2010, *The Undefended Leader*, Carlisle: Piquant Editions.

# 9

# Discerning Direction:
# Leadership and Vision

*Change is the province of leaders. It is the work of leaders to inspire people*
*to do things differently, to struggle against uncertain odds and to persevere*
*towards a misty image of a better future.*[1]

## The inevitability of change

Despite the breadth of, and at times apparently contradictory, definitions
of leadership, there does seem to be one assumption on which leadership
theorists are generally agreed: leadership is concerned substantially with
enabling new and different behaviours. The role of the individual leader
in the change process might be understood variously, but by and large all
would endorse Kouzes and Posner's suggestion that change is the province
of leaders. This is evidenced by the proliferation of leadership literature
over the last 50–60 years and the shift in emphasis from management,
with its focus on present activities, sometimes caricatured as 'doing things
right', to leadership, with its future focus on 'doing the right things'. For
Heifetz and others this shift is significantly due to the pace and nature of
change in contemporary life. Many of the challenges faced by organizations
today are profoundly different from those experienced previously. Simple
management, the deployment of existing insights and knowledge, is not sufficient to address these adaptive problems. What is required is an innovative
approach, enabling the organization to go where it has never gone before.
Leadership is the discipline that is particularly concerned to facilitate this.

Churches and other Christian organizations are by no means immune
to the impact of external or societal change. Faithful imitation of the
example of Christ will always involve faithful contextualization, allowing the unchanging good news to be incarnated in forms and expression
that communicate clearly to contemporary culture. While there will always
be elements of the Christian gospel that are a stumbling block to those
currently outside the Church, it is never appropriate to allow unhelpful
cultural preferences, often associated with nostalgia for a previous era, to
get in the way of people coming to faith in Christ. Churches can never
afford simply to do what they have always done in the hope that society will
accommodate itself to us. They too need help in facing some of their own
adaptive challenges. Perhaps it is awareness of this need that has stimulated

the growth in interest in leadership within the contemporary Church, and a realization that the exercise of leadership is one of the core responsibilities of those who hold office in the Church.

In some ways, churches, of all organizations, ought to be most comfortable with the notion of change and forward movement. In an earlier chapter we noted that the Church is an eschatological society, a people with a unique sense of the trajectory of history towards its fulfilment in Christ. Discontented with our present, sin-spoiled age, we live in the confident hope that God will ultimately act to renew all things. Furthermore, our understanding of the work of Christ, and our experience of the outpouring of the Spirit, convinces us that something of the transformative power of the future has broken, ahead of time, into the present age. Our confident prayer, therefore, as we await the fulfilment of God's purposes, is that God will bring his heavenly rule to bear on earth in fuller measure,[2] effecting change in human lives and situations, bringing them more and more into line with his own will and purposes. Meanwhile, in this interim period, our energies are directed towards seeing the goals and values of that coming kingdom worked out *today* in the spheres of everyday life in which we are involved. Our efforts are fuelled by a conviction that our work towards the establishment of God's kingdom on earth in this present age has an eternal quality and significance, and in some way contributes to the hastening of its consummation.[3] In short, we are all about seeing positive change achieved.

Perhaps this is why journey is such a popular and helpful metaphor for understanding Christian life. It bears witness to the fact that Christian people, Christian churches and Christian organizations must always be on the move, resisting the temptation to settle down in comfortable resting places along the way, striving to see God's kingdom come.[4] This being the case, it follows that one of the key responsibilities of a Christian leader is to encourage and help those for whom they have oversight to keep moving forward. Christian leaders do this, first, by stimulating a church, or other group, to discern what God's specific direction might be for them. In the light of this understanding, leaders, second, enable the members of the group to take suitable action towards the pursuit of this direction and the accomplishment of its associated goals.

## Organizational life cycles

If organizational change is a response to external factors, such as changes within external environments and, for churches, the eschatological direction of history, it is also stimulated by factors internal to the organization itself.

We are very familiar with the notion that living organisms undergo what might be described as a life cycle. The cycle begins with birth, continues with growth and development, and, in due course, the organism comes to maturity and functions at its highest capacity. However, this third phase does not last for ever. Mature organisms eventually begin to decline in both capacity and efficiency, and this decline will ultimately end in death. What is less obvious to us, often because we tend to see organizations in more mechanistic rather than organic ways, is that organizations follow similar life cycles. This can be represented as follows:

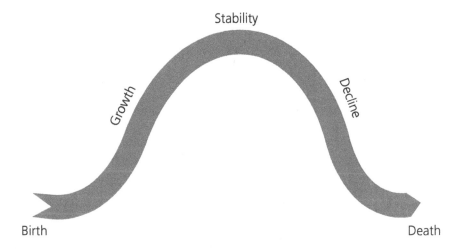

Figure 4. Organizational life cycle

Many of us will have been involved in the launch of new ministries, churches or other initiatives. This birth phase is usually characterized by excitement as something new comes into being, but also by anxiety as the tender new shoot is somewhat vulnerable. As the ministry grows, energy is generated and adaptability is required as things progress in previously unforeseen ways. The transition into maturity or stability is often gradual but this phase represents the ministry or organization functioning at its highest level of effectiveness. Resources have been secured, working practices are established, those involved have gained experience, and threats and challenges can be sustained. The temptation is to assume that we can now breathe a huge sigh of relief in the confidence that things will continue to progress happily ad infinitum, the ministry having gained some momentum and equilibrium. If only life were so straightforward and predictable.

Evidence suggests that, in organizational life, periods of stability and maximum fruitfulness last usually for periods of three to five years. After this, without further intervention, the period of stability will always be followed by one of deepening decline. One reason for this is that the energy and adaptability required to respond to changing internal and external environments, which contributed to fruitfulness in the growth phase, tends to be suppressed by the experience of stability. Furthermore, the experience of fruitfulness breeds resistance to change: why would we even need to contemplate change when things are clearly going so well?

Research undertaken in the commercial world into why successful companies begin to lose momentum suggests that 87 per cent of the reasons for stalls lie within the capacity of companies to pre-empt or address.[5] Although decline is often attributed to factors beyond our immediate control, the research suggests that this is rarely the case. The four principal reasons for stalling were identified in the research as follows (it is worth noting that although this research was conducted within the world of business, churches and voluntary sector organizations are very likely to succumb to similar tendencies):

1 *Complacency, especially surrounding the advantage we hold because of our position or because of our previous experience of success.* It is not uncommon for churches within historic denominations to assume that our privileged status will somehow make us immune from decline. Or it may be that our memory of being fruitful and influential in the past, in the community that we serve, leads us to presume that our current, less hopeful experience, is merely a temporary blip and that normal service will be resumed in due course.

2 *Unwillingness to innovate, and failure to explore opportunities for creativity.* Some organizations, and churches are notable examples of this, are shackled by an inappropriate weddedness to tradition that drives them to focus on preserving the past rather than creating the future. They find it hard to contemplate engaging in anything that has no place within the past history of their church and thus become backward rather than forward facing. In the worst cases, such churches retreat into a nostalgic bubble, congratulating themselves on their faithfulness to the past while managing steady decline. Although we believe it to be vital to hold fast to the tradition we have received, and especially that contained in the Scriptures, we recognize too that the contexts in which this tradition needs to be lived out are constantly changing and that loyalty to the tradition consists in faithful and fresh improvisation rather than simple repetition.

3 *Paralysis in the face of threats and challenges.* Churches seem to have a tendency to assume that changes in society, or in attitudes towards the Christian faith, must inevitably compromise our capacity to sustain fruitfulness in ministry. The assumption is that there is nothing we can do about this, other than to hope that attitudes will one day change again such that the climate becomes more amenable to receiving the witness and ministry of the Church as it currently exists.

4 *Lack of leadership with suitable strategic skills.* Organizations tend to recruit leaders to suit paradigms that are seen as desirable in the present

rather than required for the future. Churches have been notoriously slow in recruiting or developing entrepreneurial leaders with the capacity to help churches improvise ministry and leadership afresh in a changing context. Mercifully, there are signs in the Church of England that this is beginning to change to some extent, but the instinct to recruit those who might represent our best hope of maintaining the status quo is still potent.

These are all, in different ways, symptoms of organizations that have become so comfortable with stability that they have failed to give attention to future progress. The inevitable consequence of this is that the period of stability does not continue unchecked but gradually tails off into decline. Many of us will very likely find ourselves in situations of responsibility for churches that are facing different degrees of decline. Our task will be to initiate appropriate interventions to stimulate new energy and fresh growth. The following model[6] helpfully outlines some different strategies to be deployed according to the particular place within the life cycle at which the organization currently finds itself.

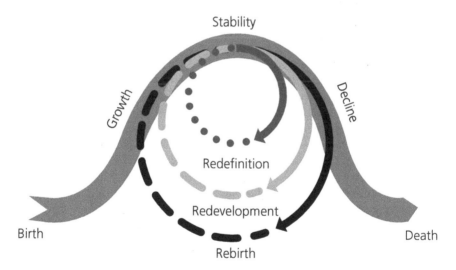

Figure 5. Congregational life cycle

Where a church has become too comfortable with its own status quo, or where the strategies and activities that have served it well in the past now appear to be less fruitful or suitable, then the task of the leader is to facilitate what we might call redefinition. Redefinition implies that the basic vision for the church or ministry is still largely valid, but, in the light of organizational and environmental changes, in the light of positive and negative experiences, successes and failures, the church needs to conduct a thorough review of what it is doing. It may be that this leads to the conclusion that some things need to continue in the same vein, though the review process will mean that these tasks are undertaken with renewed energy and conviction. However, in order for the church to accomplish its goals in the coming season, there may be activities that need to be adjusted or stopped, and new strategies that might need to be adopted.

Redefinition was exactly what was required when I arrived as vicar of All Saints Marple in the autumn of 2001. The church had for several decades enjoyed fruitfulness in its mission and ministry to the community in which it was set. There was reasonable clarity in terms of its vision and values, and the church had a well-formed understanding of its identity and calling, reinforced by a wonderful legacy of effective biblical teaching. However, the church was tired; it had experienced numerical decline and disappointment in its recent history; and it was struggling with the reducing impact of its previously fruitful ministries. The key question facing us was, 'What do we need to do in order more effectively to fulfil our widely owned vision?' The redefinition process took a relatively short time to undertake but resulted in sweeping changes to our structures and activities, our attitude to training and development, and to the ways in which resources were allocated. Over the next four years the church experienced dramatic numerical growth and significant growth in depth of spiritual life and in numbers of people engaging in mission and ministry.

With reference to the organizational cycle, Handy insists that wise organizations should ideally begin to embark on fresh thinking about future initiatives and to contemplate change towards the end of the growth phase and before stability begins to set in (point A in Figure 6).[7] In this way, change is initiated when levels of morale, energy and resources are high. The reality in most organizations is that openness to new thinking often only comes about when an organization is beginning to come to terms with decline following a period of growth and stability (point B in Figure 6). Usually both morale and levels of energy are lower at this point. Moreover, the growing urgency to act in the face of steepening decline may mean that panic measures set in and poorer or less well-considered decisions are taken. Handy's work has been represented (as set out in Figure 6) by what has become known as the sigmoid curve, a process that gives an organization the capacity to sustain growth and development over an extended period of time and to maintain adaptability in the face of ever-changing circumstances.

Rather than succumbing to the perils of stability, Handy's model illustrates a process of repeated redefinition as a proactive step towards continued fruitfulness, rather than as a remedial measure in the face of present decline. One of the principal responsibilities of leadership is to be proactive in holding before the wider organization the requirement to reflect afresh on future direction even when things appear to be going well in the present. Handy does not underestimate the challenges for a leader in seeking to

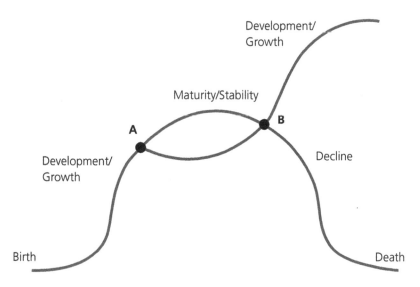

Figure 6. Sigmoid curve

initiate change at point A, observing that the intervening period between the commencement of the process and the growth that follows as a result is often one of confusion and uncertainty as change is embraced.

When a stable or declining organization fails to engage with redefinition, then the inevitable consequence is further decline. What is required in this situation is what might be described as redevelopment.

If redefinition involves finding new ways of fulfilling existing legitimate goals, often by recourse to new information or resources, redevelopment goes rather deeper and involves the discerning of new vision and direction. Redevelopment raises questions about the legitimacy of the activities in which we are engaged, and even about our core purpose as an organization. Emmanuel Church Saltburn, where I served my first incumbency, was not untypical of many more traditional Anglican churches in having maintained, largely unchanged for much of its 125-year history, both a particular style of worship and a particular understanding of what it means to be a parish church. The steady decline experienced in its recent history and the sense of disconnect with its surrounding community were not going to be addressed by simply tweaking the way some things were done. One of the key mind-shifts that needed to take place involved enabling the church to move from a self-understanding that revolved around the preferences of its members to one that was more distinctively missional and that focused on reaching out to the least and the lost within the community. What was to be a lengthy process, lasting several years, began with a PCC awayday in which, through examination of some of the early narratives in the Acts of the Apostles, we sought to build up a picture of how God might imagine his Church. Over the next few months we asked what it might mean for us to replicate in our own church life the key features of life in this early apostolic community. This then became the blueprint that determined what new things we might undertake and what existing practices and activities we might stop doing. Because the changes involved in this process were significantly to do with the culture of the church, these were very painful for many and represented a break with some cherished traditions. Although the process was ultimately very fruitful and resulted in fresh growth and vitality for the church and blessing to the wider community, like most processes of redefinition, progress was slow, especially in the initial stages. The challenge for leaders in these situations is to hold their nerve and to encourage those others who are uncertain of the value of the journey they are undertaking.

In some cases, decline has gone so far, or the imagination of a group has atrophied to such an extent, that redefinition is no longer possible. In this situation what is required is rebirth. It is not that the original aims and objectives of the church or group are necessarily misplaced, but rather that they are now completely incapable of being fulfilled by the group themselves as they currently exist. Something quite new is required.

Rebirth can take a number of different forms. In some cases it will involve enabling the old entity to come to a formal end and to give it a decent burial before launching something entirely new in its place. St Andrew's Church Marple had been planted in the 1980s from All Saints, the parish church, with the aim of reaching people living in a distinct area of the community where levels of social deprivation were higher, and where the parish church had little impact. For the first few years of its existence, St Andrew's enjoyed real fruitfulness and grew significantly. However, with the departure of the curate, under whose leadership it had grown, and other key figures, and with some complexities to do with its leadership team and their relationship with that of the parish church, steady decline began to set in. When I arrived as vicar, the church was roughly one-third the size it had been in its heyday. It had a wonderfully committed, capable, yet exhausted team of leaders whose role had increasingly become that of facilitating worship, teaching and pastoral care for a diminishing number of predominantly elderly church members. Given the determination of this team to see the church's ministry revived, we worked hard together to this end. After 12 months the team reflected that, while their passion for reaching unchurched people in that area of the parish remained undimmed, the resourcing of a separate worship centre with all that this entailed was perhaps no longer the best way of accomplishing those missional aims. Perhaps the best way forward would be to bring St Andrew's to a formal close (after some months of careful preparation we did this with a closing service of thanksgiving for all that God had accomplished through us over the preceding years, and a community barbecue), and to relaunch our ministry in that community with a renewed focus on work in the local school, the launch of some missional cell groups, and other initiatives.

The closure of a relatively informal, though well-established, church plant, meeting in a school cafeteria, might be somewhat easier than that of a church located in a historic building. Nevertheless, in situations where what currently exists hinders the accomplishment of pressing missional purposes, churches need courage to bring terminally declining ministries to a conclusion in order that new things might be brought to birth.

Facilitating appropriate organizational change is thus central to the exercise of leadership. In particular, effective leaders will be concerned to facilitate the discernment of appropriate direction, or vision, for the organization, and to enable all involved to act towards the accomplishment of that vision.

## Discerning direction

Perhaps the single biggest obstacle, within any organization, to forward progress is lack of clarity about the direction of travel. Without a proper sense of where we should be heading, we lack a clear rationale for determining priorities and often end up simply repeating the things we have always done, regardless of whether or not they are still either fruitful or appropriate. Churches can be particularly culpable in this respect. Giving time and energy to discerning future direction can be neglected due to busyness (We'll think of doing it when the immediate pressure of urgent demands decreases), past or current fruitfulness (Why even think of changing something that has produced good results?), fear of being tied down to a specific direction (Isn't it better just to be open to what the Spirit, or circumstances, might bring to us in the future?), or lack of clarity about what our priorities should be, leading to a sense of inertia when it comes to planning. Not a few churches would subscribe to the view that paying attention to the future in this kind of way is not an appropriate activity for a church and is, rather, a practice that is better confined to the corporate world. The kind of visioning process that we are considering in this chapter is dismissed by such churches as unspiritual.

Whatever the reason, neglect in this area will always hinder a church in its mission and ministry and will very likely cause it to miss out on what the Spirit might have in mind for it. The problem is not simply that there is an absence of vision in terms of future direction, it is equally that there may exist a number of implicit or assumed rival visions each held by a range of different people. Although these are often assumed rather than articulated, the variations in expectation around what the church is here for and what activities it should engage in can lead to unhelpful conflict and the dissipation of energy. By contrast, when a church gains a settled understanding of the specific journey on which it is being called by God, over the course of the next few years and months, and when that understanding is widely shared among church members, then the church gains energy and momentum in its progress along that journey. As Senge observes:

If any one idea about leadership has inspired organisations for thousands of years, it's the capacity to hold a shared picture of the future we seek to create. One is hard pressed to think of any organisation that has sustained some measure of greatness in the absence of goals, values and missions that become deeply shared throughout the organisation.[8]

## Defining terms

Although vision is perhaps the term most commonly associated with thinking about the future, churches and organizations tend to use it somewhat loosely to cover a multitude of related ideas. It is also the case that, in order to be able to discern vision or direction, we need first to have found answers to a number of other, related questions. It will probably be helpful, for the sake of clarity, to offer definitions for some of the key concepts associated with the process of discerning direction. The model in Figure 7 is a very helpful guide to the wider vision process.[9]

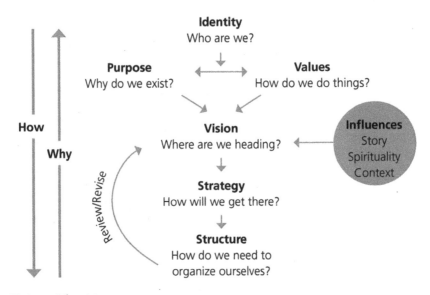

Figure 7. The vision process

## Identity

The direction of travel for a church, or any other organization for that matter, is significantly shaped by the way in which the church understands its own identity. Whereas in the world of commerce, or in the voluntary sector, the question of *who we are* might to an extent be determined by the organization itself, the question of identity for a church is determined by

God. However, the extent to which a local church has understood its true identity is something that needs to be examined. I suspect that if quizzed about this, members of the church where I served my first incumbency, at least at the time of my appointment, might have understood themselves to be a society with shared concern for, and appreciation of, a particular form of worship. It was certainly this concern that determined what activities the church would prioritize and how resources were allocated. One of the first tasks I felt it important to undertake on being appointed was to enable the church members to embrace a more authentically biblical understanding of our corporate identity. I sought to do this by teaching a series of sermons on biblical images of the Church, exploring what it means to be the body of Christ, his contemporary physical representation on earth, the people of God, the bride of Christ, and so on. We also spent some time examining how these self-understandings affected the way in which the earliest church sought to order its life, using this as a pattern for assessing our own corporate life and its faithfulness to God's expectations for his Church. Churches, in my experience, need to be frequently reminded about our true identity in Christ. One of the key leadership responsibilities is continually to refresh the church's memory about who we are.

## Purpose

Purpose answers the question, 'What are we here for', or, 'Why do we exist?' Whereas an organization's vision tends to be somewhat time limited and can change in the light of other external factors, purpose is a far more enduring facet of an organization's being. As is the case with its identity, a church's purpose is also given to it by God. While it might have a specifically local dimension that makes reference, perhaps, to the specific community in which it is located, the Church exists to share with God in the mission of his kingdom on earth. Once again, churches are prone to lose sight of their core purpose, substituting for it a more comfortable and less demanding one, often focused on providing for the pastoral, and other, needs of those who are its members. This is rarely due to a deliberate choice but is rather something into which a church drifts over a period of time. Faithful leaders will continually remind the church of its missional purpose and of the fact that it is constituted by God to be a sign, foretaste and instrument of his kingdom.[10]

## Values

Values are the guiding principles that shape the way in which we undertake all our activities and that determine what attitudes and behaviours are acceptable within an organization. Once again, the answer to the question

'How do we do things?' can, for a church, be answered very simply: we do all things in the way in which Jesus would do them. Values, as we observed in an earlier chapter, usually rest upon a set of shared, though implicit, assumptions or beliefs, and are reinforced by behaviours and practices that are congruent with those assumptions. They are thus, in many ways, more visceral and less accessible to rational investigation than are tenets of identity or purpose. As with other cultural factors in the life of an organization, the leader has a vital role in shaping values through modelling, teaching and reinforcing Christlike behaviours and attitudes. It is not uncommon for churches to develop value statements in which a small number of values in particular are brought to the fore. Although, at one level, such selectivity might be questioned given that there is a requirement that disciples of Christ adopt all the values that he himself both modelled and taught, nevertheless there is some merit in a church highlighting especially those values that it feels are most vulnerable to being neglected, or whose practice enables other values to flourish. For a number of years, one church of which I was vicar emphasized five broad values in particular as a way of intentionally fashioning its life. The first of them ('All involved') emphasized the fact that every single member of the body of Christ is enlisted by Jesus to share in his mission and ministry. This value forced us to consider not only how we provided opportunities for all church members to engage in service, but also how we valued the different contributions of various members, including children, how we encouraged especially those who were most diffident about contributing, and how we ensured that our structures and systems fostered rather than hindered this. The intentional focus on this value in turn resulted in other associated values being practised.

### Vision

A church's vision answers the question, 'What are we called to do, within a particular time frame, and in the light of our unique context, in order to express faithfully our identity, calling and values?' It is well described by Gibbs:

> Vision is the interpretation and application of mission into a specific context. In the church, vision sees, with an eye of faith, the ways that we can turn the Great Commission into a reality. Vision also motivates us, convicting us as Christians to accept our identity as God's agents of change and transformation.[11]

Vision is a picture of God's preferred future for us, which is more attractive and compelling than present reality, and which is both realistic (as opposed to being merely aspirational) and attainable, God being our helper. Vision will always be reasonably specific and will be shaped by a number of local factors. Even though all churches share a common identity and purpose, the contexts in which they are located may vary enormously. An identical, faithful outworking of our identity and purpose may result in a church situated in an urban housing estate, with significant levels of social deprivation, engaging in very different activities from one located in a small, rural village. Every church has a different story: a church of several hundred people will be expected to have a far more extensive vision than one comprising a handful of people. A church that has just given away a group of people and associated resources to plant a new church, or revive a declining one, may well have, for the next season, rather less capacity as compared to a similarly sized church that has recently experienced a significant growth spurt.

Kotter suggests that a good and effective vision will have six characteristics:[12]

### Imaginable

A vision describes what our church will be doing, or what we will look like at some stage in the future. It must be clear enough to be grasped by church members. A vision that lacks clarity will not fire anyone's imagination, and will lead to confusion, thus hindering, rather than stimulating, action.

### Desirable

A desirable vision is one that appeals to the legitimate aspirations of group members. This is not, of course, about pandering to self-interest or balancing the particular preferences of members. The legitimacy of aspirations is significantly determined by reflection on questions to do with identity, purpose and values. Aspirations will thus largely be to do with how we are to live faithfully as the people of God and how we might enable others to encounter him. A good vision gives hope to people that some of their as yet unfulfilled longings, to do with the ministry of the kingdom, might be accomplished.

### Feasible

What distinguishes a vision from an aspirational pipe dream is that it appears to be capable of being achieved, even if this will stretch both our faith and our resources. A vision to reach our entire community for Christ may be noble, but will very likely not spur anyone into meaningful action as its accomplishment is way beyond us. However, a vision to see our church grow numerically by 10 per cent over the course of the next two years may well focus our attention and galvanize us into action, as this, God being our helper, is a realistic and attainable goal.

## Focused

Many vision statements are rendered less than useful by their vagueness. A 'vision' to love God and to love others is clearly not open to challenge in terms of its biblical credentials, and may well be generally inspiring. However, most churches struggle not with convincing their members that loving others is a good thing but rather with identifying specific ways in which they might be called to display that love to others. So a more useful vision might express an intention to extend practical care to those groups in the community who have been identified as being in particular need. A vision to provide support to isolated single parents, to homeless young people or the housebound elderly will be far more effective in motivating people to fulfil the Great Commandment.

## Flexible

Despite having a clear focus, a vision must never become a straitjacket that restricts the capacity of the church and its members to respond to changing or unforeseen circumstances. It is sometimes the case that, while our ultimate destination or goal will not change, the journey involved in reaching that goal may turn out to be different from that which we anticipated. Bonem rightly warns:

> It is a mistake to think that God will unveil a complete plan before starting a process of transformation. Throughout the book of Acts, Paul and other leaders stepped out in faith without knowing where the journey would lead ... I believe that Christian leadership may be filled with even more short-term uncertainty than secular leadership because God wants us to learn to be dependent upon him, not on our own plans, and to demonstrate this dependence to others.[13]

When All Saints Marple set out on the journey of planting a new church in a neighbouring estate of significant social deprivation, one of our primary goals was to build relationships with those in the community. A key part of our vision was about establishing a coffee shop in the shopping precinct on the estate, and to this end we trained a couple of the team members as baristas. Imagine our frustration when, as we were about to move into our shop unit, we were informed that the whole building was now scheduled for demolition in order to make way for a new supermarket. Perhaps partly out of a sense of having let us down, the landlord offered us the use of an alternative building on the estate, which couldn't be used as a coffee shop but could be used for other purposes. The drop-in centre that we subsequently established there was hugely successful and became a significant community hub, in ways in which a coffee shop never could have been. It enabled us to build relationships with groups of people we had previously not imagined as being those whom God was bringing across our path. Without a sense of flexibility, and willingness to improvise a little within the broad parameters of our overarching vision, we may have ended up being thwarted in our overall mission.

## Communicable

For a vision to be widely shared it needs to be capable of being communicated easily, and for a vision to be communicable it needs to be relatively simple to understand. A leader who fails to communicate clearly gives the impression that she does not fully grasp the vision herself and thus undermines, rather than engenders, confidence in it. A vision that is communicable is not only passed on effectively from leaders to others, but is also reinforced as it is rehearsed in conversations between group members.

Those with a particularly visual imagination will perhaps already have seen that the diagram in Figure 7 looks a little like a mobile one might hang from a ceiling. Identity is the point that anchors the mobile and from which is derived purpose and values. These three factors together provide the framework upon which everything else hangs. The mistake that some leaders or organizations make is to seek to form vision without first working to make sure that appropriate answers can be given to the foundational questions to do with identity, purpose and values. Deficiencies in these areas will usually lead to inappropriate or inadequate determinations about future direction for the organization. Even if, by chance, good decisions are made about where we are heading, and about what we are to do, without the supporting rationale and associated impetus provided by sound convictions about identity, purpose and values, it is unlikely that the vision will be sustained. Even more catastrophic is the tendency of some to seek to begin by changing the structures of a church, whether those associated with organization or, more usually, those to do with worship, without first addressing the issues further up the 'mobile' and that give support to those below. In this sense, the two arrows to the left-hand side of the mobile indicate the relationship between the different elements in the mobile. Answers to questions about *why* we are engaging in this particular activity are provided by the supporting elements above. So rationale for this particular way of organizing ourselves is given by reference to the strategy we have chosen to adopt and that requires this structure for its accomplishment. The rationale for this strategy is provided by the requirements of the vision we have embraced, and so on. Answers to questions about *how* we will accomplish what we have determined are provided by going down the mobile. The question of how we will see our vision move from the realm of an aspirational idea to that of accomplishment is answered by devising a strategy suitable for the vision's implementation.

How that strategy is to be accomplished is determined by the construction of structures that will enable rather than hinder this.

## What vision contributes

We have already hinted at some of the ways in which a clear vision benefits any organization. These are some of the most obvious contributions it makes.

### 1 Sets direction

Vision has sometimes been likened to a compass; it gives an indication of the direction of travel we are to follow towards our desired destination. As Shawchuck and Heuser observe:

> The congregation's corporate vision becomes a path where there is no pathway; it brings clarity where there is obscurity and provides the impetus to keep going no matter how formidable the roadblocks ... it lifts people to new realisations of possibilities, it generates enthusiasm and power, it aligns the thoughts, emotions and actions of people in pursuit of a common and compelling purpose.[14]

Not only does it help us start out on the journey but it also helps us to hold our course steady when we face challenges and distractions. As Senge notes, 'Without a pull toward some goal which people truly want to achieve, the forces in support of the status quo can be overwhelming.'[15] A clear vision keeps us from wandering aimlessly in the hope that we might stumble upon some method of achieving our goals. It also rescues us from the dangerous tendency some have of jumping on the latest bandwagon or slavishly copying the practices of other, apparently successful, churches without thought as to their suitability for us.

### 2 Generates hope

Because a vision is a picture of a different future that is attainable, it has the capacity to bring hope and encouragement to those who have previously felt that their aspirations were out of reach. One of the clearest biblical examples of this is described in the book of Nehemiah.

Perhaps the lowest point in the history of God's people, Israel, was the period of 70 years they spent in exile in Babylon, a consequence of their disobedience towards God. Their city of Jerusalem and its glorious Temple, a sign of God's holy presence on earth, lay in ruins. Apparently forsaken by God, it seemed to Israel that God's calling upon them to be a light to other nations had now been forfeited. The period of exile came to an abrupt end when Babylon was in turn conquered by the armies of the Persian emperor Cyrus. Under this new regime, previously displaced peoples were encouraged to return to their native lands. Israel headed back to Jerusalem to rebuild their city, full of confidence that God was renewing his purposes for them.

The tribes who had, during the previous 70 years, occupied the area surrounding Jerusalem, and their leaders in particular, were rather less enthusiastic about the return of Israel to the land. Israel's initial hopes of a new beginning were soundly dashed when these local rulers opposed their attempts to rebuild the city walls of Jerusalem, through threats of violence and by enlisting the political support of the Persian authorities. The people of Jerusalem were condemned to live among the rubble of their ruined walls, longing for restoration but with no expectation that this might come to pass.

Nehemiah, at this time, was a high-ranking servant in the Persian emperor's court. Upon hearing news of the sorry plight of the returned exiles, Nehemiah is overcome with emotion. After a lengthy period of prayer and fasting he manages to secure his master's permission to go himself to Jerusalem, ultimately to serve there as governor, with resources to rebuild the city. With reference to our earlier discussion, we might suggest that, for Nehemiah, it would be inconceivable that Israel could inhabit their identity as God's people and their divine purpose, to be a sign of God's living presence on earth, in the absence of a rebuilt Jerusalem.

Nehemiah's rallying speech to the dispirited people of Jerusalem is reported in the briefest of terms.[16] He is profoundly realistic about the situation facing the people, describing the full extent of the damage to the city walls. However, it seems that he offers a vision for rebuilding in which the efforts of every group in Jerusalem society might be coordinated. No doubt he taps into a forgotten sense of the calling and destiny of Israel, and gives an account of the dramatic ways in which he has already experienced God's favour in his planning. The impact of his speech is profound. The people want to start rebuilding straight away. Hope is rekindled and fresh energy rises up. The coming days and weeks were full of challenge and of significant threats from Israel's opponents. Nevertheless, in the remarkably short period of 52 days, through the coordinated efforts of the whole population from the least to the greatest, the work was completed and the wall and its gates entirely restored. As Gibbs notes, 'In the midst of chaos leaders provide vision that rises beyond present circumstances that threaten to overwhelm and capsize the movement. Such vision provides a sense of purpose, resilience and exuberance.'[17]

### 3 Provides clarity

A coherent vision clarifies what we are planning to do and how we will go about it, but also clarifies what we are not going to do. Such a vision enables an organization to maintain focus and to resist the temptation to be side-tracked by less consequential matters. It guides the organization in terms of how resources might be allocated and people deployed. Senge draws attention to the anxiety that is often felt in organizations when change is contemplated.[18] This is especially the case when such change appears to threaten some of the cherished cultural artefacts of any organization. A clear vision, he suggests, sets parameters to the scope of the intended change. The proposed change is thus seen as purposeful and, by identifying those aspects of organizational life that are not to be changed, reassurance is provided.

### 4 Creates ownership

Individual members of a church may well have privately entertained hopes and dreams about the birth of new ministries or the development of particular initiatives, but have never acted on them, or even shared them, because they had no idea as to how these dreams might be realized or because they seemed so unlikely to succeed. A shared vision that is properly articulated has the capacity not only to draw support from such people, as it taps into their particular concerns, but also to engage others and to enlist their active support. Senge observes:

> A shared vision is not an idea but rather a force in people's hearts, a force of impressive power. It may be inspired by an idea but once it goes further – if it is compelling enough to acquire the support of more than one person – then it is no longer an abstraction. It is palpable. People begin to see it as if it exists. Few if any forces in human affairs are as powerful as shared vision.[19]

Although, as we will see, leaders do not have the sole responsibility for creating vision, the role of leader in constantly articulating the vision and commending it to others is critical. As Kouzes and Posner suggest:

> Leaders need to get others to see the exciting future possibilities. They breathe life into visions. They communicate hopes and dreams so that others clearly understand and share them as their own. They show others how their values and interests will be served by the long-term vision of the future.[20]

## How vision is discerned

The discernment of direction or vision comes about through a process that can well be described as one of threefold listening: to God, to our context and to other people.

Few of those who might go down in Christian history as visionary figures would ever have regarded themselves as original or creative thinkers. Most seem to describe themselves as simply operating under God's direction and seeking to fulfil his will. Jesus himself insisted that he did nothing on his own initiative but had come, rather, to do the will of the Father.[21] Nehemiah describes some of his actions as being the consequence of what God put into his heart to do.[22] The vision that Moses communicates to the Hebrew slaves in Egypt, and throughout their wilderness wanderings, of what it means to be a people uniquely belonging to God, inhabiting a land currently occupied by hostile, pagan tribes, and of being a means of blessing to all the peoples on earth, is not one that he has dreamed up himself but rather one that God has imprinted upon his heart and imagination. Because the whole of life matters to God, those who exercise influence in any way, in any sphere of life, will always be concerned to discern God's specific will and purpose for their workplace, church, ministry, community or family, in this particular season. Often this is discerned as we reflect afresh on the biblical narrative and specifically in relation to those fundamental questions to do with identity, purpose and values. Vision is often discerned as we ponder what a faithful improvisation around God's unchanging narrative might look like in our present situation.

On one PCC awayday, as a means of initiating a process of redefinition, I asked those gathered to imagine that Jesus had moved into our community six months previously. We then broke into groups and spent the rest of the morning asking what he had been doing for the last six months, where, and with whom. It was a simple but very effective way of exercising our corporate imagination as to what the body of Christ ought to be prioritizing in this community, based on what we knew about Jesus' practice and the needs of our community. Richard Niebuhr once observed that 'The great Christian revolutions came not by the discovery of something that was not known before. They happen when someone takes radically something that was always there.'[23]

Vision is never abstract or disembodied, nor should it ever be an off-the-peg replication of what someone else has done to good effect in some other place. Vision is always specific to the context out of which it arises, emerging out of an imagining of that context in the light of God's story. When Nehemiah came to Jerusalem, fired by a longing to see God's purposes for his people re-established and his city restored, before he contemplated addressing the disheartened inhabitants of the city, he undertook a clandestine survey of the city walls in order to get a proper understanding of the nature of the task ahead.[24] When he subsequently addressed the local community and their leaders, he was able to offer a vision that was both informed and realistic. Each of these qualities is vital to the success of any vision. A vision needs to be properly informed in order to be seen as a viable way of addressing needs and issues that are regarded as of importance to the wider group. Equally a vision needs to be realistic if it is to be credible. For a vision to be realistic it must take seriously, rather than minimize or ignore, the challenges it seeks to address. Holding out false hopes and minimizing threats serves as a disincentive to engagement with vision[25] and is demotivating to people. By contrast, facing up to the realities of the situation may well provide the incentive to pursue a vision that offers the hope of a solution to those challenges. In his research into the failure of change initiatives, Kotter identifies eight principal errors to which organizations succumb and which prevent change from being achieved.[26] The first of these he identifies as complacency in the face of challenge. This complacency militates against organizations pursuing change as a matter of necessity. Kotter insists that to overcome this, leaders need to create a sense of urgency. They do this by highlighting the seriousness of current challenges, thus creating impetus for change. Nehemiah begins his vision casting by referring to 'the bad situation we are in'.[27]

'Inspecting the walls' will involve contemporary leaders in gathering as much information about our own contexts as possible. A wealth of research-based information about our communities is usually freely available from statutory bodies, shedding light on demographics, social need and so on. In my previous parish we found it illuminating to conduct door-to-door questionnaires from time to time in different parts of our community, in which we invited comment on, among other things, perceptions about local need and the role of the church in the community. Conversation with organizations such as local schools, GP surgeries, police and other community groups is often a fruitful way of gaining a more informed picture of local issues and concerns. At the same time, church members must be given opportunity to contribute their own insights into the church's local context and current priorities and opportunities. Once a year we asked members of our midweek 'Lifegroups' to give time and space to reflect together on what new initiatives we felt God might be asking us to consider. Any ideas that a group felt might have validity were fed back to the church leadership team for fuller consideration. Some of our most significant new initiatives were birthed this way. They were dreamed of by those who, because of their own life place, saw particular needs or situations to which others might have been oblivious.

This third aspect of listening, listening to others, is vital for two reasons. First, as noted already, it enables the vision process to possess wider scope as it embraces insights and reflections not available to those at the centre of the organization. Second, engaging others in the process at an early stage creates commitment to the vision itself: people are always more likely to feel greater ownership of a vision in whose formation they have been invited to play some part. As Senge notes:

> The practice of shared vision involves the skills of unearthing shared 'pictures of the future' that foster genuine commitment and enrolment rather than compliance. In mastering this discipline, leaders learn the counterproductiveness of trying to dictate a vision, no matter how heartfelt.[28]

This thinking runs somewhat counter to that advocated in some of the literature, both from the world of business and that of church leadership, and which tends to elevate the role of the CEO, or senior church leader, as the originator of vision. It is certainly the case that the leader is called to be the catalyst for the formation of vision, ensuring that churches pay regular attention to forming and refreshing vision. The leader is also called to be the principal advocate for and champion of the agreed vision, taking responsibility for its clear and constant communication so that it is widely understood and acted out by the whole church. Bennis and Nanus point out:

> It usually turns out that the vision did not originate with the leader personally, but rather from others. The leader may have been the one who chose the image from those available, articulated it, gave it form and legitimacy, and focused attention on it, but the leader only rarely was the one who conceived the vision in the first place.[29]

With this in mind, one of the most frequently asked questions concerns which groups of people should be involved in this process of vision formation and in what particular ways. We have found the model in Figure 8 helpful in offering a rationale for differing levels of involvement in the vision process.[30]

The essential point that the model affirms is that a person's level of involvement in the vision-forming process should be commensurate with their perceived level of commitment to the organization. The model suggests that we might think in terms of five categories of people. In a local church, the category into which people fit will be determined to an extent by the size of the church; in smaller churches a higher proportion of church members will find themselves exercising higher levels of involvement in the more advanced stages of the vision process.

The first group of people with the lowest level of commitment to the life of the church can simply be told what the vision is. This group will include fringe members, occasional worshippers and others whose involvement in the life and ministry of the church is partial or uncertain. It may well be the case that these are people who have little expectation of being involved in shaping the trajectory of the church's life and are happy to receive vision formed by responsible others.

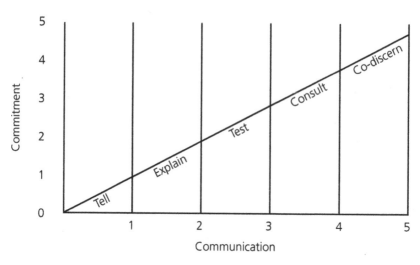

Figure 8. Levels of involvement

The second category might well involve more regular worshippers, members of small groups and those who make regular financial gifts or otherwise clearly identify as members of the church. In a larger church this will include quite a number of church members. In a smaller church, there may be very few people who fall into this category as those who are clearly committed to the church also have particular responsibilities entrusted to them and thus fit into different categories higher up this scale. Those in this second group are not content simply to be told what the vision is but need to be 'enrolled' into embracing the vision. The leader thus needs to explain the vision carefully to them, offering a clear rationale for proposed actions and seeking to demonstrate how their own appropriate aspirations might be met by this vision. The goal of the explanation process is not simply to gain grudging compliance but a level of enthusiasm for the vision whereby those enthused begin to share a sense of responsibility for its accomplishment. This process may well be a discursive one that offers people opportunity to question and otherwise engage with the vision. I have often found it helpful, when in the process of explaining a vision, to offer opportunity for church members to discuss proposals with me either in the context of informal, mid-sized meetings or personal appointments. The task of explaining the rationale for a particular vision is an ongoing one. Wise leaders will continually draw attention to the agreed direction of travel and to the rationale for it, repeatedly underlining its importance to the church or organization.

Simple explanation of the vision will not, however, be sufficient for those whose perceived level of commitment is higher. This category of people will include, for example, those who exercise oversight of areas of ministry and small-group leaders. In a larger church this group might include PCC members or deacons. In a much smaller church, where everyone understands themselves to be a key stakeholder, this might include the whole congregation. In order to gain commitment, vision needs to be tested with this group of people. Testing is a process in which a proposed vision is offered for scrutiny before being released more widely. Those who are invited to test the vision would usually be those who are most directly affected by its ramifications. So before launching a radical new restructuring of small groups, a strategy dreamed up by the church leadership team after feedback and encouragement from small-group leaders, the new proposals were presented to those same small-group leaders in draft form. This group of people were invited to comment on them, point out shortcomings and potential difficulties and offer suggestions for improvement. When changes to patterns of Sunday worship were mooted by the PCC of that same church, the whole congregation (who would have seen themselves as key stakeholders in this) were given opportunity to complete a detailed questionnaire in which preferences could be expressed on some of the details to do with the proposed changes, and other comments offered, including suggestions for improving the proposed scheme. Although not all suggestions could necessarily be acted upon, all were considered, and the fact that all those with a significant stake in the outcome had been enlisted in its *testing* meant that the new scheme was embraced enthusiastically.

The consulting phase of the vision process is conducted with those who, by virtue of their position or level of responsibility, are regarded as meriting involvement in the early stages of vision formation. In a smaller or mid-sized church this will include the PCC; in a larger church the staff team or heads of ministry areas. This is the phase of the process in which we are seeking together to form a vision that will enable us to address those issues that are agreed to be most pressing for us. While it is always appropriate to give people from across the organization opportunity to contribute to vision thinking (for example, as mentioned earlier, by inviting reflections from small-group members that might then be fed into the wider process), in the consulting phase all such contributions are weighed and the draft vision is formulated for wider testing. In a previous parish, one such consultation process was initiated at the conclusion of a year that had been spent reviewing purpose and values, and in which there had been significant changes to the church's leadership team. Prior to spending a day away together, the new team were each asked to write a letter to a former colleague who had recently moved on. The letter was dated five years in the future, and people were asked to describe, to our former colleague, some of the key things that had taken place in the life of the church in the intervening years since his departure. As the letters were read out at the awayday, a picture was gradually built up of what the immediate future of the church might look like. Different ideas were weighed and further refined, or in some cases dismissed, and out of the day a draft vision document emerged, which was then further tested by the PCC, before becoming the foundation for our activities for the next season in the church's life. The advantage of engaging in such a process with an appropriate and reasonably small group of people is that it stimulates proper creativity and also enables fuller consideration to be given to ideas that might otherwise be dismissed as fanciful or inappropriate.

The fifth category of people will always be the smallest group within the process. These are those who are responsible for co-discerning with the leader the direction of travel. If consulting involves finding an appropriate response to challenges and opportunities, co-discerning is more about identifying what those challenges are in the first place. Other senior staff, churchwardens, elders and those in similar positions of leadership will be those with whom we instinctively co-discern. In many ways this group sets the agenda and defines the areas of permission within which others will operate.

This model is helpful in suggesting how different groups of people might be appropriately engaged in the vision process. One of the reasons for the failure of such processes is often the failure of the leader to engage people in appropriate ways, often by communicating with them at a level that is not commensurate to their perceived level of commitment. So a leader who simply tells other staff or PCC members what the vision is that she has dreamed up should not be surprised to encounter resistance towards that vision from those who feel that their role merits some contribution to the formation of the vision. A forceful leader may eventually obtain compliance with an imposed vision but will rarely secure the commitment that is required for that vision to succeed and be fruitful. As Kouzes and Posner wisely observe:

> Too often leaders assume that it is their sole responsibility to be the visionaries ... Leaders are expected to be forward-looking, but not expected to impose their vision of the future on others ... People want to view themselves in the picture of the future that the leader is painting. The key task for leaders is inspiring a shared vision, not selling their own idiosyncratic view of the world. What this requires is finding common ground among those people who have to implement the vision ... This means that you can't adopt the view that visions came from the top down. You have to start engaging others in a collective dialogue about the future, not delivering a monologue.[31]

Wise leaders understand their calling to be catalysts who enable churches and other organizations to respond to God's summons to press on with him. They take seriously their calling to coordinate and facilitate the efforts of their people to discern and formulate a compelling vision for the future. They understand their role as champions and communicators of the vision that has been discerned, tested and embraced corporately by the whole church, realizing that effective communication is the key to enabling others to act upon that vision. Such leaders also cultivate a proper humility before God, recognizing the limitations of their own human wisdom and seeking to encourage a continual openness and responsiveness to the leading of God's Spirit.

Carefully planned strategies will only get us so far in understanding God's way forward. This is not to diminish their importance in any way. Christian leaders have a God given responsibility to use their power of reason, imagination and intellect. But the experience of God's people again and again has been that it is God's surprises rather than their own plans that open up the future in remarkable ways ... God is a God of life and growth, and growth is irregular and unpredictable, but also irrepressible and thrillingly beautiful. If things point in one direction, but God seems to be leading somewhere else, our advice is go for God every time.[32]

---

## Leadership on the ground

St George's Church has been serving the community of Everton, Liverpool, for more than two centuries. It is known locally as the Iron Church, due to its unique, cast-iron interior framework, and when Kate Wharton was appointed as the church's new minister in March 2009 both church and community were facing huge uncertainty.

The Church Urban Fund data for that year identified St George's parish as the fifth poorest of all 12,760 parishes in England, highlighting numerous significant social challenges for the area. The worshipping congregation at St George's had declined significantly during the previous five years, a consequence in part of a very lengthy vacancy followed by the very short incumbency of Kate's predecessor. Around 25 faithful people gathered for worship each Sunday morning, with a further handful of elderly people attending a traditional evening service. Just managing to hold on, and with very little hope of anyone else being willing to come to serve as incumbent, the shrinking congregation had begun to face the possibility that, once numbers fell below 20 at the morning service, it might be time to close the church. The building itself was in a poor state of repair; half a million pounds would be required to repair the dilapidated roof and to prevent the waterfalls that cascaded into the building at times of heavy rain.

Having served a curacy in a similarly challenging inner urban parish, Kate's call to St George's Everton began to grow in her even before the church became vacant. Under no illusion concerning the size of the task facing her, it was this overwhelming sense of vocation, and a confidence in God's faithfulness, that fuelled Kate's enthusiasm and excitement for the work ahead. Recognizing the poverty of resources to hand, as she prayed for her new church, Kate had a strong sense of God saying that the people whom he would use to build his church in Everton were not yet there. While praying that God might quickly provide some 'scaffolding' for the work, a few people who knew what they were doing and who might be able to contribute to ministry activities fairly quickly, Kate also realized that those 'not yet there' would be largely those not yet belonging to Christ and yet to be reached for him.

Kate's overriding concern from the outset was to enable a more positive and kingdom-orientated culture to form within St George's. Although she did not set out with a clear blueprint for the future of St George's, over the preceding years, through observation of and engagement with other friends in church leadership and through her involvement with the New Wine Network of churches, Kate had come to some settled convictions as to what were some of the practices that were both signs of healthy church culture but that also contributed to its formation. Indeed, perhaps one of the reasons for Kate's effectiveness during her years in Everton can be attributed to the clarity of these convictions and her resolution in holding on to them and being guided by them, even if she had less clarity as to how they might be worked out. She speaks of always knowing where she wanted to go even if she had less idea as to how to get there. At the outset of her time in Everton, Kate wrote down a list of around 30 activities that she felt were essential signs of church health. These ranged from the fairly obvious (including organize proper preparation for those seeking baptism or marriage, introduce a time in each service when the presence of the Spirit is welcomed, initiate formal times of corporate prayer), the widely espoused (set up a network of small groups with a focus on empowering people for mission, develop links with the local schools and take assemblies there), to the less obvious (have an annual PCC awayday, establish an informal midweek group at the vicarage in order to grow the spiritual life of the church).

## Encountering God

Kate's longing was for people within the church family and beyond to encounter something more of the transforming presence and power of

God. As well as instituting the weekly 'Open to God' vicarage group, where people could experience Spirit-led worship (using a worship DVD), engage with Scripture in a meaningful way, and grow in experience and practice of prayer ministry, Kate set about changing Sunday worship. Her aim was that this should be both a place where there was an expectation of meeting with God and also somewhere that was welcoming and accessible to newcomers. The very limited resources available to her restricted the scope of what was going to be possible, but Kate realized that worship that was both more visual and more informal might be more culturally appropriate. The introduction of regular interviews and the reporting of testimonies (people were invited to comment on 'Where have you seen God's fingerprints this week?'), and encouragement to the congregation to share prophetic words, pictures and other insights, led to a far more interactive feel to worship and much fuller engagement, with 'ordinary' people sensing for the first time that they had a role to play in the church's ministry.

Kate recognized that Sunday evenings could be used more profitably for activities that might build up and resource the life of the church. The small evening congregation, though initially resistant, were eventually persuaded by Kate that their traditional service might be moved to an early morning slot. Sunday evenings were now available for Alpha courses, informal prayer gatherings and other training events. At the same time, Kate looked for opportunities to take church members to local New Wine celebration and training events as a way of enlarging their expectation and experience of what was possible with God, and of planting a vision of what St George's itself could look like.

## Growing leaders

Longing to see local people play a full part in the leadership of the church, and convinced that God's Spirit equips every member of the church for ministry, Kate nevertheless faced some significant challenges as she sought to develop other people. Most of those in the community, because of factors to do with personal background and life experiences, lacked any confidence in their own capacity to serve in any way. Kate's first task was to encourage others to share her own conviction that every life is capable of being redeemed and restored by God. She looked for those who demonstrated what she saw as particular potential and then, gradually, began to entrust them with leadership responsibility, setting appropriate expectations for them and offering a good deal of support.

A number of those who ultimately emerged as leaders first came to Kate's attention as they attended Alpha courses. Of the three people, all with some previous involvement with St George's, who attended the first Alpha course Kate led, one went on to lead a newly formed prayer ministry team and eventually became a Reader. Kate was disappointed by the next Alpha course. None of the several people who had signed up came along to the first meeting. This one-to-one course proved to be very fruitful, however. The solitary attendee came to faith, experienced release from longstanding issues to do with addiction, and ultimately became one of the key lay leaders in the church.

Much of the leadership formation was undertaken on a one-to-one basis as each emerging leader had their own unique formation needs. One resource that proved to be useful as a group exercise, however, was the SHAPE course.[33] Through reflection on the spiritual gifts, passions, experiences and other dimensions of participants' lives, the course enables people to discern, with others, those areas of service to which they are most suited and for which they are best shaped. Running this course built up those who took part and was a catalyst for the establishment of new missional ministries, including 'Signpost', a weekly drop-in for coffee, advice and skills training.

Kate also looked for externally resourced activities that might provide training opportunities for church members. Engaging in the diocesan child-friendly church award provided a context in which church members might reflect on aspects of their own leadership practice and became a useful tool for leadership development.

Kate was willing to take risks with a number of people, fully understanding that some would thrive and some would not. While fully prepared to live with initial failure, and always willing to allow people to progress at their own pace, she was not prepared to tolerate behaviour that was destructive or damaging towards other people. Gradually a culture was emerging in which people were honoured and all were enabled to thrive.

## Building community

If people were to be added to the church, the church community had to be one that was attractive and to which others wanted to belong. As well as paying attention to the attractional qualities of Sunday worship, Kate initiated a number of regular social events, mainly held at the vicarage, there being no other suitable public space, including 'Fireworks and Food', a Light Party (as an alternative to Halloween), an Easter egg hunt, and other fun events for all ages. These were publicized through the local school, with whom ever stronger links were being developed and which Kate saw as a gateway into the wider community. An annual holiday club was organized in conjunction with the school, and the school community began to come into church for worship every Wednesday. As the church grew in confidence in its calling, they began to take their place more intentionally at the heart of the community, organizing street parties in celebration of the Queen's Diamond Jubilee, events to tie in with the Paralympic Games and, in conjunction with English Heritage and a local historian and author, local history days at which the story of the church and its surrounding community was told. Increasingly, more and more of those who had been contacted through occasional offices, or those who had simply wandered in off the street out of curiosity or looking for help, stayed connected with St George's and joined the worshipping family.

## Self-sustenance

Ministry in inner-city areas is demanding for all manner of reasons, not least because of the challenge of living in an isolated vicarage that is not infrequently the target of vandals. Kate Wharton is a remarkably resilient leader. This is in no small part the consequence of paying serious attention to personal formation. Throughout her time in Everton, Kate made sure that she took advantage of opportunities for personal resourcing through her involvement with the New Wine Network, enrolling on the Arrow Leadership programme,[34] and by seeking spiritual direction and mentoring. A lifelong learner, she looked for opportunities to gain from the experience of others in similar contexts and who shared similar spiritual ambitions and aspirations, and for inspiration from those whose context might be different but from whose example she might learn. Kate has always recognized the wisdom of seeking out trusted friends who might offer advice, personal care and prayer support, acknowledging that ministry and leadership is never a solitary activity but always undertaken in fellowship with others.

### Leaving well

By the time Kate left Everton, after eight years as vicar of St George's, she left behind a church community that now encompassed over 100 people. Planning very intentionally for the season that would follow her moving on, Kate began to gather a nascent team of those who held responsibility for key areas of ministry and to prepare them for leading the church in the future. The challenges of inner-city ministry never diminish. However, St George's Everton seems today to be facing them more hopefully, and with more developed leadership resources, than do many similar churches.

## Questions to aid reflection

1  Of all the various strategies that Kate deployed in order to move St George's forward, are there particular ones that might be helpfully replicated or adapted for use in your own context?

2  Kate came to her new position with a number of settled convictions about what a healthy church might look like. What do you think might be the strengths and weaknesses of such an approach?

3  What might we learn from Kate's example about growing and developing a work in a context so seriously lacking in resources?

## Notes

1 Kouzes, J. and Posner, B., 2012, *The Leadership Challenge*, 5th edn, San Francisco, CA: Jossey-Bass, p. 1.

2 Matthew 6.10.

3 It seems likely that it was convictions such as these that formed the basis of Jesus' instructions to his first followers in the period between his resurrection and ascension (Acts 1.3) as he prepared them for the work of proclaiming the presence of God's kingdom to the ends of the earth.

4 1 Timothy 4.10.

5 Olsen, M. S., Van Bever, D. and Verry, S., 2008, 'When Growth Stalls', *Harvard Business Review*, March 2008.

6 The original provenance of this model is, we think, The Episcopal Church of the USA.

7 Handy, C., 1995, *The Empty Raincoat*, London: Random House, chapter 3.

8 Senge, P., 2006, *The Fifth Discipline: The Art and Practice of the Learning Organisation*, rev. edn, London: Random House, p. 9.

9 I am grateful to my CPAS colleague James Lawrence, who originally crafted this model.

10 Newbigin, L., 1953, *The Household of God*, London: SCM Press.

11 Gibbs, E., 2005, *Leadership Next*, Leicester: InterVarsity Press, p. 133.

12 Kotter, J. P., 2012, *Leading Change*, Boston, MA: Harvard Business Review Press, p. 74.

13 Bonem, M., 2012, *In Pursuit of Great and Godly Leadership*, San Francisco, CA: Jossey-Bass, p. 197.

14 Shawchuck, N. and Heuser, R., 1993, *Leading the Congregation*, Nashville, TN: Abingdon Press, p. 140.

15 Senge, *The Fifth Discipline*, rev. edn, p. 195.

16 Nehemiah 2.17–18.

17 Gibbs, *Leadership Next*, p. 59.

18 Senge, *The Fifth Discipline*, rev. edn, p. 335.

19 Senge, *The Fifth Discipline*, rev. edn, p. 192.

20 Kouzes and Posner, *The Leadership Challenge*, p. 100.

21 John 6.38.

22 Nehemiah 7.5.

23 Quoted in Hirsch, A. and Catchim, T., 2012, *The Permanent Revolution*, San Francisco, CA: Jossey-Bass, p. 97.

24 Nehemiah 2.11–12.

25 Collins, J., 2001, *Good to Great*, London: Random House, p. 74.

26 Kotter, *Leading Change*, pp. 37–52.

27 Nehemiah 2.17.

28 Senge, *The Fifth Discipline*, rev. edn, p. 9.

29 Bennis, W. and Nanus, B., 2007, *Leaders: Strategies for Taking Charge*, 2nd edn, New York: HarperCollins, p. 88.

30 This is a further development of a model outlined in Senge, P. et al., 1994, *The Fifth Discipline Fieldbook*, London: Nicholas Brealey Publishing, pp. 312–28.

31 Kouzes and Posner, *The Leadership Challenge*, p. 116.

32 Booker, M. and Ireland, M., 2003, *Evangelism – Which Way Now?*, London: Church House Publishing, p. 188.

33 Although originating from Saddleback Church in Southern California (further information about this resource from Saddleback Church can be found at https:// saddlebackchurch.teachable.com/p/understandingshape), a number of versions of this course are now available, revised in order to fit better within a British context. Kate used that offered by the Diocese of Carlisle. It is available at www.cumbria christianlearning.org.uk/shape-2018 (accessed 25 November 2019).

34 Arrow is a leadership formation process for younger leaders, run in the UK under the auspices of CPAS. Further details may be found at www.cpas.org.uk/ events-and-programmes/equipping-leaders/arrow-leadership-programme.

# The Spirituality of Christian Leadership

*The first act of Jesus' ministry recorded by Mark shows him identifying with the people. The second shows him receiving an anointing by the Spirit for his work. Incarnation and anointing are both vital aspects of Christian service. One shows how we must be committed to people whilst the other shows how we must derive our strength from God. Sometimes people recognised as 'Spirit-filled' are insensitive to culture and to human need and their ministries suffer as a result. But a more serious problem is when people who wisely identify with people and adopt the right methods are nevertheless not spiritually powerful because they rely more on their methods than on the Spirit's power.*[1]

One of our aims in the preceding chapters has been to bridge the gap that sometimes exists between sacred and secular leadership theory. With the caveat that leadership is inevitably contextual and teleological (shaped by the purpose of the host organization), we have sought to demonstrate that many leadership insights that originate from secular contexts are perfectly consistent with Christian leadership understanding and praxis. This being the case, as a way of drawing together our leadership reflections it may be appropriate to ask: In what ways might Christian leadership be distinct from any other exercise of leadership? Is Christian leadership merely secular leadership informed by a different set of values, or is there more to its distinctiveness? Are there ways in which leadership is conceived and undertaken differently by those who inhabit, and are shaped by, an authentically Christian spirituality? The answer to these questions, we suggest, is to be found in considering the motivation for, and goal of, Christian leadership, and the particular manner in which it is undertaken and resourced.

## Miletus: Spring AD 57

Towards the conclusion of his third missionary journey, hastening from Greece, via Asia Minor, to Jerusalem, in the hope of arriving there in time for the feast of Pentecost in May, the apostle Paul meets at Miletus, for the last time, with the elders of the Ephesian church. This has been a church with which he has enjoyed a deep and relatively unproblematic relationship. His farewell to them is an emotional one for both parties. In many ways, Luke's account of Paul's farewell speech[2] represents the passing of the apostolic baton from Paul not simply to the group who are assuming responsibility for the Ephesian church but to those leaders, raised up by Paul, who would now take oversight of the wider Christian community. In a passage strikingly resonant with the teachings we encounter in the Pauline epistles, Luke summarizes Paul's leadership in a way that, almost more than any other biblical passage, gives us a blueprint for an authentically Christian understanding of leadership. As we conclude our own exploration of the key elements of Christian leadership, we will use some of Paul's statements in this passage as a summary.

## A gift from God

The pivot around which this whole passage revolves appears to be verse 24. Paul explains that his only ambition is to complete the course God has set for him and to fulfil the ministry 'which I received from the Lord Jesus'. Perhaps what most distinguishes Christian leadership from any other form of leadership is the understanding that it is received from God as a gift. Leadership undertaken in any context is, for the Christian, a vocation, a sacred trust from God.

For Paul, this sense of vocation was that which gave impetus to his life and leadership. In a similarly autobiographical passage he explains to the Philippian Christians that it is the surpassing worth of knowing Christ, and of being called by him, that gives him the motivation to keep pressing on, despite challenges, uncertainties and difficulties, to 'lay hold of that for which also I was laid hold of by Christ Jesus'.[3] This historic sense of being called by Christ is reiterated as a daily reality through the work of the indwelling Spirit, who directs Paul in a compelling way.[4] Understanding that we have been called to belong to God, and that as a consequence every aspect of our life, including work, family, relationships, leisure and church membership, is to be lived as a vocational activity, invests the whole of life with a sense of purpose and responsibility. Every aspect of life is seen as something that matters to God and in which he longs to be intimately involved. When it comes to leadership, people may assume responsibility for many different reasons, some noble and altruistic, others less so. However, for the Christian, over and beyond any other reason, is a conviction that God has called me to take on this role, and that in doing so I am in some way sharing with him in his oversight of my company, church, group or organization. Indeed, because my fundamental commitment is to seek his will and surrender every aspect of my life to the leading of his Spirit, that which determines what I will do, and what I will decline to do, is not any concern for material gain self-aggrandisement or any other form of self-ambition but rather a concern to please and obey him. Because our responsibility is towards God, Christian leaders understand that we are first and foremost accountable to him for the way in which we discharge what is entrusted to us. Any sense of accountability towards others, whether those whom we manage, company shareholders, those who benefit in other ways from the activities of our organization, church members or other stakeholders, is eclipsed by this greater sense of accountability to God.

The understanding of leadership as a gift from God, and the concomitant sense of accountability towards him, leads to a number of other consequences for leadership and the way in which we exercise it.

## Humility

Perhaps in contrast to some of the false apostles and other purportedly spiritual leaders with whom he had to contend in some of the churches, Paul is adamant that he has always sought to conduct himself with humility (*tapeinophrosunē*) in his dealings with the Ephesians. Words of this group are frequently used in the New Testament to denote an attitude that is pleasing to God because it implies a proper understanding of our true position before him. It is the disposition of Mary that leads to her being raised up by God as an acceptable servant,[5] is used by Jesus to describe his own submissiveness to God,[6] and is regarded by Paul[7] as that quality that led to Jesus' willingness to suffer crucifixion and death out of obedience to God's will. By extension, words of this group also imply a willingness to serve others, as opposed to lording it over them. Such humility, or meekness, does not imply powerlessness. Rather, it sets the appropriate context in which power might be exercised. As MacManus observes:

> To be meek is to have controlled strength ... We cannot be entrusted with authority over others if we cannot be trusted to live under the authority of others. That's one reason why children who are never taught to honour and submit to their parents make such poor adults.[8]

Christian leaders understand that their power and authority come from God. It is given for the blessing and flourishing of others and must never be subverted for other, selfish purposes. It is as we submit to his authority, and conduct ourselves in an attitude of appropriate humility towards him, that we are enabled to be truly fruitful and powerful in accomplishing his work.

## Kingdom-focus

We have referenced on more than one occasion the contextual nature of Christian leadership. The broad context in which all Christian leadership is exercised is the arena of this world in which God is at work to bring in his kingdom. It is an appreciation of this wider context that informs our understanding of Christian leadership no matter what the specific outworking of it might be. Paul's understanding that in Jesus God had acted definitively to inaugurate his end-time kingdom in this age, thereby turning back the tide of sin and evil that had engulfed and spoiled God's good creation, gave shape to everything he did. The ministry he received from Christ (Acts 20.24) was to testify to the gospel of God's kingdom. He insists that he never shrank from teaching anything that was profitable about this kingdom, urging people to respond appropriately in repentance and faith (vv. 20–21), as he sought to remind people (v. 27) of the whole purpose of God.

The kingdom, or rule, of God might be described as what life looks like when God is ordering things. It is a realm in which those far from God are invited to be reconciled to him, where the sick are healed and those in spiritual or material bondage are set free, where God's justice prevails and where human injustice is overcome. In short, it is a realm in which those created in God's image flourish and prosper in relationship with their Creator.

These kingdom values are helpfully reflected, as a manifesto for the Church, in the Five Marks of Mission, adopted in the closing years of the last century by the Anglican Communion:

- To proclaim the Good News of the Kingdom
- To teach, baptize and nurture new believers
- To respond to human need by loving service
- To transform unjust structures of society, to challenge violence of every kind and to pursue peace and reconciliation
- To strive to safeguard the integrity of creation and sustain and renew the life of the earth.

Together these declarations set something of an agenda for the Church and its activities as we seek faithfully to work with God for the growth of his kingdom. We might reasonably expect them to be explicit in the different aspects of the life of local churches, and they provide a schema within which those exercising leadership in the Church might operate. However, they also give something of a framework for understanding the goals to which Christian leadership might address itself in any and every context. Opportunities for overt proclamation of the gospel might be excluded from many workplaces and other contexts, in some cases through legislation. Similarly, the baptism and discipling of new believers may not be something that might naturally take place on the factory floor. However, Christian leaders will still be concerned to conduct themselves, and to lead in such a way, that these missional aims might be furthered rather than thwarted. The way we treat other people has the capacity to speak eloquently of a God who is concerned for them and who values them. A Christian employer, or manager of others, can work hard to ensure that employees and staff are treated with dignity, are fairly remunerated for their labour, and their various contributions to the organization properly affirmed and recognized. The way we model Christian values and practices can be an enormous encouragement to those who are setting out on the path of discipleship themselves as we offer an example to follow. Albert Schweitzer once observed, 'One other thing stirs me when I look back at my youthful days, the fact that so many people gave me something or were something to me without knowing it.'

Christian leaders understand that the activities in which they are involved, such as the employment of others, or oversight of the provision of services for the benefit of others, are not activities that are morally neutral or somehow removed from God's concern. Every human affair is important to him. Therefore, one good question that every leader might ask themselves, no matter what their level of responsibility, is, 'How might I exercise my own leadership in a way whereby the purposes of God's kingdom are advanced?'

## Perseverance

Leadership, when undertaken conscientiously, is always demanding and often costly to the person exercising it. Quite apart from the sense of responsibility for other people and for their well-being, which can at times be overwhelming, Christian leaders understand that the progress of God's kingdom is not uncontested. Those who stand with and for God are more than likely to experience challenges and opposition of both human and spiritual origin. So Paul is keen to remind the Ephesian elders of the trials, hostile scheming on the part of Jewish authorities, and the tears that were a constant accompaniment to his ministry (Acts 20.19). These themes are expounded much more fully in Paul's second letter to the church at Corinth. Here he describes opposition from various quarters during his ministry in Ephesus, persecution experienced generally as the normal backdrop to his ministry, as well as some of the denigration of his own ministry arising from certain quarters within the Corinthian church. In a remarkably honest letter, Paul admits to almost being crushed by the extent of the difficulties he faced, describing his experience as being 'burdened excessively, beyond our strength, so that we despaired even of life'.[9] The reason Paul gives for being able to stay the course and to be sustained in his leadership is that the ministry he fulfils is one he has received through God's mercy. Therefore, he insists, 'we do not lose heart'.[10]

Leadership is a demanding activity. One of the things that gives me great cause for concern is the number of younger church leaders who are withdrawing from local church leadership in order to pursue other ministries or occupations. In conversation with some of them it seems that one of the reasons many give for seeking a move out of church leadership is that the role is simply more demanding than they had realized. In the hardest times I have experienced in church leadership, the apostle Paul, and especially his Corinthian correspondence, has been the greatest encouragement to press on. The understanding that our call is from God becomes an imperative to persevere that transcends the struggles and challenges of the present time. It is this understanding that has provided the impetus for many of the celebrated heroes of the faith in times past, and an infinitely greater number of completely unknown, though no less significant in God's eyes, faithful Christian leaders. Their only desire was to finish the course set before them by God. This is the goal of all Christian leadership and thus becomes its key to perseverance no matter what challenges it faces.

## Integrity

Paul is at pains to remind the Ephesians that he never sought to use his own leadership as something from which to profit personally. He insists that he never coveted any person's material possessions, nor sought to be remunerated for his ministry among the Ephesians. Indeed, he engaged in manual labour as a way of sustaining not only himself but also those who were serving as his co-labourers in the work of the gospel.[11] Although elsewhere in the New Testament Paul upholds the principle that it is appropriate that those who serve the Lord should be properly maintained so as to be able to discharge their responsibilities unhindered (even though he chose not to benefit from such provision himself), what he seems to have in mind here is using a leadership position for selfish or inappropriate gain.[12]

The industrialist Sir John Laing (1879–1978) presided for many years over his family's firm, Laing Construction. A deeply committed Christian, Laing always regarded his chairmanship as a stewardship entrusted to him by God. Long before the advent of the welfare state, Laing ensured that his workers received an adequate wage, that they were given paid holidays and sick leave, and that working conditions were safe and fair. Despite the multi-million-pound turnover of the company, Laing chose to pay himself a modest salary (it is said that on his death the total value of his personal possessions amounted to less than £1,000), preferring to give away as much of the company profit as possible to Christian charities.

Laing's attitude, sadly, stands in sharp contrast to that of many others throughout human history. The Old Testament prophets frequently berate God's people for the ways in which they tolerate the injustice of the powerful who exploit their position to gain materially while the powerless are consigned to poverty.[13] In recent decades in the UK, the gap between rich and poor has increased alarmingly. A 2018 report by the Institute for Public Policy Research (IPPR) Commission on Economic Justice[14] revealed that there is now a sixfold difference between the income of the top 20 per cent of households and that of the bottom 20 per cent. More than one-fifth of all households are now judged to be below the poverty line, even though most of those households are in work, and one in three children are deemed to live in poverty. Forty-four per cent of the UK's wealth is owned by just 10 per cent of the population, five times the total wealth owned by the poorest half. Even though levels of remuneration may legitimately be set by company boards, if these privilege the powerful to the detriment of others, then those who collude in such practices may well be guilty of coveting material possessions that ought properly to belong to others. Christian leaders will not only refuse to enter into such collusion, but integrity requires them to do all within their power to ensure that those for whom they are responsible are adequately provided for in a manner that accords with God's understanding of justice.

Of course, our capacity to benefit financially from our leadership, especially if that leadership is undertaken in the sphere of the Church, may be very limited. However, there are other ways in which we can fall into the trap of using our position for personal gain. For some, holding position in and of itself satisfies an unmet need within us. We are hungry for status and the recognition it brings, whether in our own eyes or in those of followers. Our motives for seeking leadership position and for holding on to it means that our capacity to discharge that leadership with integrity is compromised. We are more concerned to maintain our status, or to secure the affirmation and approval of others, than we are always to do what God might require of us. Worse still, we can become threatened by, and grow jealous of, the success of others to the extent that we become reluctant to see others develop and grow, out of fear that they might outshine us. All of these temptations are significantly diminished when we understand our leadership to be a gift that we hold at God's pleasure until asked to lay it down, and when we come to realize that God values and affirms us not on the basis of our accomplishments or achievements but rather because we are found in Christ. As Walker so helpfully explains:

> It seems to me that what I need to be free as a leader is to be loved. My problem is that I am insecure; I have unmet needs; needs for approval, status, affirmation, success. As long as I have these unmet needs, I will use people around me, including those I lead, to meet my needs. How can I be set free? The answer lies in being secured by a loving, unconditional, gracious and yet directional relationship in which my needs are met.[15]

Conducting ourselves as leaders with integrity becomes more possible when we lead from a position of security in Christ, rather than as a means to obtain some form of security through the exercise of that leadership.

One of the great contrasts in leadership described in Scripture is that between the first two kings of Israel, Saul and David. Saul is a complex and flawed figure beset by a host of personal insecurities. Facing the first major crisis of his reign, Saul finds it impossible to trust in God's promises to act on behalf of his people, and acts in a way that is tantamount to trying to force God's hand, taking upon himself responsibility that properly belongs to God.[16] It is because of this act of disobedience, which indicates that Saul is not truly a person 'after God's own heart', that God determines to replace him with a more reliable leader. The subsequent acts of Saul's reign represent a downward spiral into self-destruction as he increasingly exercises his monarchy in a self-seeking and self-reliant fashion. He treats lightly the specific instructions given him by God and is relatively unconcerned about pursuing God's will, choosing instead a course of action that holds out the promise of personal material benefit.[17] Far from seeking God's honour, Saul becomes concerned more about his own status in the eyes of others, drawing attention to himself by erecting a monument to his achievements.[18] Worst of all, obsessed with holding on to power and establishing his own dynasty through his son Jonathan, Saul is jealous of the success of David, his erstwhile servant now perceived as a rival, and seeks to kill him.[19] Despite a dramatic call from God to his leadership role, and significant experiences of God's anointing and equipping, Saul very quickly loses any sense of leadership as being a gift from God and regards it far more as a personal possession.

David, on the other hand, at least during the first half of his career, stands as an example of what leadership looks like when exercised as a gift from God. David's trust in God to fulfil his purposes is first evidenced by his attitude towards his showdown with the Philistine champion Goliath.[20] Concern for God's honour, and confidence in God's ability to keep his promises, means that David declines the offer of borrowed armour (representing reliance on natural resources) and goes out in the knowledge that 'the battle is the LORD's'.[21] Later, when faced with opportunity to kill his persecutor Saul, and thereby to step into his own calling as the new king of Israel,[22] David refuses to take matters into his own hands and to accomplish God's purposes by inappropriate means. Even when, ultimately, he has enjoyed considerable success as the ruler of Israel, and when the kingdom is finally established, David's concern is to erect an appropriate sign to the glory of God rather than a monument to his own glory.[23] His prayer of thanksgiving is a glorious expression of gratitude to God for his favour,[24] an acknowledgement that it is God who has accomplished the success of Israel rather than David, and continuing trust in God to work through David for the blessing of the people.

## Succession planning

What is most striking about the assembly at Miletus is that, in gathering these leaders together, Paul is completing the process of planning for succession, which he began in the early stages of his ministry in Ephesus. He entrusts to them the responsibility he himself has held for overseeing the Ephesian church[25] and commends them to God's grace for their future leadership (Acts 20.32). Paul is far less concerned about holding a particular leadership position than he is about securing the long-term health of the work he has initiated. Having led many of these elders to Christ, discipled and nurtured them and given them a vision for ministry and leadership, he is now delighted to entrust his own responsibility fully to them.

One of the leadership emphases that stands out in each of the leaders who form the subjects of case studies included in this book is their commitment either to raise up and release successors or to enable good succession to take place. Each seem more concerned for the ongoing vitality of their organization than for their own reputation. When we see leadership as a gift from God, and ourselves as stewards, we will find it easier to see ourselves merely as temporary custodians of our sphere of leadership responsibility, and to see that part of this responsibility involves doing whatever lies within our capacity to enable positive leadership beyond our own incumbency.[26]

## The strength that God supplies

In highlighting some of the virtues integral to Christian leadership, we are not implying that these are the sole preserve of those who are Christians. Because every exercise of leadership is a sharing in a responsibility entrusted to the human race by God, any leadership has the capacity to manifest those virtues and qualities that reflect the image of God in humankind. Moreover, Christian leaders do not have a monopoly on virtues like perseverance or even integrity; the same qualities may well be demonstrated even more powerfully by other leaders, though on the basis of a different motivation. What we are saying is that these virtues are integral to Christian leadership, and without them leadership may not properly be described as Christian. We are also suggesting that, for the Christian, these qualities are not innate or natural, but rather arise in response to the call of God and as a result of the operation of his Spirit in the life of the believer. This leads us to the second principal distinctive of Christian leadership, which is to do with the manner in which it is resourced.

In an earlier chapter we drew attention to the charismatic nature of Christian leadership whereby leadership is understood as an outworking (*energēmatōn*)[27] of the indwelling Spirit through the life of a believer. Both Old and New Testaments are full of examples of relatively ordinary people, none of whom might ever have aspired to leadership on the basis of their own natural abilities or qualities, and yet who were used powerfully by God and exercised significant influence for him. The astonishment of the Jerusalem Council at the eloquence and confidence of Peter and John, who have been summoned to answer before them, is palpable as they understand that these are simple, uneducated and untrained fishermen.[28] Luke's delightfully pregnant comment that 'they began to recognise them as having been with Jesus' indicates where the source of their power and competence lay. Christian leaders understand that their capacity to undertake that which has been entrusted to them, the wisdom and courage and all other qualities they require, is to be found in God and in the power of his Spirit. Our understanding of what might be possible for us and for our organization is determined not simply by virtue of what resources, material and other, we currently have at our disposal. Rather, our expectation and ambition is shaped by our confidence in God's capacity to provide all that is needed to accomplish what he has called us to undertake. One of the key responsibilities of a Christian leader is not only to lead out of faith in God, rather than fear of failure, but equally to enable others to share such confidence.

Given that Christian leadership is a gift from God and a sharing in his grace, it becomes clear that if we wish to grow in our leadership capacity, as well as apply ourselves to honing leadership skills and competencies, we must even more apply ourselves to grow in our walk with God. This seems to be the lesson that Jesus is keen to impress upon the first disciples. Their frustration at their own lack of capacity to cast out a demon from a young man leads them to question Jesus about this.[29] His reply that this kind 'does not go out except by prayer and fasting' is not to advocate a particular exorcism technique as yet unknown to the disciples. Jesus has just released the young man through a simple word of command. It seems that what he is commending here is the regular practice of prayer and fasting as a means to grow in closeness with God and in consecration to his will. Those who consecrate themselves to God have, he suggests, access to deeper resources in him. This is of a piece with some of the final instructions Jesus passes on to those same disciples on the evening of his betrayal. In a purple passage of Scripture, Jesus declares himself to be the true vine (by deploying this ancient symbol describing God's people Israel Jesus is identifying himself as the epicentre of God's purposes on earth, and his followers as sharing significantly in the furtherance of those purposes) and likens his followers to branches within the vine.[30] The secret to any branch becoming fruitful is that it remain (older and more poetic translations prefer the word 'abide') within the vine. Fruitfulness in leadership, as in any other activity, is directly linked to remaining close to Christ so that we draw on the resources only available to those who cultivate such closeness.

We began our exploration of leadership by commenting on the widespread desire for leadership that we see expressed in so many different spheres of contemporary life. Our journey has ended with a reflection on the kind of leadership that the world most needs. This is leadership that is inspired and shaped by God, that has a concern for human flourishing at its heart, that is empowered by the Holy Spirit, and that is undertaken in close partnership with Jesus Christ. Our prayer is that this authentically Christian leadership might be more widely and more intentionally practised by those Christians who lead in all manner of different contexts, and that it might increasingly become the pattern to which all leadership conforms.

## Notes

1 Fernando, A., 2002, *Jesus Driven Ministry*, Leicester: InterVarsity Press, p. 29.

2 Acts 20.17–35.

3 Philippians 3.12.

4 Acts 20.22.

5 Luke 1.48.

6 Matthew 11.29.

7 Philippians 2.3.

8 MacManus, E. R., 2003, *Uprising*, Nashville, TN: Thomas Nelson, p. 60.

9 2 Corinthians 1.8.

10 2 Corinthians 4.1.

11 Acts 20.33–34.

12 1 Corinthians 9.7–14.

13 Isaiah 1.23; Amos 8.4–6; Micah 6.11–12.

14 The Institute for Public Policy Research Centre for Economic Justice, *Prosperity and Justice: The Final Report of the IPPR Commission on Economic Justice*, www.ippr.org/cej/reports/.

15 Walker, S. P., 2005, *Subversive Leadership*, Oxford: The Leadership Community, p. 91.

16 1 Samuel 13.8ff.

17 1 Samuel 15.1–9.

18 1 Samuel 15.12.

19 1 Samuel 18.10–17.

20 1 Samuel 17.

21 1 Samuel 17.47.

22 1 Samuel 24.

23 2 Samuel 7.

24 2 Samuel 7.18ff.

25 Acts 20.28.

26 For a more detailed discussion of ideas to do with succession planning, see Parkinson, I., 2017, *Enabling Succession*, Cambridge: Grove Books.

27 1 Corinthians 12.6.

28 Acts 4.13.

29 Matthew 17.14–21.

30 John 15.1–17.

# References and Further Reading

Adair, J., 2001, *The Leadership of Jesus*, Norwich: Canterbury Press.

Adair, J., 2005, *How to Grow Leaders*, London: Kogan Page.

Advisory Council for the Church's Ministry, 1987, *Education for the Church's Ministry: The Report of the Working Party on Assessment*, London: ACCM.

Allen, R., 2006, *The Spontaneous Expansion of the Church – And the Causes which Hinder It*, Cambridge: Lutterworth Press.

Allen, R., 2011, *Missionary Methods: St Paul's or Ours*, Mansfield Centre, CT: Martino Publishing.

Alvesson, M., 2013, *Understanding Organisational Culture*, 2nd edn, London: Sage.

Ancona, D., Malone, T. W., Orlikowski, W. J. and Senge, P., 2007, 'In Praise of the Incomplete Leader', *Harvard Business Review*, February 2007.

Avis, P., 2015, *Becoming a Bishop: A Theological Handbook of Episcopal Ministry*, London: Bloomsbury.

Banks, R., 1994, *Paul's Idea of Community*, Peabody, MA: Hendrickson.

Banks, R. and Ledbetter, B. M., 2004, *Reviewing Leadership*, Grand Rapids, MI: Baker.

Barth, K., 1975 [1936], *Church Dogmatics 1/1*, trans. G. Bromiley, Edinburgh: T & T Clark.

Barth, M., 1974, *Ephesians: Introduction, Translation and Commentary on Chapters 4–6*, Anchor Bible Commentary, vol. 34a, New York: Doubleday.

Bass, B. M., 1985, *Leadership and Performance beyond Expectations*, New York: Free Press.

Bass, B. M., 1998, 'The Ethics of Transformational Leadership', in Ciulla, J. (ed.), *Ethics: The Heart of Leadership*, Westport, CT: Praeger, pp. 169–92.

Bass, B. M., 2008, *The Bass Handbook of Leadership*, 4th edn, New York: The Free Press.

Bass, B. M. and Avolio, B. J. (eds), 1994, *Improving Organizational Effectiveness through Transformational Leadership*, Thousand Oaks, CA: Sage.

Bass, B. M. and Riggio, R. E., 2006, *Transformational Leadership*, 2nd edn, Mahwah, NJ: Psychology Press.

Beeley, C. A., 2012, *Leading God's People*, Grand Rapids, MI: Eerdmans.

Bennis, W. and Nanus, B., 2007, *Leaders: Strategies for Taking Charge*, 2nd edn, New York: HarperCollins.

Beyer, H. W., 'διακονεω, διακονια διακονος', in Kittel, G. (ed.), 1964, *Theological Dictionary of the New Testament*, vol. 2, Grand Rapids, MI: Eerdmans, pp. 81–93.

Blake, R. R. and Mouton, J. S., 1964, *The Managerial Grid*, Houston, TX: Gulf Publishing.

Bolden, R., 2004, *What is Leadership?*, Leadership South West Research Report, Exeter, www.leadershipsouthwest.com.

Bonem, M., 2012, *In Pursuit of Great and Godly Leadership*, San Francisco, CA: Jossey-Bass.

Booker, M. and Ireland, M., 2003, *Evangelism – Which Way Now?*, London: Church House Publishing.

Boyatzis, R. and McKee, A., 2005, *Resonant Leadership*, Boston, MA: Harvard Business School Press.

Bruce, F. F., 1961, *The Epistle to the Ephesians*, London: Pickering and Inglis.

Burns, J. MacGregor, 1978, *Leadership*, New York: Harper and Row.

Cain, S., 'Not Leadership Material? Good. The World needs Followers', *New York Times*, 24 March 2017.

Caird, G. B., 1976, *Paul's Letters from Prison*, Oxford: Oxford University Press.

Campbell, R. A., 1994, *The Elders: Seniority within Earliest Christianity*, Edinburgh: T & T Clark.

Carey, G., 1986, 'Reflections Upon the Nature of Ministry and Priesthood in the Light of the LIMA Report', *Anvil* 3(1).

Carroll, L., 2015 [1872], *Alice's Adventures in Wonderland and Through the Looking Glass*, London: Penguin.

Chand, S., 2010, *Cracking Your Church's Culture Code*, San Francisco, CA: Jossey-Bass.

Clarke, A. D., 2008, *A Pauline Theology of Church Leadership*, London: T & T Clark.

Clapp, R., 1996, *A Peculiar People*, Downers Grove, IL: Inter Varsity Press USA.

Coenen, L., 'ἐπισκοπος, πρεσβυτερος', in Brown, C. (ed.), 1975, *New International Dictionary of New Testament Theology*, vol. 1, Exeter: Paternoster Press, pp. 188–201.

Cole, N., 2009, *Organic Leadership*, Grand Rapids, MI: Baker.

Collins, J., 2001, *Good to Great*, London: Random House.

Collins, J. N., 1990, *Diakonia: Re-interpreting the Ancient Sources*, Oxford: Oxford University Press.

Cottrell, S., 2009, *Hit the Ground Kneeling*, London: Church House Publishing.

Croft, S., 2016, *The Gift of Leadership*, Norwich: Canterbury Press.

Dansereau, F., Graen, G. B. and Haga, W., 1975, 'A Vertical Dyad Linkage Approach to Leadership in Formal Organisations', *Organizational Behavior and Human Performance* 13, pp. 46–78.

De Rond, M., 2012, *There Is an I in Team*, Boston, MA: Harvard Business Review Press.

Dugan, John P., 2017, *Leadership Theory: Cultivating Critical Perspectives*, San Francisco, CA: Jossey-Bass.

Dunn, J., 1995, *The Effective Leader*, Eastbourne: Kingsway.

Dunn, J. D. G., 1975, *Jesus and the Spirit*, London: SCM Press.

Dunn, J. D. G., 2003, *The Theology of Paul the Apostle*, London: Bloomsbury.

Eichrodt, W., 1970, *Ezekiel*, London: SCM Press.

Eisenhardt, K. M., Kahwajy, J. L. and Bourgeois, L. J., 1997, 'How Management Teams can have a Good Fight', *Harvard Business Review*, July 1997.

Faier, E., 'Is Leadership Greater than the Sum of Its Parts?', unpublished manuscript, c. June 2002.

Faith and Order Commission of the Church of England, 2015, Senior Church Leadership, Archbishops' Council.

Ferguson, A. and Moritz, M., 2016, Leading, London: Hodder & Stoughton.

Fernando, A., 2002, Jesus Driven Ministry, Leicester: InterVarsity Press.

Georgi, D., 1987, The Opponents of Paul in Second Corinthians, Edinburgh: T & T Clark.

Gibbs, E., 2005, Leadership Next, Leicester: InterVarsity Press.

Gill, R., 2011, Theory and Practice of Leadership, London: Sage.

Goethals, G. R. and Sorenson, G. L. J. (eds), 2006, The Quest for a General Theory of Leadership, Cheltenham: Edward Elgar.

Goffee, R. and Jones, G., 2006, Why Should Anyone be Led by You?, Boston, MA: Harvard Business School Press.

Goleman, D., Boyatzis, R. and McKee, A., 2004, Primal Leadership: Learning to Lead with Emotional Intelligence, Boston, MA: Harvard Business School Press.

Greene, M., 2014, Fruitfulness on the Frontline, Nottingham: InterVarsity Press.

Greenleaf, R. K., 2002, Servant Leadership: A Journey into the Nature of Legitimate Power and Greatness, 25th anniversary edn, New York: Paulist Press.

Greenwood, R., 1995, Transforming Priesthood, London: SPCK.

Greenwood, R., 2009, Parish Priests for the Sake of the Kingdom, London: SPCK.

Grint, K. (ed.), 1997, Leadership: Classical, Contemporary and Critical Approaches, Oxford: Oxford University Press.

Grint, K., 2005, Leadership: Limits and Possibilities, Basingstoke: Palgrave Macmillan.

Handy, C., 1995, The Empty Raincoat, London: Random House.

Harris, J., 'Where's Jeremy Corbyn? Lost in a Rose-tinted Vision of Labour's Past', The Guardian, 25 June 2018.

Hawkins, P. and Shohet, R., 2012, Supervision in the Helping Professions, 4th edn, Maidenhead: Open University Press.

Heifetz, R., 1994, Leadership without Easy Answers, Cambridge, MA: The Belknap Press of Harvard University Press.

Heifetz, R. A. and Linsky, M., 2002, Leadership on the Line, Boston, MA: Harvard Business School Press.

Hersey, P. and Blanchard, K. H., 1993, Management of Organizational Behavior: Utilizing Human Resources, 6th edn, Englewood Cliffs, NJ: Prentice Hall.

Hess, K., 'διακονεω', in Brown, C. (ed.), 1975, New International Dictionary of New Testament Theology, vol. 3, Exeter: Paternoster Press, pp. 544–9.

Hirsch, A. and Catchim, T., 2012, The Permanent Revolution, San Francisco, CA: Jossey-Bass.

Hobbes, T. and Tuck, R. (eds), 1991, Hobbes: Leviathan, Cambridge: Cambridge University Press.

Hollander, E. P. and Julian, J. W., 1969, 'Contemporary Trends in the Analysis of Leadership Processes', Psychological Bulletin 71(5), pp. 387–97.

Hollmann, J., Carpes, A. d. M. and Beuron, T. A., 2010, The DaimlerChrysler Merger – A Cultural Mismatch?, www.spell.org.br/documentos/download/5150.

House, R. J., 1971, 'A Path Goal Theory of Leader Effectiveness', *Administrative Science Quarterly* 16, pp. 321–8.

Hurst, D. K., 2012, *The New Ecology of Leadership*, Chichester: Columbia University Press.

Hybels, B., 2002, *Courageous Leadership*, Grand Rapids, MI: Zondervan.

Jacobsen, E. O. (ed.), 2009, *The Three Tasks of Leadership*, Grand Rapids, MI: Eerdmans.

Jagelman, I., 1998, *The Empowered Church*, Adelaide: Openbook.

Janis, I. L., 1982, *Groupthink: Psychological Studies of Policy Decisions and Fiascoes*, Boston, MA: Houghton Mifflin.

Katz, R. L., 1955, 'Skills of an Effective Administrator', *Harvard Business Review* 33(1).

Katzenbach, J. R. and Smith, D. K., 1993, *The Wisdom of Teams*, Boston, MA: Harvard Business School Press.

Kellerman, B., 2008, *Followership*, Boston, MA: Harvard Business Review Press.

Kotter, J. P. and Heskett, J. L., 1992, *Corporate Culture and Performance*, New York: The Free Press.

Kouzes, J. and Posner, B., 2012, *The Leadership Challenge*, 5th edn, San Francisco, CA: Jossey-Bass.

Ladkin, D., 2010, *Rethinking Leadership*, Cheltenham: Edward Elgar.

Laloux, F., 2014, *Reinventing Organizations*, Brussels: Nelson Parker.

Lamdin, K., 2012, *Finding Your Leadership Style*, London: SPCK.

Lawrence, J., 2004, *Growing Leaders*, Oxford: Bible Reading Fellowship.

Lawrence, J., 2020, *Leading Well with Others*, Cambridge: Grove Books.

Lederach, J. P., 2003, *The Little Book of Conflict Transformation*, Intercourse, PA: GoodBooks.

Lencioni, P., 2002, *The Five Dysfunctions of a Team*, San Francisco, CA: Jossey-Bass.

Lewis, R. and Cordeiro, W., 2005, *Culture Shift*, San Francisco, CA: Jossey-Bass.

Lincoln, A. T., 1990, *Ephesians*, Word Biblical Commentary, vol. 42, Nashville, TN: Thomas Nelson.

Loew, L. and O'Leonard, K., 2012, *Leadership Development Factbook 2012: Benchmarks and Trends in US Leadership Development*, Bersin by Deloitte report, Oakland CA: Bersin by Deloitte.

Maccoby, M., 2007, *The Leaders We Need*, Boston, MA: Harvard Business School Press.

Mackay, J., 1958–59, 'The Form of a Servant', *Theology Today* 4, p. 304.

MacManus, E. R., 2003, *Uprising*, Nashville, TN: Thomas Nelson.

MacMillan, P., 2001, *The Performance Factor*, Nashville, TN: Broadman and Holman.

McChrystal, S., 2018, *Leaders: Myth and Reality*, London: Portfolio Penguin.

Meindl, J. R., Ehrlich, S. B. and Dukerisch, J. M., 1985, 'The Romance of Leadership', *Administrative Science Quarterly* 30, pp. 521–51.

Nash, S., Pimlott, J. and Nash, P., 2008, *Skills for Collaborative Ministry*, London, SPCK.

Newbigin, L., 1953, *The Household of God*, London: SCM Press.
Northouse, P. G., 2010, *Leadership Theory and Practice*, London: Sage.
Nouwen, H., 1981, *The Way of the Heart*, New York: Seabury.
Nouwen, H., 1989, *In the Name of Jesus*, London: Darton, Longman & Todd.

Olsen, M. S., Van Bever, D. and Verry, S., 2008, 'When Growth Stalls', *Harvard Business Review*, March 2008.
Orwell, G., 2003, *Shooting an Elephant and Other Essays*, London: Penguin.

Padfield, J., 2019, *Hopeful Influence: A Theology of Christian Leadership*, London: SCM Press.
Parkinson, I., 2015, *Reignite*, Oxford: Monarch.
Parkinson, I., 2017, *Enabling Succession*, Cambridge: Grove Books.
Pentland, A., 2012, *The New Science of Building Great Teams*, Boston, MA: Harvard Business Review.
Percy, M., 2017, *The Future Shapes of Anglicanism*, Abingdon: Routledge.
Pickard, S., 2009, *Theological Foundations for Collaborative Ministry*, Farnham: Ashgate.
Plato, 2007, *The Republic*, London: Penguin Classics.
Prior, S., 2017, *Effective Line Management in Ministry*, Cambridge: Grove Books.

Ramsay, M., 1990 [1936], *The Gospel and the Catholic Church*, London: SPCK.
Rath, T., 2007, *Strengthsfinder 2.0*, New York: Perseus-Gallup Press.
Roxburgh, A. and Romanuk, F., 2006, *The Missional Leader*, San Francisco, CA: Jossey-Bass.

Sample, S. B., 2002, *The Contrarian's Guide to Leadership*, San Francisco, CA: Jossey-Bass.
Schein, E., 2010, *Organizational Culture and Leadership*, 4th edn, San Francisco, CA: Jossey-Bass.
Schillebeeckx, E., 1981, *Ministry: Leadership in the Community of Jesus Christ*, New York: Crossroad Publishing.
Schultz, R., 1996 (i), 'שפט' in VanGemeren, W. A. (ed.), 1996, *New International Dictionary of Old Testament Theology and Exegesis*, vol. 4, Carlisle: Paternoster Press, pp. 213–20.
Schultz, R., 1996 (ii), 'עבד' in VanGemeren, W. A. (ed.), 1996, *New International Dictionary of Old Testament Theology and Exegesis*, vol. 4, Carlisle, Paternoster Press, pp. 1183–98.
Schwarz, C. A., 1996, *Natural Church Development Handbook*, Moggerhanger, Bedford: British Church Growth Association.
Selznick, P., 1957, *Leadership in Administration: A Sociological Interpretation*, New York: Harper.
Senge, P., 2006, *The Fifth Discipline: The Art and Practice of the Learning Organisation*, rev. edn, London: Random House.
Senge, P. et al., 1994, *The Fifth Discipline Fieldbook*, London: Nicholas Brealey Publishing.
Shawchuck, N. and Heuser, R., 1993, *Leading the Congregation*, Nashville, TN: Abingdon Press.

Sinclair, A., 2007, *Leadership for the Disillusioned*, Crows Nest, NSW: Allen & Unwin.

Smircich, L., 1983, 'Concepts of Culture and Organisational Analysis', *Administrative Science Quarterly* 28, pp. 339–58.

Smircich, L. and Morgan, G., 1982, '"Leadership": The Management of Meaning', *Journal of Applied Behavioral Science* 18(3), pp. 257–73.

Snyder, H., 1980, *The Radical Wesley*, Downers Grove, IL: InterVarsity Press.

Snyder, H., 1983, *Liberating the Church*, Downers Grove, IL: InterVarsity Press.

Snyder, H., 1997, *Signs of the Spirit*, Eugene, OR: Wipf and Stock.

Stark, R., 1997, *The Rise of Christianity*, New York: HarperCollins.

Stodgill, R. M., 1948, 'Personal Factors Associated with Leadership: A Survey of the Literature', *Journal of Psychology* 25, pp. 35–71.

Stodgill, R. M., 1974, *Handbook of Leadership*, New York: Free Press.

Stuart, D., 1987, *Word Biblical Commentary: Hosea–Jonah*, Waco, TX: Word Books.

Timmis, S., 2012, *Gospel-centred Leadership*, Epsom: The Good Book Company.

Tomlin, G., 2014, *The Widening Circle*, London: SPCK.

Vergauwe, J., Wille, B., Hofmans, J., Kaiser, R. B. and de Fruyt, F., 2017, 'Too Much Charisma Can Make Leaders Look Less Effective', *Harvard Business Review*, September 2017.

Voas, D. and Watt, L., 2014, *From Anecdote to Evidence*, The Church Commissioners for England.

Volf, M., 1998, *After Our Likeness: The Church as the Image of the Trinity*, Grand Rapids, MI: Eerdmans.

Von Eicken, E. and Lindner, H., 'ἀποστελλω', in Brown, C. (ed.), 1975, *New International Dictionary of New Testament Theology*, vol. 1, Exeter: Paternoster Press, pp. 126–8.

Walker, S. P., 2005, *Subversive Leadership*, Oxford: The Leadership Community.

Walker, S. P., 2010, *The Undefended Leader*, Carlisle: Piquant Editions.

Western, S., 2013, *Leadership: A Critical Text*, 2nd edn, London: Sage.

Willimon, W., 2015, *Pastor*, Nashville, TN: Abingdon Press.

Wright, W. C., 2000, *Relational Leadership*, Carlisle: Paternoster Press.

# Index of Biblical References

# Index of Names and Subjects